HEART FAILURE IN CLINICAL PRACTICE
SECOND EDITION
Volume 3 Treatment

HEART FAILURE IN CLINICAL PRACTICE
SECOND EDITION
Volume 3 Treatment

Edited by

John JV McMurray BSC MBCHB MD FRCP FESC FACC
Honorary Professor and Consultant Cardiologist
Western Infirmary, Glasgow, UK

John GF Cleland MD FRCP FESC FACC
Professor and Honorary Consultant Cardiologist
Academic Unit
Department of Cardiology
University of Hull
Hull, UK

Presented as a service to medicine by

 NOVARTIS

MARTIN DUNITZ

This copy of *Heart Failure in Clinical Practice* is given as a service to medicine by Novartis Pharmaceuticals (UK) Ltd. The views expressed herein are not necessarily those of Novartis Pharmaceuticals (UK) Ltd.

Although every effort has been made to ensure that drug dosages and other information are presented accurately in the publication, the ultimate responsibility rests with the prescribing physician. Neither Novartis Pharmaceuticals (UK) Ltd, the publishers nor the authors can be held responsible for errors or for any consequences arising from the use of information contained herein. Any product mentioned in this publication should be used in accordance with the prescribing information prepared by the manufacturers. No claims or endorsements are made for any drug or compound at present under clinical investigation

© Martin Dunitz Ltd 1999, 2000

First published in the United Kingdom in 1996 by

Martin Dunitz Ltd
The Livery House
7–9 Pratt Street
London NW1 0AE

Second Edition 1999, 2000

A CIP record for this book is available from the British Library.

ISBN 1-84184-006-8

Composition by Wearset, Boldon, Tyne and Wear, UK
Printed and bound in Spain by Grafos SA. Artes Sobre papel

CONTENTS

Contributors

Farqad Alamgir MBBS
University of Hull
Castle Hill Hospital
Castle Road
Cottingham
Kingston-upon-Hull
UK

Inder S Anand FRCP DPhil(oxon) FACC
Staff Physician VA Medical Center and
Professor of Medicine
University of Minnesota Medical School
Minneapolis MN 55417
USA

Y Chandrashekar MD DM
Staff Physician VA Medical Center and
Assistant Professor of Medicine
University of Minnesota Medical School
Minneapolis MN 55417
USA

John GF Cleland MD FRCP FESC FACC
Professor of Cardiology
University of Hull
Castle Hill Hospital
Kingston-upon-Hull
UK

Stuart M Cobbe MD FRCP FESC
Walton Professor of Medical Cardiology
Department of Medical Cardiology
Royal Infirmary
Glasgow
UK

Julian Collinson MBBS MRCP
Clinical Trials and Evaluation Unit
Royal Brompton Hospital and
Imperial College School of Medicine
London
UK

Robert Neil Doughty MB MRCP FRACP
New Zealand National Heart
Foundation BNZ Senior Fellow
Department of Medicine
Faculty of Medicine and Health Science
University of Auckland
Auckland
New Zealand

Marcus D Flather MBBS MRCP
Clinical Trials and Evaluation Unit
Royal Brompton Hospital and
Imperial College School of Medicine
London
UK

Marvin A Konstam MD FACC
Division of Cardiology
Department of Medicine and Radiology
Tufts University School of Medicine
New England Medical Center
Boston MA 02111
USA

Andrew C Rankin MD FRCP
Senior Lecturer in Medical Cardiology
Department of Medical Cardiology
Royal Infirmary
Glasgow
UK

Michael W Rich MD
Associate Professor of Medicine
Director, Geriatric Cardiology Program
Barnes-Jewish Hospital
Washington University School of
Medicine
St Louis MO 63110
USA

Norman Sharpe MD FRACP FACC
Professor, Department of Medicine
Faculty of Medicine and Health Science
University of Auckland
Auckland
New Zealand

John J Smith MD PhD FACC
Division of Cardiology
Department of Medicine and
Department of Pharmacology and
Experimental Therapeutics
Tufts University School of Medicine
New England Medical Center
Boston MA
USA

Stephen Westaby BSc FRCS MS
Consultant Cardiac Surgeon
Oxford Heart Centre
John Radcliffe Hospital
Headley Way
Headington
Oxford
UK

VOLUME 3

TREATMENT

13

Clinical trials of ACE inhibitors in heart failure and other cardiovascular indications
Julian Collinson and Marcus D Flather

Introduction

Angiotensin-converting enzyme (ACE) inhibitors are a group of compounds discovered in the early 1970s. Their structures and functions are based on teprotide, a component of the venom of the snake *Bothrops jararaca*.[1,2] The principal action of ACE inhibitors is blockade of the enzyme responsible for conversion of angiotensin I to angiotensin II in the serum as well as in local tissues. ACE inhibitors cause arterial and venous dilatation that decreases peripheral vascular resistance and cardiac pre- and afterload. These haemodynamic effects are thought to be responsible for many of the beneficial effects of ACE inhibitors. ACE inhibitors cause an increase in bradykinin that may mediate some of their effects on blood pressure and on the renin–angiotensin system.[3] This in turn may give rise to some of their clinical benefit, together with decreased sodium retention or effects on left ventricular remodelling.[4] Other novel mechanisms that are under investigation may also play a part, including antithrombotic and antiatherogenic effects, regulation of smooth muscle proliferation, improved endothelial function and the effect of ACE inhibitors on the rate of sudden death.[5–7]

Angiotensin-converting enzyme inhibitors are among the most successful therapies for cardiovascular diseases. They are the cornerstone of therapy in heart failure and are commonly used in the treatment of hypertension, myocardial infarction (MI) and diabetic renal disease.[8] About 150 000 patients have been randomized in placebo-controlled trials of ACE inhibitors in heart failure, myocardial infarction, hypertension or diabetes. A further 100 000 or so are involved in ongoing randomized trials in diabetes, vascular protection or comparisons with other agents including angiotensin II receptor antagonists. In this chapter we concentrate on trials of ACE inhibitors in heart failure and left ventricular dysfunction. We conclude by briefly reviewing other cardiovascular indications including myocardial infarction, hypertension, diabetes and vascular protection.

Effects of ACE inhibitors in patients with heart failure

Several studies in the early 1990s evaluated the effects of ACE inhibitors on survival in patients with both symptomatic and asymptomatic left ventricular systolic dysfunction (see Table 13.1).[9–12]

The CONSENSUS (Co-operative North Scandinavian Enalapril Survival Study)[9] trial recruited 253 patients in a double-blind study. Enalapril, or matching placebo, was started at a dose of 5 mg twice daily and increased to a

Trial	Design	Eligibility	Agent and regimen	Average follow-up	Death/numbers randomized (%) Treatment	Death/numbers randomized (%) Control	OR (95% CI)	P
CONSENSUS[9]	Double-blind	NYHA 4	Enalapril or placebo 5 mg bd titrated to 20 mg bd, initial dose reduced to 2.5 mg bd	188 days	33/127 (26%)	55/126 (44%)	0.59	0.002
SOLVD-Treatment[10]	Double-blind	Heart failure (NYHA 2/3), ejection fraction <0.35	Enalapril or placebo 2.5/5 mg bd titrated to 10 mg bd	41.4 months	452/1284 (35.2%)	510/1285 (39.7%)	0.84 (0.74–0.95)	0.0036
SOLVD-Prevention[11]	Double-blind	Ejection fraction <0.35, no heart failure treatment	Enalapril or placebo 2.5 mg bd titrated to 10 mg bd	37.4 months	313/2115 (14.8%)	334/2113 (15.8%)	0.92 (0.79–1.08)	0.30
V-HeFT II[12]	Double-blind	Men aged 18–75, chronic heart failure	Enalapril 5 mg daily titrated to 20 mg daily or hydralazine (37.5 mg titrated to 300 mg daily) with isosorbide dinitrate (40 mg titrated to 160 mg)	24 months	132/403 (32.8%)	153/401 (38.2%)	0.72	0.08
SAVE[14]	Double-blind	LVEF <40%, 3–16 days post-MI	Captopril or placebo 12.5 mg initial dose, titrating up to 25–50 mg tid	42 months	228/1115 (20.5%)	275/1116 (24.6%)	0.79 (0.68–0.97)	0.019
AIRE[15]	Double blind	Clinical heart failure, 3–10 days post-MI	Ramipril or placebo 2.5 mg bd initial dose, titrating up to 5 mg bd for at least 6 months	15 months	170/1004 (16.9%)	222/982 (22.6%)	0.70 (0.60–0.89)	0.002
TRACE[16]	Double-blind	Wall motion index <1.2 (LVEF <35%), 3–7 days post-MI	Trandolapril or placebo 1 mg od initial dose, titrating up to 4 mg od	36 months	304/876 (34.7%)	369/873 (42.3%)	0.73 (0.67–0.91)	0.001

CONSENSUS: Cooperative North Scandinavian Enalapril Survival Study; SOLVD: Studies of Left Ventricular Dysfunction; V-HeFT: Veterans Administration Cooperative Vasodilator-Heart Failure Trial; SAVE: Survival and Ventricular Enlargement; AIRE: Acute Infarction Ramipril Efficacy; TRACE: Trandolapril in patients with reduced left ventricular function after AMI
tid: three times daily; bd: twice daily; od: once daily.

Table 13.1
ACE Inhibitors in heart failure and left ventricular dysfunction: summary of large long-term trials

maximum of 40 mg per day depending on side-effects and clinical response. At the start of the study, all patients were in NYHA (New York Heart Association) functional class IV. There were no specific ejection fraction (EF) criteria for enrolment. There was a mean follow-up of 188 days (range 1 day–20 months). After 6 months, mortality (the primary endpoint) was 26% (33 deaths) in the enalapril group compared to 44% (55 deaths) in the placebo group (risk reduction (RR) 40%, P = 0.002). At 12 months, mortality was 39% (50 deaths) in the enalapril group and 54% (68 deaths) in the placebo group (RR 31%, P = 0.001). The benefits appeared to be due to a reduction in progression of heart failure. The mean age for patients enrolled into the study was about 70 years, which is older than patients enrolled in other survival studies.

In the SOLVD (Studies of Left Ventricular Dysfunction) treatment[10] trial, 2569 patients with NYHA class II and III heart failure with an EF no more than 35% were recruited. Patients were given either enalapril, starting at 2.5 mg and increasing to 20 mg per day, or matched placebo. Mean follow-up was 41.4 months (range 22–55 months). At the end of the study, there had been 510 deaths in the placebo group (39.7%) compared with 452 (35.2%) in the enalapril group (RR 16%, 95% confidence interval (CI) 5–26%, P = 0.0036). Again, the largest effect seemed to be because of a reduction in progressive heart failure.

In the SOLVD prevention trial,[11] 4228 patients with EF no more than 35% who had not received treatment for heart failure were recruited. Enalapril or placebo was given at a dose of 2.5–20 mg. Mean follow-up was 37.4 months. All-cause mortality was 15.8% (334 deaths) in the placebo group and 14.8% (313 deaths) in the enalapril group (RR 8%, 95% CI 8–21%, P = 0.30). When death was combined with first admission to hospital, there was a reduction from 24.5% (518 events) in the placebo group to 20.6% (434 events) in the enalapril group (RR 20%, 95% CI 9–30%, P < 0.001).

The V-HeFT II (Second Vasodilator–Heart Failure Veterans Affairs Cooperative Study Group) trial[12] reported on 804 men receiving digoxin and diuretic therapy for heart failure. Patients were randomized to 20 mg enalapril or a combination of 300 mg hydralazine with 160 mg isosorbide dinitrate (a combination that had previously been shown to reduce heart failure mortality). After 2 years, mortality was 18% (132 deaths) for those taking enalapril and 25% (153 deaths) for those on hydralazine and isosorbide dinitrate (RR, 28%, P = 0.016).

A systematic overview of randomized trials of ACE inhibitors compared to control in heart failure (EF ≤40%) was carried out by Garg and Yusuf.[13] A total of 34 trials was identified evaluating a variety of different ACE inhibitors, of which 12 studies followed patients beyond 90 days and seven beyond 6 months. At any follow-up, there had been 611 deaths among 3870 (15.8%) patients allocated to the ACE inhibitor group and 709 deaths among 3235 (21.9%) control patients (odds ratio (OR) 0.77, 95% CI 0.67–0.88, P < 0.001). Data on hospitalization were available for most patients. There were 22.4% patients who died or had a hospital admission in the ACE inhibitor group compared to 32.6% in the control group (OR 0.65; 95% CI 0.57–0.74, P < 0.001). The individual trials and the overview provide substantial evidence of benefit for ACE inhibitors in patients with heart failure.

Treatment of LV dysfunction and heart failure following myocardial infarction

Three large long-term randomized controlled trials of ACE inhibitors in patients with LV dysfunction or heart failure following myocardial infarction (MI) have been published: SAVE (Survival and Ventricular Enlargement),[14] AIRE (Acute Infarction Ramipril Efficacy)[15] and TRACE (Trandolapril in patients with reduced left ventricular function after AMI).[16] The main design features and results of these trials are summarized in Table 13.2.

The SAVE study enrolled 2231 patients with EF no more than 40%, without clinical evidence of heart failure or ongoing ischaemia.[14] Patients were randomized between 3 and 16 days (mean 11 days) after MI to either captopril (titrating up to a maximum dose of 50 mg three times daily) or matching placebo. Treatment was continued for a mean of 42 months (range 24–60 months). At the last study visit, 70% of survivors in the captopril group were taking study treatment compared to 73% in the placebo group, and of these 79% and 90%, respectively reached the target dose of 150 mg daily. There were 228 (20.5%) deaths out of 1115 patients in the captopril group compared to 275 (24.6%) deaths out of 1116 patients in the placebo group (OR 0.79, 95% CI 0.68–0.97, $P = 0.019$). A similar reduction was observed when cardiovascular deaths (84% of the total) were compared and significant benefits of captopril were observed on the incidence of heart failure requiring hospitalization. A 25% risk reduction was also observed in the rate of fatal or nonfatal recurrent MI (133 in the captopril group and 170 in the placebo group; 95% CI 5–40%, $P = 0.015$).

The AIRE study[15] randomized 2006 patients with clinical evidence of heart failure (based on clinical examination or chest X-ray) to ramipril (target dose 5 mg twice daily) or matching placebo commencing 3–10 days after acute MI. Average length of follow-up was 15 months (range 6–30 months). All-cause mortality in the ramipril group was 17% (170 deaths out of 1014) compared to 23% in the control group (222 deaths out of 992 patients; OR 0.70, 95% CI 0.60–0.89, $P = 0.002$). A risk reduction of 19% was observed in the rate of the secondary outcome cluster (first event of death, severe resistant heart failure, MI or stroke) in the ramipril group compared to placebo (95% CI 5–31%, $P = 0.008$). An analysis of cause of death demonstrated that sudden death accounted for 54% of all deaths and 93% of out-of-hospital deaths.[6] The group randomized to ramipril had a reduction in the risk of sudden death of 30% (95% CI 8–47%, $P = 0.011$). In the AIRE extension study, longer-term follow-up to about 5 years was obtained for 603 patients randomized in 30 UK centres.[17] All-cause mortality was 27.5% originally allocated to the ramipril group and 38.9% in those originally allocated control (RR 36%, 95% CI 15–52%, $P = 0.002$).

The TRACE study[16] randomized 1749 patients with echocardiographic wall motion abnormality consistent with an EF less than 35% to either trandolapril (maximum dose of 4 mg daily) or matching placebo 3–7 days after MI.[16] Length of follow-up was 24–50 months. All-cause mortality in the trandolapril group was 34.7% (304 deaths out of 876 patients) compared to 42.3% in the placebo group (369 deaths out of 873 patients; relative risk of death 0.74, 95% CI 0.67–0.91, $P = 0.001$). There were similar reductions in the rates of other secondary outcomes including deaths from cardiovascular causes (RR 0.75, 95% CI

Trial	Design	Eligibility	Time of first dose after AMI (hours)	Agent, regimen, and follow-up	Average follow-up	Deaths/numbers randomized (%)		OR (%) (95% CI)	P
						Treatment	Control		
CONSENSUS-II[20]	Double-blind	ST elevation, Q waves or raised cardiac enzymes	<24	Enalapril or placebo initial iv infusion of 1 mg enalapril at over 2 h, then 2.5 mg oral enalapril titrating up to 10 mg daily	6 months	312/3044 (10.25%)	286/3046 (9.40%)	1.10 (0.93–1.29)	0.26
GISSI-3[21]	Open	ST elevation or depression	<24	Lisinopril or control 5 mg initial dose, titrating up to 10 mg daily	6 weeks	597/9435 (6.33%)	673/9460 (7.11%)	0.88 (0.79–0.99)	0.03
SMILE[24]	Double-blind	Anterior MI, no thrombolysis	<24	Zofenopril or placebo 7.5 mg initial dose, titrating up to 30 mg bid	6 weeks	38/772 (4.9%)	51/784 (6.5%)	0.75 (0.40–1.11)	0.19
ISIS-4[22]	Double-blind	Suspected AMI	<24	Captopril or placebo 6.25 mg initial dose, titrating up to target of 50 mg bid	4 weeks	2088/29028 (7.19%)	2231/29022 (7.69%)	0.93 (0.87–0.99)	0.02
CCS-1[23]	Double-blind	Suspected AMI	<36	Captopril or placebo 6.25 mg initial dose then 12.5 mg tid	4 weeks	617/6814 (9.05%)	654/6820 (9.59%)	0.94 (0.84–1.05)	0.3

CONSENSUS II: Cooperative New Scandinavian Enalapril Survival study; GISSI-3: Gruppo Italiano per lo Studio della Sopravvivenza nell'Infarto Miocardico; SMILE: Survival of Myocardial Infarction Long term Evaluation; ISIS-4: Fourth International Study of Infarct Survival; CCS-1: Chinese Cardiac Study. AMI: Acute myocardial infarction; iv: intravenous; bid: twice daily; tid: three times daily. OR: odds ratio; CI: confidence interval.

Table 13.2
Large trials of ACE inhibitors started in the acute phase of MI

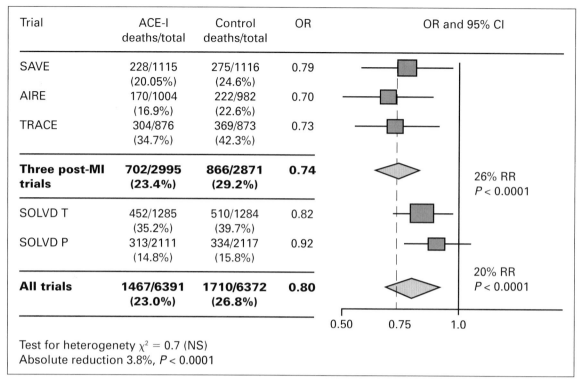

Trial	ACE-I deaths/total	Control deaths/total	OR	OR and 95% CI
SAVE	228/1115 (20.05%)	275/1116 (24.6%)	0.79	
AIRE	170/1004 (16.9%)	222/982 (22.6%)	0.70	
TRACE	304/876 (34.7%)	369/873 (42.3%)	0.73	
Three post-MI trials	**702/2995 (23.4%)**	**866/2871 (29.2%)**	**0.74**	26% RR $P < 0.0001$
SOLVD T	452/1285 (35.2%)	510/1284 (39.7%)	0.82	
SOLVD P	313/2111 (14.8%)	334/2117 (15.8%)	0.92	20% RR $P < 0.0001$
All trials	**1467/6391 (23.0%)**	**1710/6372 (26.8%)**	**0.80**	

Test for heterogenety $\chi^2 = 0.7$ (NS)
Absolute reduction 3.8%, $P < 0.0001$

Figure 13.1
Meta-analysis of large long-term studies of ACE inhibitors in heart failure and LV dysfunction (SAVE, AIRE, TRACE, SOLVD). Squares represent the point estimate of odds ratios and horizontal lines the 95% confidence intervals of the estimates. The size of the squares approximates to the amount of statistical information in the trial. Diamonds represent the summary statistics and their 95% confidence intervals using the Yusuf–Peto modification of the Mantel–Haenszel method.[50]

0.63–0.89, $P = 0.001$), sudden death (RR 0.76, 95% CI 0.59–0.98, $P = 0.03$) and progression to severe heart failure (RR 0.71, 95% CI 0.56–0.89, $P = 0.03$). There was no apparent reduction in the rate of fatal or nonfatal recurrent MI. The TRACE study group carefully screened 6676 consecutive patients with confirmed MI entering the coronary care units of participating hospitals for entry into the study. Of these about 25% were entered into the trial, which is a relatively high proportion of patients screened compared to other clinical trials.

In a systematic overview of these three trials, the proportion of deaths in the ACE inhibitor group was 23.4% compared to 29.1% in the control group (OR 0.74, 95% CI 0.66–0.83, $P < 0.0001$; (see Figure 13.1).[18] The proportion of patients admitted to hospital for heart failure was 11.9% and 15.5% respectively (OR 0.73, 95% CI 0.63–0.85, $P < 0.0001$). Recurrent nonfatal MI occurred in 10.8% of the ACE inhibitor group compared to 13.2% of controls (OR 0.80, 95% CI 0.69–0.94 $P < 0.01$) which supports previous observations of prevention of myocardial ischaemic events.[10,11,14] There was no difference in the proportion of strokes which occurred in 4.0% and 3.7% respectively (OR 1.10, NS). Previous reports had suggested that the beneficial effects of ACE inhibitors could be reduced by the coadministration of aspirin. In the systematic overview, the OR of all-cause mortality among patients taking aspirin at baseline was 0.74 ($P < 0.0001$ for the comparison of ACE inhibitor versus control), and was 0.73 for patients not taking aspirin at baseline ($P = 0.004$ for the comparison of ACE inhibitor versus control). These data confirm that the proportional benefits of ACE inhibitors are very similar in patients taking aspirin compared to those not taking aspirin at baseline, and suggest that coadministration of aspirin and ACE inhibitors does not significantly attenuate the effects of either beneficial agent. Regression analysis of the odds ratio of mortality in the ACE inhibitor group compared to control and baseline ejection fraction shows a highly significant relationship with greater relative benefit accruing in those patients with lower ejection fractions. The long-term post-MI trials have shown convincing and consistent risk reductions in mortality (of the order of 20 to 25%) in patients with a history of chronic heart failure, or objective evidence of impaired left ventricular function. The estimated number of lives saved per 1000 patients treated for 2–3 years is between 40 and 70.

The issue of optimal dose of ACE inhibitors in heart failure was addressed in the NETWORK study.[19] A total of 1532 patients with clinical evidence of heart failure (no EF parameters were specified) were randomized in a double-blind manner to one of three doses of enalapril: 2.5 mg twice daily, 5 mg twice daily or 10 mg twice daily for 6 months. The primary outcome of death, hospital admission for heart failure or worsening heart failure occurred in 12.3%, 12.9% and 14.7% respectively (relative risk of events comparing low dose to high dose 1.20; 95% CI 0.88–1.64). The study was not able to comment on the most appropriate dose of enalapril in heart failure. The ATLAS (Assessment of Treatment with Lisinopril and Survival) study randomized 3164 patients to low-dose (2.5 or 5.0 mg daily versus 32.5 or 35 mg daily) or high-dose lisinopril for 3 years. The study was presented at the meeting of the American College of Cardiology (Atlanta, 1998), but has not yet been published. Compared to the low dose, after 3 years, high-dose lisinopril resulted in a 12% risk reduction for the combined endpoint of all-cause death plus all-cause hospitalization ($P = 0.002$) and a 15% risk reduction in the combined endpoint of all-cause death plus hospitalization for heart failure ($P = 0.001$).

Trials of ACE inhibitors started in the acute phase of MI

The design aspects, drug regimens and mortality results for the five large acute phase, short-term trials are summarized in Table 13.2.[20–24] A systematic overview (meta-analysis) of these trials has recently been published. Data for the systematic overview were available for nearly 100 000 patients from four trials. Overall 30-day mortality was 7.1% in the ACE inhibitor group patients and 7.6% in the control group (RR 7%, 95% CI 2–11%, $P < 0.004$). This represents the avoidance of about five deaths for every 1000 patients treated for 30 days, and most of the benefit was observed in the first week. Overall, 239 deaths were avoided in the first few weeks in the group randomized to ACE inhibitor therapy. Of these, 96 deaths (40% of total benefit) were avoided during days 0–1, 104 deaths (44%) avoided during days 2–7, and just 39 (16%) during days 8–30(76). Thus the benefits of starting ACE inhibitors in the early phase of MI are mostly observed in the first week, even in a relatively unselected population. Most of the benefit appears to be concentrated in patients with greater LV damage at randomization including anterior MI (11 deaths avoided per 1000 patients treated) compared to other sites of MI (one death avoided). Similarly patients in Killip class 2 or 3 appeared to have greater benefit (14 deaths avoided per 1000 patients) compared to Killip class 1 (three deaths avoided per 1000 patients). Larger benefits were also observed in patients with higher heart rates and diabetics compared to nondiabetics. Beneficial effects were not apparently observed in patients older than 75 years (about 15% of the total) perhaps because of a higher incidence of adverse effects such as hypotension and renal dysfunction. The simple interpretation that greater benefits occur in patients with more ventricular damage at baseline, although attractive, should be treated with caution since it relies on subgroup analyses in the overview which may be unreliable. Despite early hypotension with the use of ACE inhibitors in the acute phase of MI, the lives saved in GISSI-3 and ISIS-4 during the first few days[22,25] underscore the importance of this strategy. Further support is provided by a more recent mechanistic study in which the HEART (Healing and Afterload Reducing Therapy) investigators showed that early use of an ACE inhibitor was associated with prompt improvements of LV function.[26] There is good evidence to start low-dose ACE inhibitors in the early phase of MI particularly in those with large MI, heart failure or objective evidence of impaired LV function, as long as systolic blood pressure is maintained over 100 mmHg.

Studies comparing ACE inhibitors with angiotensin II antagonists

Several studies comparing angiotensin II receptor antagonists with ACE inhibitors are underway. ELITE (Evaluation of Losartan in the Elderly) was a blinded study that randomized 722 patients to a maximum of losartan 50 mg daily or captopril 50 mg three times daily for about a year.[27] The main eligibility criteria were age over 65 years, EF no more than 40%, and no previous exposure to ACE inhibitors. A persistent increase in serum creatinine, the primary outcome, occurred in 10.5% in each group. Significantly fewer patients on losartan discontinued therapy because of side-effects compared to captopril (12.2 versus 20.8%, respectively, $P = 0.002$). Death or hospital admission for heart failure was 9.4% in the losartan group compared to 13.2% in the captopril group ($P = 0.075$). This difference was mainly due to an unexpected reduction in all-cause mortality seen in the losartan group (4.8 versus 8.7% for captopril, RR 46%, 95% CI 5–69%, $P = 0.035$). The hypothesis that losartan may reduce mortality and major morbidity is being tested in the ongoing ELITE-2 study of 2600 patients with heart failure. The study will report after 510 deaths have occurred.

The RESOLVD (Randomised Evaluation of Strategies for Left Ventricular Dysfunction) study randomized 768 patients between enalapril, candesartan or their combination. The primary outcomes were the distance walked during 6 minutes, and the effects on neurohormones. The trial also evaluated the role of metoprolol. There were several treatment combinations and the study was not powered to evaluate clinical outcomes.[28] The study has not yet been published. Candesartan is being investigated further in the large CHARM programme consisting of three trials in different groups of heart failure patients (low ejection fraction and intolerant of ACE inhibitors, low ejection fraction and treated with ACE inhibitor, and preserved ejection fraction not treated with an ACE inhibitor).

The OPTIMAAL (Optimal Trial in Myocardial Infarction with Angiotensin II Antagonist Losartan) is a large study of more than 5000 patients with evidence of a recent large MI, or post-MI heart failure. Patients are randomized to losartan or captopril for an expected 18 months of treatment. The trial is in progress and will report after 937 deaths have occurred.[29]

Another angiotensin II receptor antagonist is being used in two other large trials. The VAL-HeFT (Valsartan in Heart Failure) trial will recruit approximately 4000 patients and randomize them to valsartan or placebo. Patients will be in NYHA class II–IV and will be treated with standard treatments including an ACE inhibitor. The primary endpoint is all-cause mortality. The VALIANT (Valsartan in Acute Myocardial Infarction) trial will recruit approximately 14 500 patients who are post-MI and have either clinical or radiological evidence of heart failure or left ventricular dysfunction. Valsartan will be assessed in comparison to, as well as in combination with, captopril. The endpoint is all-cause mortality and the trial will be completed in late 2003.

In a recent study, Hamroff et al randomized 33 patients on maximal doses of ACE inhibitors to losartan 50 mg or placebo.[30] At 6 months, peak aerobic capacity increased from 13.5 ± 0.6 ml/kg/min to 15.7 ± 1.1 ml/kg/min ($P = 0.02$) in the group receiving losartan. There was no significant change in those taking placebo (peak aerobic capacity 14.1 ± 0.6 ml/kg/min at baseline, 13.6 ± 1.1 ml/kg/min at follow-up). These data support a rationale for investigating further the combination of angiotensin II antagonists and ACE inhibitors.

Newer studies of ACE inhibitors in hypertension and diabetes

The recent CAPPP (Captopril Prevention Project) study compared captopril with conventional therapy (thiazide diuretics, beta-blockers or both) in 10 985 patients with uncomplicated hypertension over about 5 years of treatment.[31] The study was prospective, randomized and open with blinded endpoint evaluation. The primary outcome of death, myocardial infarction and stroke occurred in 363 of the captopril group (11.1 per 1000 patient-years) and 335 (10.2 per 1000 patient-years) in the conventional therapy group (RR 1.05, 95% CI 0.90–1.22, $P = 0.52$). Cardiovascular mortality was lower with captopril (76 versus 95 deaths, RR 0.77, 95% CI 0.57–1.04, $P = 0.07$) and fatal and nonfatal strokes were more common (189 versus 148 events, RR 1.25, 95% CI 1.01–1.55, $P = 0.044$). The subgroup of patients with diabetes had significantly better outcomes on captopril than the conventional group. At randomization and during the trial blood pressure was lower in the conventional group than the captopril group. Treatment was also open-label which raises the possibility of bias in reporting of outcomes. These limitations do not allow CAPPP to provide definitive information on the effects of ACE inhibitors compared to diuretics and beta-blockers in hypertension.

Activation of the renin–angiotensin system and raised glomerular capillary pressure cause worsening renal dysfunction in patients with diabetes. ACE inhibitors decrease glomerular capillary pressure by dilating efferent arterioles and reducing arterial blood pressure. ACE inhibitors have been shown to slow the decline of renal function in diabetic nephropathy and slow the progression from microalbuminaemia to frank proteinuria.[32] This is reflected in a maintained creatinine clearance and reduced progression to dialysis, transplantation and death.[33,34] ACE inhibitors also prevent worsening proteinuria and decline in glomerular filtration rate in patients with established proteinuria.[35] A further study demonstrated that these protective effects were apparent in a range of renal diseases except for polycystic renal disease. Protection appeared independent of the pre-existing degree of renal insufficiency. ACE inhibitors have also been shown to reduce progression to retinopathy, even in normotensive patients.[36]

The ABCD (Appropriate Blood Pressure Control in Diabetes) study compared enalapril with the calcium channel blocker nisoldipine in 470 hypertensive patients with noninsulin dependent diabetes over a 5-year treatment period.[37] The primary outcome was change in renal function measured by creatinine clearance. Secondary outcomes included clinical events (death, myocardial infarction, stroke and heart failure). A recent report gave information on clinical events. Blood pressure control was similar in the two groups. A reduction in the incidence of fatal and nonfatal MI was observed in the enalapril group compared to nisoldipine (5/235 (2.1%) versus 25/235 (9.8%), $P = 0.001$). The rate of other clinical outcomes was also lower in the enalapril group.

The FACET (Fosinopril versus Amlodipine Cardiovascular Events Randomized Trial) study enrolled 380 hypertensive patients with noninsulin dependent diabetes.[38] Patients were excluded if they had coronary artery disease or significant renal dysfunction. Patients were randomized to open-label fosinopril (20 mg/day) or amlodipine (10 mg/day) and followed for up to 3.5 years. If blood pressure was not controlled, the other study drug was added. At the end of follow-up, there was no difference in the primary of outcomes of effects on lipids or diabetic control. Patients taking fosinopril had a lower risk of the combined outcome of acute MI, stroke, or hospitalization for angina than those receiving amlodipine (14/189 versus 27/191; hazard ratio 0.49, 95% CI 0.26–0.95). Although the number of patients enrolled is small, this study suggests that fosinopril should be preferred to amlodipine for the first line treatment of hypertensive patients with diabetes.

The UKPDS (United Kingdom Prospective Diabetes Study) group enrolled 4297 patients of whom 1148 had hypertension and were included in the hypertensive substudy.[39,40] Overall, these two studies demonstrated that tight control of blood pressure (aiming for a blood pressure less than 150/85 mmHg) resulted in reduced progression to microvascular and macrovascular complications. However, there were no apparent differences between those randomized to captopril (25 mg twice daily, increasing to 50 mg twice daily) and atenolol (50 mg, increasing to 100 mg) in terms of blood pressure control (blood pressure reduced to a mean of 144/83 mmHg compared to 143/81 mmHg, respectively). Similar proportions in the two groups showed deteriorating retinopathy (31% for captopril versus 37% for atenolol) and developed clinical albuminuria (5 and 9% respectively). These studies suggest that it is the amount by which blood pressure is lowered and not the particular drug used that is important.

Vascular protection

There is accumulating evidence that angiotensin II may promote or activate vascular smooth muscle growth, superoxide anion generation (adversely effecting nitric oxide production), adhesion molecules and inflammation, macrophages and plasminogen activator inhibitors.[41] Inhibition of angiotensin II by ACE inhibitors should help to reverse or inhibit those processes that are thought to contribute to atherosclerosis and ischaemic vascular events. In animal models of atherosclerosis, ACE inhibitors reduce the incidence of vascular lesions.[42] An alternative hypothesis is that supra-therapeutic doses were used in some of the animal models resulting in suppressed appetite, leading to reduced progression of atherosclerosis. ACE inhibitors have also been shown to normalize endothelial dysfunction in patients with diabetes, hypertension or coronary artery disease.[43] The mechanism is unclear, although the inhibition of angiotensin II may reduce the production of superoxide radicals and nitric oxide production is increased, possibly by a bradykinin-dependent mechanism. These effects may add to the already established benefits of ACE inhibitors on blood pressure, neurohormonal modulation, haemodynamics, renal function and cardiac remodelling.

The SOLVD and SAVE trials demonstrated a reduction in myocardial infarction in patients with LV dysfunction.[10,14] These observations, along with the potential beneficial mechanisms summarized above, have generated the hypothesis that ACE inhibitors may provide protection against vascular events in high-risk patients without LV dysfunction. Several studies are investigating the mechanistic effects of ACE inhibitors on progression of vascular lesions.[44] The recently reported SCAT trial (Simvastatin Coronary Atherosclerosis Trial) randomized 460 patients with atherosclerotic coronary lesions to simvastatin, enalapril, both or neither in a 2×2 factorial design. The results were presented at the meeting of the American College of Cardiology (New Orleans, March 1999). Average follow-up was 48 months. Patients receiving simvastatin had significantly less progression of lesions compared to placebo, while there appeared to be no such benefits in patients receiving enalapril compared to placebo. The QUIET trial enrolled 1750 patients with coronary artery disease and enrolled them to 3 years of treatment with quinapril or placebo. There was a nonsignificant reduction in major vascular events. The study entered low-risk patients and was too small to make any clear statement about the efficacy of ACE inhibitors in this setting.

There are three large ongoing randomized trials evaluating the effects of ACE inhibitors in patients at high risk of vascular events either because of pre-existing cardiovascular disease or diabetes. The main features of these trials are summarized in Table 13.3.

The HOPE (Heart Outcomes Protection Evaluation) has randomized 9541 patients (including 2500 women, 3600 diabetics and 5200 $\geqslant$65 years) to ramipril, vitamin E, both or neither in a 2×2 factorial design.[45] Preliminary results show a substantial and significant reduction in the primary end-point of cardiovascular death, myocardial infarction or stroke with ramipril. The PEACE (Prevention of Events with Angiotensin Converting Enzyme Inhibition) study will also follow patients randomized to trandolapril or placebo for about 5 years.[46] The third study is the EUROPA (European Trial on Reduction of Cardiac Events with Perindopril in Stable Coronary Artery Disease) trial evaluating perindopril in 10 500 patients.[47] These three trials will provide clear information about the effects of ACE inhibitors on vascular protection and represent the next chapter in the unfolding story of these exciting therapeutic agents.

New developments

Omapatrilat is a new type of agent that is an ACE inhibitor which also blocks neutral

Trial	Treatment groups	Eligibility	Sample size	Main outcomes	Follow-up	Expected year of report
HOPE	2 × 2 factorial of ramipril (2.5 mg titrated to 10 mg) versus placebo and vitamin E (400 U per day) versus placebo	High risk for cardiovascular events	9541	Death		2000
PEACE	Trandolapril 2 mg, titrated to 4 mg versus placebo	Stable coronary disease — prior MI or >50% coronary vessel stenosis	8000	Cardiovascular mortality, nonfatal MI, revascularization	5 years	2002
EUROPA	Perindopril 4–8 mg daily versus placebo	Stable coronary disease without evidence of heart failure	10 500	Composite of death, MI, unstable angina, cardiac arrest	Minimum 3 years	2003

HOPE: Heart Outcomes Prevention Evaluation; EUROPA: European Trial on Reduction of Cardiac Events with Perindopril in Stable Coronary Artery Disease; PEACE: Prevention of Events with Angiotensin Converting Enzyme Inhibition.

Table 13.3
Ongoing studies of ACE inhibitors in coronary artery disease

endopeptidase thereby blocking natriuretic peptide breakdown. These properties give it potent antihypertensive effects.[48] It is being investigated for other indications including heart failure and diabetic renal disease.

Conclusions

The beneficial role of long-term treatment with ACE inhibitors in heart failure and LV systolic dysfunction is established. There is evidence that they are underused and under-dosed.[49] This aspect needs further urgent evaluation and correction. ACE inhibitors should be started early in the acute phase of MI in patients with a systolic blood pressure greater than 100 mmHg and evidence of moderate to severe myocardial damage. ACE inhibitors are also clearly indicated in diabetic renal disease and for patients with diabetes and hypertension. They can be used as first line treatment in a broad range of hypertensive patients, in particular those with LV damage, LV hypertrophy and renal disease. ACE inhibitors have become the bench mark for comparisons of new promising agents such as angiotensin II antagonists. The new and exciting possibility of vascular protection in patients at high risk of cardiovascular events, but with preserved LV function, is being tested in ongoing trials that should report over the next 2 to 3 years.

References

1. Ondetti MA, Williams NJ, Sabo EF et al. Angiotensin converting enzyme inhibitors from the venom of *Bothrops jararaca*: isolation, elucidation of structure, and synthesis. *Biochemistry* 1971; **10**: 4033–4039.

2. Ondetti MA, Rubin B, Cushman DW. Design of specific inhibitors of angiotensin converting enzyme: a new class of orally active antihypertensive agents. *Science* 1977; **196**: 441–444.

3. Gainer JV, Morrow JD, Loveland A et al. Effect of bradykinin-receptor blockade on the response to angiotensin-converting-enzyme inhibitor in normotensive and hypertensive subjects. *N Engl J Med* 1998; **339**: 1285–1292.

4. Baur LH, Schipperheyn JJ, van der Wall EE et al. Beneficial effect of enalapril on left ventricular remodelling in patients with a severe residual stenosis after acute anterior wall infarction. *Eur Heart J* 1997; **18**: 1313–1321.

5. Lonn EM, Yusuf S, Jha P et al. The emerging role of angiotensin converting enzyme inhibitors in cardiac and vascular protection. *Circulation* 1994; **90**: 2056–2069.

6. Cleland JG, Erhardt L, Murray G et al. Effect of ramipril on morbidity and mode of death among survivors of acute myocardial infarction with clinical evidence of heart failure. A report from the AIRE Study Investigators. *Eur Heart J* 1997; **18**: 41–51.

7. Ferrari R, Bachetti T, Agnoletti L et al. Endothelial function and dysfunction in heart failure. *Eur Heart J* 1999; **19**: G41–G47.

8. Brown NJ, Vaughan DE. Angiotensin-converting enzyme inhibitors. *Circulation* 1998; **97**: 1411–1420.

9. The CONSENSUS Trial Study Group. Effects of enalapril on mortality in severe congestive heart failure. Results of the Cooperative North Scandinavian Enalapril Survival Study (CONSENSUS). *N Engl J Med* 1987; **316**: 1429–1435.

10. The SOLVD Investigators. Effect of enalapril on survival in patients with reduced left ventricular ejection fractions and congestive heart failure. *N Engl J Med* 1991; **325**: 293–302.

11. The SOLVD Investigators. Effect of enalapril on mortality and the development of heart failure in asymptomatic patients with reduced left ventricular ejection fractions. *N Engl J Med* 1992; **327**: 685–691.

12. Cohn JN, Johnson G, Ziesche S et al. A comparison of enalapril with hydralazine-isosorbide dinitrate in the treatment of chronic congestive heart failure. *N Engl J Med* 1991; **325**: 303–310.

13. Garg R, Yusuf S. Overview of randomized trials of angiotensin-converting enzyme inhibitors on mortality and morbidity in patients with heart failure. Collaborative Group on ACE Inhibitor Trials [published erratum appears in *JAMA* 1995; **274**: 462] [see comments]. *JAMA* 1995; **273**: 1450–1456.

14. Pfeffer MA, Braunwald E, Moye LA et al. Effect of captopril on mortality and morbidity in patients with left ventricular dysfunction after myocardial infarction. Results of the survival and ventricular enlargement trial. The SAVE Investigators [see comments]. *N Engl J Med* 1992; **327**: 669–677.

15. AIRE Study Investigators. Effect of ramipril on mortality and morbidity of survivors of acute myocardial infarction with clinical evidence of heart failure. *Lancet* 1993; **342**: 821–828.

16. Kober L, Torp-Pedersen C, Carlsen JE et al. A clinical trial of the angiotensin-converting-enzyme inhibitor trandolapril in patients with left ventricular dysfunction after myocardial infarction. *N Engl J Med* 1995; **333**: 1670–1676.

17. Hall AS, Murray GD, Ball SG, on behalf of the AIREX Study Investigators. Follow-up study of patients randomly allocated ramipril or placebo for heart failure after acute myocardial infarction: AIRE Extension (AIREX) Study. *Lancet* 1997; **349**: 1493–1497.

18. Flather MD, Kober L, Pfeffer MA et al. Meta-analysis of individual patient data from trials of long-term ACE-inhibitor treatment of acute

myocardial infarction (SAVE, AIRE, and TRACE studies). *Circulation* 1997; **96**: I–706 (Abst).

19. The NETWORK investigators. Clinical outcomes with enalapril in symptomatic chronic heart failure; a dose comparison. *Eur Heart J* 1998; **19**: 483–489.

20. Swedberg K, Held P, Kjekshus J et al. Effects of the early administration of enalapril on mortality in patients with acute myocardial infarction. Results of the Cooperative New Scandinavian Enalapril Survival Study II (CONSENSUS II) [see comments]. *N Engl J Med* 1992; **327**: 678–684.

21. Gruppo Italiano per lo Studio della Streptochinasi nell'Infarto Miocardico (GISSI). GISSI-3: effects of lisinopril and transdermal glyceryl trinitrate singly and together on 6-week mortality and ventricular function after acute myocardial infarction. *Lancet* 1994; **343**: 1115–1121.

22. ISIS-4 (Fourth International Study of Infarct Survival) Collaborative Group. ISIS-4: a randomised factorial trial assessing early oral captopril, oral mononitrate, and intravenous magnesium sulphate in 58 050 patients with suspected acute myocardial infarction. *Lancet* 1995; **345**: 669–685.

23. Chinese Cardiac Society Collaborative Group. Oral captopril versus placebo among 13 634 patients with suspected acute myocardial infarction: Interim report from the Chinese Cardiac Study (CCS-1). *Lancet* 1995; **345**: 686–687.

24. Ambrosioni E, Borghi C, Magnani B. The effect of the angiotensin-converting-enzyme inhibitor zofenopril on mortality and morbidity after anterior myocardial infarction. The Survival of Myocardial Infarction Long-Term Evaluation (SMILE) Study Investigators [see comments]. *N Engl J Med* 1995; **332**: 80–85.

25. Latini R, Maggioni A, Flather M et al. ACE inhibitor use in patients with myocardial infarction. *Circulation* 1995; **92**: 3132–3137.

26. Pfeffer MA, Greaves SC, Arnold JM et al. Early versus delayed angiotensin-converting enzyme inhibition therapy in acute myocardial infarction: the healing and afterload reducing therapy trial. *Circulation* 1997; **95**: 2643–2651.

27. Pitt B, Segal R, Martinez FA et al. Randomised trial of losartan versus captopril in patients over 65 with heart failure (Evaluation of Losartan in the Elderly Study, ELITE). *Lancet* 1997; **349**: 747–752.

28. Struthers AD. Angiotensin II receptor antagonists for heart failure. *Br J Cardiol* 1999; **6**: 75–79.

29. Dickstein K, Kjekshus J, for the OPTIMAAL Study Group. Comparison of the effects of losartan and captopril on mortality in patients after acute myocardial infarction: the OPTIMAAL trial design. *Am J Cardiol* 1999; **83**: 477–481.

30. Hamroff G, Katz SD, Mancini D et al. Addition of angiotensin II receptor blockade to maximal angiotensin-converting enzyme inhibition improves exercise capacity in patients with severe congestive heart failure. *Circulation* 1999; **99**: 990–992.

31. Hansson L, Lindholm LH, Niskanen L et al. Effect of angiotensin-converting enzyme inhibition compared with conventional therapy on cardiovascular morbidity and mortality in hypertension: the Captopril Prevention Project (CAPPP) randomised trial. *Lancet* 1999; **353**: 611–616.

32. Ravid M, Brosh D, Levi Z et al. Use of enalapril to attenuate decline in renal function in normotensive normoalbuminuric patients with type 2 diabetes mellitus. A randomized, controlled trial. *Ann Intern Med* 1998; **128**: 982–988.

33. The EUCLID Study Group. Randomised placebo-controlled trial of lisinopril in normotensive patients with insulin-dependent diabetes and normoalbuminaemia or microalbuminaemia. *Lancet* 1997; **349**: 1787–1792.

34. Laffel LM, McGill JB, Gans DJ. The beneficial effect of angiotensin-converting enzyme with captopril on diabetic nephropathy in normotensive IDDM patients with microalbuminaemia. North American Microalbuminuria Study Group. *Am J Med* 1995; **99**: 497–504.

35. The GISEN Group (Gruppo Italiano di Studi Epidemiologici in Nefrologia). Randomised placebo-controlled trial of effect of ramipril on decline in glomerular filtration rate and risk of terminal renal failure in proteinuric, non-

diabetic nephropathy. *Lancet* 1997; **349**: 1857–1863.

36. Chaturvedi N, Sjolie AK, Stephenson JM et al. Effect of lisinopril on progression of retinopathy in normotensive people with type 1 diabetes. The EUCLID Study Group. *Lancet* 1998; **351**: 28–31.

37. Estacio RO, Jeffers BW, Hiatt WR et al. The effect of nisoldipine as compared with enalapril on cardiovascular outcomes in patients with non-insulin dependent diabetes and hypertension. *N Engl J Med* 1998; **338**: 645–652.

38. Tatti P, Pahor M, Byington RP et al. Outcome results of the Fosinopril Versus Amlodipine Cardiovascular Events Randomized Trial (FACET) in patients with hypertension and NIDDM. *Diabetes Care* 1998; **21**: 597–603.

39. UK Prospective Diabetes Study Group. Tight blood pressure control and risk of macrovascular and microvascular complications in type 2 diabetes: UKPDS 38. *BMJ* 1998; **317**: 703–713.

40. UK Prospective Diabetes Study Group. Efficacy of atenolol and captopril in reducing risk of macrovascular and microvascular complications in type 2 diabetes: UKPDS 39. *BMJ* 1998; **317**: 713–720.

41. Dzau VJ. Mechanisms of protective effects of ACE inhibition on coronary artery disease. *Eur Heart J* 1998; **19**: J2–J6.

42. Chobanian AV, Haudenschild CC, Nickerson C, Drago R. Anti-atherogenic affect of captopril in the Watanabe heritable hyperlipidemic rabbit. *Hypertension* 1990; **15**: 327–331.

43. Mancini GB, Henry GC, Macaya C et al. Angiotensin-converting enzyme inhibition with quinapril improves endothelial vasomotor dysfunction in patients with coronary artery disease: the TREND (Trial on Reversing Endothelial Dysfunction) Study. *Circulation* 1996; **94**: 258–265.

44. Yusuf S, Lonn E. Anti-ischaemic effects of ACE inhibitors: review of current clinical evidence and ongoing clinical trials. *Eur Heart J* 1998; **19**: J36–J44.

45. The HOPE study investigators. The HOPE (Heart Outcomes Prevention Evaluation) Study: the design of a large, simple randomized trial of an angiotensin-converting enzyme inhibitor (ramipril) and vitamin E in patients at high risk of cardiovascular events. *Can J Cardiol* 1996; **12**: 127–137.

46. Pfeffer MA, Domanski M, Rosenberg Y et al. Prevention of events with angiotensin-converting enzyme inhibition (the PEACE study design). Prevention of Events with Angiotensin-Converting Enzyme inhibition). *Am J Cardiol* 1998; **82**: 25H–30H.

47. Fox KM, Henderson JR, Bertrand ME et al. The European trial on reduction of cardiac events with perindopril in stable coronary artery disease (EUROPA). *Eur Heart J* 1998; **19**: J52–J55.

48. Trippodo NC, Robl JA, Asaad MM et al. Effects of omapatrilat in low, normal, and high renin experimental hypertension. *Am J Hypertens* 1998; **11**: 363–372.

49. McMurray JJV. Failure to practice evidence-based medicine: why do physicians not treat patients with heart failure with angiotensin-converting enzyme inhibitors? *Eur Heart J* 1998; **19**: L15–L21.

50. Yusuf S, Peto R, Lewis J et al. Beta blockade during and after myocardial infarction: an overview of the randomised trials. *Prog Cardiovasc Dis* 1985; **27**: 335–371.

14

Angiotensin II receptor blockers for heart failure: the current state of play

John GF Cleland and Farqad Alamgir

Introduction

Angiotensin-converting enzyme (ACE) inhibitors have revolutionized our understanding and treatment of chronic heart failure (CHF). The wealth of evidence indicating that ACE inhibitors are effective suggests that caution should be exercised in substituting them with any new class of agent unless and until substantial evidence of benefit with the new class of agent can be demonstrated.

Several angiotensin II receptor blockers (ARBs) have been licensed for use in hypertension and have been shown to be at least as effective as ACE inhibitors in reducing blood pressure.[1-5] ARBs have also been shown to have an excellent side-effect profile with fewer withdrawals for adverse events than placebo and no increase in troublesome cough as with ACE inhibitors.[6,7] However, relatively few countries have licensed ARBs for the management of CHF and where this has occurred the terms of the licence have generally been restrictive, suggesting that the regulatory authorities believe that the evidence of benefit with ARBs for CHF is less conclusive than that for hypertension.

ARBs will undoubtedly give important insights into how ACE inhibitors work, but do they have a clinical role as an alternative or in addition to ACE inhibitors for the management of CHF? Large scale trials to address the role of ARBs for the management of CHF are underway and will begin to report their results within the next year. The purpose of this chapter is to review the existing evidence to determine whether ARBs already have a role in the management of CHF.

Organization of the renin–angiotensin–aldosterone system

The organization of the renin–angiotensin–aldosterone system (RAAS) is outlined in Figure 15.1. The ACE is responsible not only for the production of angiotensin II but also the degradation of bradykinin.[8,9] Other possible substrates for ACE include erythropoeitin and the enkephalins.

Angiotensin II has numerous actions. Acute effects include arterial and, probably, venous constriction, reduced parasympathetic and increased sympathetic nervous activity and, possibly, direct effects on the kidney resulting in salt and water retention.[10] Chronic effects include cardiac and vascular remodelling and a potential role in the genesis of atheroma.[11-13]

Less is known about bradykinin because it is difficult to measure accurately, it acts very close to its site of synthesis with little spillover to the circulation, and because pharmacological tools for manipulating its actions on its

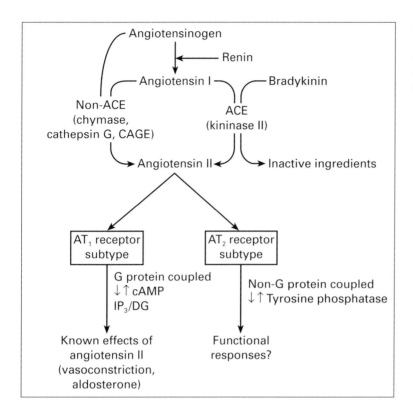

Figure 14.1
*The renin–angiotension–
aldosterone system and
angiotensin II receptor
subtypes.*

receptor site have only recently become available. In general the actions of bradykinin are opposite to those of angiotensin II and include vasodilatation, stimulation of nitric oxide and vasodilator prostaglandin production,[14] the latter being a potential mechanism for the possible interaction between ACE inhibitors and aspirin.[15] Current evidence suggests that, like angiotensin II, bradykinin may also have distinctly different acute and chronic effects.[16] Bradykinin may have favourable effects on left ventricular remodelling, endothelial function and the development of atheroma. However, bradykinin is also purported to activate the sympathetic nervous system, a potentially undesirable effect.[13,17]

Alternative pathways for the generation of angiotensin II

Chymase can convert angiotensin I to II by an ACE-independent pathway. Whether it is present in sufficient quantity to generate significant amounts of angiotensin II either systemically or at a local (tissue) level in humans is uncertain. Studies suggest that mRNA for chymase is expressed at much lower levels than ACE in human cardiac tissues,[18,19] although in rat experiments Urata et al[20] have suggested that enough chymase exists to generate a considerable amount of angiotensin II. Chymotrypsin, angiotensin-generating enzyme and cathepsin D are other pathways for angiotensin II production which are not blocked by ACE inhibitors (Figure 14.1).[21]

Angiotensin II receptor subtypes

The current principal classification in humans is into AT_1 and AT_2 receptors but it is likely that the number of receptor subtypes described will increase. AT_1 receptors are widely distributed in the heart, on the luminal surface of the vascular endothelium, noradrenergic nerve terminals, adrenal cortex and kidneys.[22] AT_2 receptor expression is high in fetal tissues and in healing wounds. In the human heart the AT_2 receptor predominates and the concentration is maintained or increased, compared to that of AT_1 receptors as CHF develops.[23–26]

The AT_1 receptor appears responsible for the mediation of all the classical effects of angiotensin II.[22,27] Stimulation of the AT_2 receptor may cause vasodilatation and have antiproliferative effects but may also stimulate apoptosis which could have adverse effects on cardiovascular remodelling.[28,29] Thus the clinical effects of selective AT_1 receptor blockade could be superior, inferior or identical to those of nonselective blockade AT receptor blockade.

ARBs: basic pharmacology

All the ARBs licensed so far are AT_1 selective. In animal models short-term administration of AT_2 receptor antagonists has not generally exerted any effect.[27] Many ARBs are prodrugs, like many ACE inhibitors, and require metabolization to the active agent, although in some cases the parent compound also has weak ARB activity. A brief summary of some of the pharmacological properties of ARBs is shown in Table 14.1.[30]

Currently, among ARBs, the greatest experience is with losartan. The parent drug has a short half-life, about 2 hours, and a relatively low potency.[31] However, losartan undergoes oxidation in the liver to a much more potent metabolite that also has a longer half-life of about 7 hours.[32] The duration of the biological activity of losartan is much longer than the plasma half-life of either the parent drug or the metabolite would suggest. This is because the metabolite is tightly bound to the receptor and therefore inhibition persists despite elimination of free drug from the plasma: 80 mg of losartan inhibits the pressor effects of exogenous angiotensin II by 94% for up to 24 hours.[33] About 1% of the population do not appear able to convert losartan to its active metabolite, the significance of which is not clear.

Hepatic disease increases oral bioavailability and increases the half-life of losartan. Dose reduction is recommended in the presence of important intrinsic liver disease.[34,35] Renal disease has little effect on the kinetics of losartan or its metabolite, even in patients requiring dialysis.[34,35] Gender and age have only modest effects on pharmacokinetics.[34] No important interactions have been noted as yet with either warfarin or digoxin and any of the ARBs.[34]

An interesting ancillary property of losartan that may not be shared by other ARBs is a uricosuric effect.[36] This may reduce the risk of gout in the long term although increased urinary urate excretion could promote uric acid nephropathy. Further long-term studies are required.

Why might the effects of ARBs and ACE inhibitors differ?

ACE 'breakthrough'

Although acute administration of an ACE inhibitor reduces plasma angiotensin II to around the limit of detection, plasma

Drug	Prodrug	Absorption (%)	Site of activation	Type of AT_1 receptor antagonism	Plasma half-life	Potency versus EXP-3174	Protein binding (%)	Hepatic clearance (%)	Renal clearance (%)	Ancillary properties	Interactions	Dose range in hypertension (mg)
Losartan (active metabolite EXP-3174)	Yes	20–35	Hepatic, cytochrome p450	Mixed	2 h for parent drug, 7 h for major metabolite	Not applicable	>98	65	35	Uricosuric	None reported	50–100
Candesartan	Yes	42	GI tract (hydrolysis)	Noncompetitive	9 h		>99	67	33			8–16
Valsartan	No	23		Mixed	5–9 h		85–98	83	13		Absorption reduced by fatty food	80–160
Irbesartan	No	60–85	Not applicable	Noncompetitive (?)	11–12 h	1.5×	90	80	20			150–300
Eprosartan		13		Competitive	5–9 h		98	90	7		Absorption reduced by fatty food	400–800
Telmisartan		40		Mixed	16–23 h		?	99	1		Absorption reduced by fatty food	20–160
Tasosartan	Yes	??		Competitive	1–7 h		?	?	?			100–1200

For references see McInnes[32].

Table 14.1
Pharmacology of AT receptor antagonists

angiotensin II (even when technically robust sampling and assay methods are used) and aldosterone are often not suppressed after several months of treatment.[37] Poor compliance might be responsible in some instances for the apparent loss of ACE inhibition but the problem appears too prevalent to be accounted for by poor compliance alone. ACE inhibition leads to an accumulation of the precursor for angiotensin II, angiotensin I. While 80% ACE inhibition may be enough to suppress angiotensin II formation at normal levels of angiotensin I, much more intense inhibition may be required in the presence of increased substrate. Thus while small doses (e.g. 5 mg of enalapril or lisinopril) of an ACE inhibitor may be adequate to suppress angiotensin II initially, much larger doses (e.g. 35 mg lisinopril or 40 mg of enalapril) may be required for long-term inhibition. Increasing levels of angiotensin I may also be converted to angiotensin II through ACE-independent pathways.[38] ARBs block the downstream effects of angiotensin II and therefore it does not matter by which route it is generated.

AT$_2$ receptor stimulation

Activation of the RAAS is normally limited by negative feedback of angiotensin II on the AT$_1$ receptor. ARBs block the AT$_1$ receptor and therefore release the RAAS from negative feedback. Accordingly plasma concentrations of angiotensin II rise and consequently stimulation of the unblocked AT$_2$ receptor may increase. Therefore, unlike ACE inhibitors, ARBs may increase stimulation of the AT$_2$ receptor which may, or may not, be beneficial (see above).

Bradykinin–prostaglandin and other pathways

ACE inhibitors, unlike ARBs, increase bradykinin[39] and hence nitric oxide and vasodilator and antiaggregatory prostaglandins. This could confer additional vasodilator, antithrombotic and antiatherogenic effects on ACE inhibitors as well as having favourable effects on cardiovascular remodelling.[16,40] However, bradykinin appears to increase cardiac sympathetic activity[17] and this could have an adverse effect on outcome, especially in the absence of a beta-blocker. Neutralization of the prostaglandin-mediated effects of ACE inhibition could account for the possible adverse interaction between aspirin and ACE inhibitors.[41]

ACE inhibitors may also inhibit other enzymes, for instance neutral endopeptidase or matrix metalloproteinases that could have beneficial effects on symptoms or cardiovascular remodelling.

Effects on haematocrit

ACE inhibitors cause haematocrit to fall, either because of haemodilution or because of a fall in red cell volume due to a decline in erythropoietin, an effect either mediated directly or through an improvement in renal blood flow.[42,43] Haemodilution, could reduce oxygen uptake and transport and detract from the benefits of ACE inhibitors on symptoms and functional capacity. However, reducing haematocrit could also reduce the risk of thrombotic events. There are data to suggest that ARBs also may reduce haematocrit.[5]

Electrophysiological and autonomic effects

One study of losartan suggests that ARBs may reduce sudden death to a greater extent than ACE inhibitors. Compared to captopril, losartan appeared to prevent progressive electrical remodelling and QT dispersion.[44] However, Binkley et al studied the effects of losartan on heart rate variability (HRV) in a double-blind placebo-controlled study of 35 patients with

CHF.[45] Losartan tended to reduce parasympathetically mediated high-frequency HRV and increase sympathetically mediated low-frequency HRV. The lack of a beneficial increase in parasympathetic activity contrasts with the effect of ACE inhibitors. Whether any superiority of ARBs on sudden death reflects an effect on arrhythmias or vascular events remains open to doubt.

Uricosuric effect

The apparently specific uricosuric effect of losartan could do more than just protect against gout. Plasma concentrations of uric acid may be a marker of oxidant stress[46] that in turn may have adverse effects on cardiac and vascular function. Whether these properties are shared by other ARBs is not clear as yet.

Tolerability

ARBs may also be better tolerated than, at least, some ACE inhibitors.[7,47] Only if a drug is taken can it be effective and therefore greater tolerability may translate into greater efficacy. ARBs have generally been better tolerated than placebo in studies of hypertension, although it should be pointed out that fewer patients have generally withdrawn from ACE inhibitors than placebo in studies of CHF.[48,49] Losartan was better tolerated than captopril in the ELITE study.[7]

Will the combination of ACE inhibitors and ARBs prove superior to either class alone?

Renin secretion is suppressed by angiotensin II and AT_1 receptor antagonists increase plasma renin by releasing it from this negative feedback loop. As renin rises so does angiotensin I and consequently angiotensin II.[50,51] Just as the effects of ACE inhibition may be overcome by competition from rising concentrations of angiotensin I so AT_1 inhibition may be overcome by rising concentrations of angiotensin II, either by displacing ARBs that bind reversibly to the AT_1 receptor or by stimulating unblocked receptors more powerfully.

Rather than being alternatives it is possible that the actions of ARBs and ACE inhibitors are complimentary. ACE inhibition could prevent the rise in angiotensin II associated with ARBs, thereby reducing competition for binding of the antagonist to the AT_1 receptor and protecting unblocked AT_1 receptors, while ARBs could block the effects of any residual angiotensin II formed despite ACE inhibition. Studies already show that the rise in angiotensin II induced by an ARB can be attenuated by ACE inhibition, at least in the short term, while addition of an ARB to an ACE inhibitor results in a further decline in aldosterone, indicating better renin–angiotensin system blockade.[52–54]

Troublesome issues

ACE inhibitors improve haemodynamics, symptoms and prognosis but the extent to which these clinical outcomes are interrelated is unclear. It is quite possible that different types of benefit with ACE inhibitors are mediated through different pathways. Demonstration that the haemodynamic actions of ACE inhibitors and ARBs are the same suggests that the haemodynamic effects of ACE inhibitors are mediated through the AT_1 receptor. However, haemodynamic equivalence cannot be assumed to indicate equivalent effects on symptoms and prognosis.

Surprisingly, after 15 years of research we still know comparatively little about the optimal dose of any ACE inhibitor for CHF.[55,56]

This is a very important issue because, when comparing the effects of two classes of drugs, it is important to know that merely changing the dose of one or other drug would not have replicated any difference observed or if no difference was observed that this did not reflect the use of an inadequate dose of one or other drug. The NETWORK study showed no difference in outcome from 2.5 mg, 5 mg or 10 mg bd of enalapril over 6 months,[57] while the ATLAS study suggested a greater morbidity/mortality benefit with 35 mg compared to 5 mg/day of lisinopril over 46 months.[58] However, these studies still do not show what the optimal long-term dose is — for instance lisinopril 20 or 100 mg/day could be the optimal dose.

Effects of AT₁ receptor antagonists in animal experiments

In animal preparations losartan inhibits the actions of angiotensin II, including vasoconstriction, increased myocardial contractility, smooth muscle cell growth, myocardial hypertrophy, collagen synthesis by myocardial fibroblasts and cardiac myocyte necrosis.[59–61] Losartan also inhibits the neuroendocrine actions of angiotensin II, including adrenal medullary release of adrenaline, noradrenaline release from sympathetic nerve terminals, renal renin release and endothelial endothelin-1 production, and angiotensin II mediated increases in proximal tubular salt and water retention.[27,62–64] In experimental CHF losartan improves central haemodynamics,[65,66] reduces atrial natriuretic peptide,[66] increases renal blood flow[66,67] and, in high cardiac output models, increases urine volume.[68]

In a murine model of myocarditis an ARB helped preserve ventricular function[69] and val-

sartan retarded adverse ventricular remodelling in a canine, coronary microembolization model of CHF.[70] Schieffer et al[71] noted similar benefits from enalapril and losartan on myocardial hypertrophy and interstitial fibrosis. In a dog model of CHF induced by repeated DC shocks, ramipril but not losartan delayed the onset of CHF; a bradykinin antagonist attenuated the benefit observed with the ACE inhibitor suggesting an important influence of bradykinin on the remodelling process.[16] Some investigators have found that antagonists of the AT₂ receptor may more closely simulate the effects of an ACE inhibitor on ventricular remodelling.[72] Also, some studies suggest that ACE inhibitors may be more effective than ARBs in reducing myocardial hypertrophy both in animals[73] and in human hypertension.[74–76] However, animal models also suggest that there may be beneficial synergistic haemodynamic effects between ARBs and ACE inhibitors.[77,78]

In a comparative study, 360 cardiomyopathic hamsters were randomized to placebo, quinapril or two different doses of losartan.[79] Survival improved only in the group treated with quinapril. Animals on high-dose losartan had reduced survival compared to placebo; low-dose losartan was neutral. Studies of murine myocarditis have also suggested less favourable effects of ARBs than ACE inhibitors on outcome.[80] However, ARBs have been shown to improve survival in some animal models of hypertension and hypertrophy.[27,35,38]

Human studies

Acute haemodynamic effects of ARBs compared to placebo in patients with CHF

A single-dose study randomized 66 patients to placebo or losartan in one of five doses

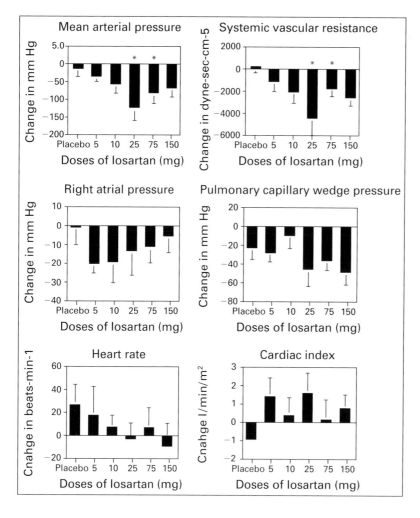

Figure 14.2

Bar graphs of change in haemodynamic parameters by area-under-the-curve analysis after administration of placebo and five doses of losartan (5 mg, 10 mg, 25 mg, 75 mg, and 150 mg). Increasing vasodilator response was noted up to a dose of 25 mg. (* – significance (P < 0.05) compared with placebo.) (From Lang et al[50])

($N = 10$ per dose).[50] Losartan 25 mg reduced systemic vascular resistance (SVR) by about 20% and arterial pressure by 10–15 mmHg. Trends to an increase in cardiac index (about 0.2 l/min/m²) and reduction in pulmonary capillary wedge pressure (placebo-corrected change 3–4 mmHg) and heart rate (3–4 bpm) were generally not significant (Figure 14.2). The effects persisted for at least 24 hours. The haemodynamic effects of losartan 5, 10, 75 and 150 mg trended in the same direction as the 25 mg dose but were generally not significantly different from placebo.

We reported a haemodynamic study before and after 3 months dosing[51] with losartan at doses of 2.5 mg, 10 mg, 25 mg and 50 mg in a substantially larger group of patients (22–29 per group). Mean arterial pressure fell by up to 10 mmHg after the 25- and 50-mg doses but otherwise haemodynamics improved little after acute dosing. Cardiac output and heart rate were essentially unchanged and mean PCWP (placebo corrected) fell acutely by no more than 3 mmHg, while SVR declined only with the 50-mg dose. However, some cases of symptomatic first-dose hypotension were noted with higher initializing doses although only partially reported in the paper.

A preliminary report from a substantial ($N = 96$) placebo-controlled study of irbesartan[81] suggested similar acute haemodynamic effects to the above, with inconsistent changes in heart rate and cardiac index. Mean arterial pressure fell by 6–8 mmHg, SVR by about 20% and PCWP by 3–7 mmHg (all placebo corrected) with doses of 100–200 mg.

In summary, the acute haemodynamic response to ARBs appears generally modest and broadly similar to that observed with ACE inhibitors. However, as with ACE inhibitors, some patients are prone to marked, symptomatic hypotension. It is not clear to what extent this can be avoided by starting with lower doses. It is also important to realize that the patients in these studies were selected for not being on an ACE inhibitor for some reason and therefore tended either to be 'new' patients, often with rather mild CHF or patients who had been withdrawn from ACE inhibitors because of side-effects. Patients with symptomatically mild CHF may have less neuroendocrine activation and less haemodynamic disturbance making it difficult to show changes even with active treatments.

Chronic haemodynamic effects of ARBs compared to placebo in patients with CHF

In our study, after 3 months therapy and 12 hours following a further dose, 25 mg of losartan reduced SVR by about 20%, PCWP by 5 mmHg, blood pressure by 6 mmHg and heart rate by 6 bpm (all placebo-corrected) and increased cardiac index (0.3–0.4 l/min/m²; Figure 14.3).[51] The 50-mg dose exerted similar, but no greater an effect. Other doses exerted less consistent effects, although it is notable that the 2.5-mg dose appeared to

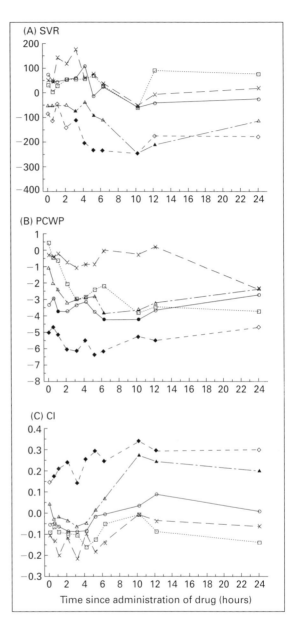

Figure 14.3

Plots of mean change from pretreatment baseline levels after 12 weeks of therapy in (A) systemic vascular resistance, (B) pulmonary capillary wedge pressure, and (C) cardiac index. Placebo; ○ losartan 2.5 mg; □ losartan 10 mg; △ losartan 25 mg; ◇ losartan 50 mg. Shaded symbols indicate a significant difference (P ≤ 0.05) between losartan and placebo groups.[51]*

retain some effect in reducing PCWP. Only the 50-mg dose reduced cardiothoracic ratio significantly over 3 months. Thus, as with ACE inhibitors the long-term haemodynamic benefits were generally modest.

Havranek et al randomized 218 patients into a 12-week study comparing 12.5 mg (presumed no effect dose), 37.5 mg, 75 mg or 150 mg irbesartan.[82] The study showed a 3–4 mmHg greater fall in PCWP with the 75–150-mg dose with variable falls in mean arterial pressure (1–5 mmHg — corrected for the fall in the lowest-dose group). Trends to a decline in heart rate and rise in ejection fraction with the higher dose were not significant. Trends to fewer discontinuations for worsening CHF were also noted with higher doses.

A 4-week study comparing lisinopril ($N = 14$) and 40 mg ($N = 19$), 80 mg ($N = 21$) or 160 mg ($N = 25$) bd valsartan and placebo also reported that valsartan reduced blood pressure by 8–11 mmHg, PCWP by 4–8 mmHg and SVR compared to placebo and increased cardiac output.[83] Lisinopril exerted similar effects.

Neuroendocrine effects

Neuroendocrine variables were measured in several of the above studies. The single-dose study of losartan showed increases in plasma renin activity and a decline in aldosterone and angiotensin II as predicted.[50] As with ACE inhibitors, inconsistent falls in plasma noradrenaline were noted with doses of 25 mg and above. The fall in aldosterone 6-hours postdosing was observed with doses as low as 10 mg. The long-term study of losartan showed reductions in aldosterone after 12 weeks of the 10-, 25- and 50-mg doses of losartan.[51] Increases in renin and angiotensin II after acute dosing were not present after 12 weeks. Norepinephrine changed little if at all (Figure 15.4). A secondary report from our

study[84] showed that the 25- and 50-mg doses of losartan reduced plasma concentrations of N-terminal proatrial natriuretic peptide and that this correlated with the decline in PCWP.

Neuroendocrine effects of ARBs have also been reported in long-term studies comparing ARBs and ACE inhibitors. Dickstein et al in a substantial study ($N = 166$) reported no difference in effect between losartan 25–50 mg/day and enalapril 20 mg/day on plasma concentrations of norepinephrine or N-terminal proatrial natriuretic peptide.[85] The ELITE study, comparing captopril and losartan over 48 weeks also showed no difference in norepinephrine.[7] A small ($N = 16$) crossover study with 3-week treatment periods suggested similar changes in aldosterone and renin activity with losartan and enalapril while trends to a greater reduction in norepinephrine with enalapril were not significantly different.[86] The RESOLVD study also suggested similar effects of enalapril and candesartan on aldosterone and norepinephrine although the combination reduced aldosterone further.[54] The RAAS-pilot study suggested that addition of losartan 50 mg to 10 mg bd of enalapril reduced aldosterone compared to enalapril 10 mg bd or 20 mg bd.[52] The higher dose of enalapril and combination therapy also tended to reduce plasma noreprinephrine more.

Effects of ARBs compared to placebo on clinical outcomes in patients with CHF

Haemodynamic studies
Data gleaned from two moderately large, medium-term haemodynamic studies in patients with treated CHF but not receiving an ACE inhibitor suggest that symptoms of CHF were improved by ARBs (Table 14.2).[51,82] Three deaths were reported in the long-term study of losartan, at least two of these on inef-

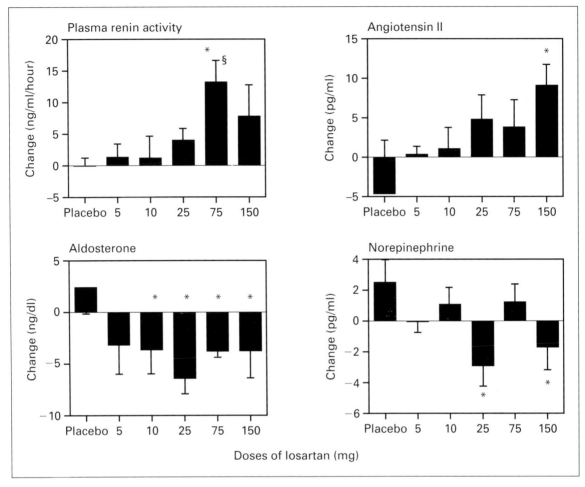

Figure 14.4
Bar graphs of neurohormonal response by area-under-the-curve analysis after administration of placebo and five doses of losartan. Logarithmic values are displayed. Plasma renin activity and plasma angiotensin II concentrations increased with increasing doses of losartan. Aldosterone and noradrenaline concentrations decreased following losartan administration.
* Significance (P < 0.05) compared with placebo;
§ significance compared with 25 mg losartan (From Lang et al[50])

fective doses of losartan (2.5 mg/day) and one on 10 mg/day. A further two deaths occurred in relation to losartan in the short-term haemodynamic study. No deaths occurred on placebo.

Exercise testing studies

A study to assess exercise capacity in the US ($N = 351$) showed a nonsignificant reduction in mortality over 12 weeks from 3.5% to 1.7%, while in an international study ($N = 385$) mortality fell from 6.9% to 1.2%

Drug	Outcome	Placebo	2.5 mg	10 mg	25 mg	50 mg
Losartan (N = 134)[51]	Worsening	Placebo 26%	NR	20%	10%	9%
	Improvement	NR	NR	NR	48%	52%
Irbesartan (N = 218)[82]	Discontinuation for worsening	Placebo Not studied	12.5 mg 9.3%	37.5 mg 11.1%	75 mg 3.6%	150 mg 1.8%
Candesartan (N = 926)[88]	Symptoms and exercise capacity	Placebo —	—	4 mg	8 mg	16 mg

Improvement in symptoms with all doses of candesartan compared to placebo. Dose-related improvement in exercise capacity

Trends to prevention of worsening with higher doses were not statistically significant in the studies with losartan and irbesartan.
NR = not reported.

Table 14.2
Dose response studies with ARBs in CHF and clinical outcome

	Placebo	Candesartan
Death	3.3%	3.4%
Myocardial infarction	5.5%	2.8%
Stroke	1.1%	0%
Symptomatic hypotension	0%	5%
All hospitalizations	18.7%	12.6%
CHF hospitalizations	12.1%	8.4%
Death or CHF hospitalization	14.5%	11.7%
Any serious adverse event	23%	18%

Table 14.3
SPICE (Study of Patients Intolerant to Converting Enzyme Inhibitors)[89]

$(P < 0.05)$.[87] A prespecified combined analysis showed a reduction in mortality and CHF-related hospitalization, although neither trial showed an improvement in exercise capacity, the primary endpoint, or symptoms. The latter may reflect the fact that only very mild patients were recruited due to concerns about placing patients on placebo for 3 months.

A large study compared the effects of candesartan and placebo on symptoms and exercise capacity.[88] Patients ($N = 926$) with CHF, ejection fraction of 30–45% but not receiving an ACE inhibitor were enrolled. Of these, 844 patients were randomly assigned to candesartan 4 mg ($N = 208$), 8 mg ($N = 212$) or 16 mg ($N = 213$) or placebo ($N = 211$) once daily for 3 months. Candesartan produced a dose-dependent increase in total exercise time compared with baseline that was statistically significant compared to placebo for the highest dose. Improvements in signs and symptoms of CHF and NYHA class were significantly greater with all doses of candesartan than with placebo ($P = 0.0001$). A similar frequency and profile of adverse events was observed in both the placebo- and candesartan-treated patients.

One small ($N = 16$) crossover study with 3-week treatment periods suggested an improvement in exercise capacity with losartan, the increase in exercise being similar to that observed on enalapril.[86] Interestingly, the improvement in exercise capacity with enalapril but not losartan was reversed with the addition of aspirin 325 mg/day.

Safety and tolerance studies
The SPICE study screened 9580 patients with CHF and ejection fraction no more than 35% to identify ACE intolerant patients. Of the patients 9% were found to be intolerant of ACE inhibitors mainly due to cough or hypotension, and 179 were randomized to candesartan (titrated to 16 mg/day) or placebo and followed for 12–14 weeks.[89] Trends in favour of candesartan were not statistically significant (Table 14.3).

Although many of the above studies missed their primary endpoint all of the above studies suggested benefit with the use of an ARB in some way or another and none suggested any adverse impact on symptoms, morbidity or mortality. Overall these data provide compelling evidence that ARBs exert clinical benefits compared to placebo in CHF although differences between ARBs may exist.

Effects of ARBs compared to ACE inhibitors on clinical outcomes in patients with CHF

Five substantial studies have compared the effects of ARBs with ACE inhibitors on exercise capacity and symptoms.[7,54,85,90,91] None has reported a significant difference in these outcomes. The ELITE and RESOLVD studies are reported in greater detail because they are the largest long-term studies reported so far.

ELITE (Evaluation of Losartan in the Elderly Study)[7]

ELITE randomized 722 patients to captopril 50 mg tid or losartan 50 mg once daily in a double-blind study of 48 weeks duration. The primary endpoint was an increase in serum creatinine of at least 26.5 µmol/l (0.3 mg/dl) which, as an index of an important adverse effect on renal function, appears arbitrary and unlikely to make most clinicians withdraw ACE inhibitor therapy or take any other action. The secondary endpoint, death and/or admission for CHF, was formulated after patient recruitment was complete after the results of other studies had become known. Analyses of all-cause mortality and hospital admission for CHF were other prespecified outcomes of interest and an analysis of all-cause hospital admission was conducted as a further exploratory analysis.

Patient selection

Patients had to be at least 65 years of age and two-thirds were at least 70 years; the mean age was 73 years. Two-thirds were in NYHA class II and one-third in class III. Only 74% of patients were receiving diuretics, a powerful stimulus to neuroendocrine activation in heart failure, the substrate upon which ARBs and ACE inhibitors probably work. Over 80% of patients were in NYHA class I or II by the study end in both groups. The mean ejection fraction was 30%. Patients with renal dysfunction (serum creatinine ≥221 µmol/l (2.5 mg/dl)) were excluded and thus a population at low risk of developing serious adverse renal events was identified. The mean baseline serum creatinine was 106 µmol/l (1.2 mg/dl). Compared to SOLVD-treatment, the ELITE population was about a decade older but appeared to have milder CHF, as the ejection fraction was considerably higher and diuretic use was lower.

Results

There was no difference in outcome with respect to changes in serum creatinine with 10.5% of patients having an increase of at least 26.5 µmol/l. There was a trend to a greater increase in serum potassium with captopril but it is not clear if this should be considered beneficial or not.

Losartan reduced overall mortality by 46% (relative risk reduction, $P < 0.04$) and this was largely due to a reduction in sudden deaths (64%, $P < 0.05$) and death due to myocardial infarction (76%, NS; Table 14.4). Death due to progressive CHF occurred in only one patient in each group, perhaps reflecting an appropriately rigid definition of death due to progressive CHF. Only 5.7% of patients in each group were hospitalized for CHF over 48 weeks suggesting that the patients in ELITE had relatively mild CHF. These data also support the view that progressive CHF is a relatively uncommon contributor to death in patients with mild CHF treated with ACE inhibitors and that losartan is as effective as an ACE inhibitor in this respect. Losartan and

	Losartan (50 mg per day)	Captopril (50 mg tid)	RR
Number	352	370	
Mortality			
Total	17 (4.8%)	32 (8.7%)	0.46 $P = 0.035$
Sudden	5 (1.4%)	14 (3.8%)	0.64 NS
Hospital admission			
Total	78 (22.2%)	110 (29.7%)	0.26 $P = 0.014$
For CHF	20 (5.7%)	21 (5.7%)	0.04 NS
Death or hospital admission for CHF	33 (9.4%)	49 (13.2%)	0.32 $P = 0.075$
Adverse events			
Renal function (rise of >26.5 µmol/l or 0.3 mg/dl)	10.5%	10.5%	NS
First dose hypotension	$N = 4$	$N = 7$	
Hypotensive symptoms	24%	24%	
Withdrawals			
Total	65 (19%)	111 (30%)	$P < 0.002$
For AE	43 (12%)	77 (21%)	$P < 0.002$
For cough	None	14 (4%)	$P < 0.002$
For renal dysfunction	5	3	
For worsening CHF	3	9	

Table 14.4
ELITE study (follow-up 48 weeks)[7]. RR = risk reduction.

captopril exerted similar benefits on symptoms. However, nine patients discontinued captopril because of worsening CHF but only three discontinued losartan. Changes in plasma norepinephrine, a potential marker of progressive ventricular dysfunction were not significantly different between groups.

Despite reducing mortality, which leaves more people at risk of hospitalization, losartan reduced all-cause hospitalization by 26% over and above any effect of captopril (Table 14.4). No specific reasons for this difference are apparent so far but perhaps this may reflect the lower side-effect profile and better tolerability of losartan. Over 70% of patients were maintained on the target dose of both losartan and captopril while 85% achieved the target dose at some time in the study. Overall, 20.8% of captopril-treated patients withdrew because of side-effects versus 12.2% of losartan-treated patients ($P < 0.002$) (Table 14.4). This difference was largely due to a lower risk of cough, taste disturbance, angiooedema and worsening CHF: 3.8% of patients discontinued captopril due to cough versus none on losartan ($P < 0.002$). There was no difference in the rate of hypotensive symptoms (24%).

Only when an effective drug is ingested can its benefits be realized. Thus losartan could have proved superior to an ACE inhibitor not because it was more effective but because it was more likely to be taken. Excluding deaths, 18.2% of patients discontinued losartan for any reason versus 28.6% of those on captopril ($P < 0.001$) but this did not account for the difference in survival (3.7 versus 8.5% for those remaining on therapy with losartan or captopril respectively, $P = 0.013$).

Health economic issues

Healthcare resource utilization data were collected during the ELITE study.[92] The mean in-trial (48 weeks) cost of the captopril treatment group was $2487 and of the losartan group $2151 (NS) although captopril was not costed at its generic price which made it a rather expensive option among ACE inhibitors. None the less, the analysis does suggest that the potential benefits of losartan in the ELITE study could be attained at little or no extra cost. Projecting beyond the trial, losartan was estimated to result in net savings of $1235 and a gain of 0.27 years per patient over a lifetime. The estimates of lifetime cost-effectiveness for losartan ranged from cost-saving to $1598 per year of life gained. The assumption that there was no further mortality benefit from losartan beyond the end of the study, which limits long-term costs (dead patients do not have continuing healthcare costs), biases the economic analysis in favour of losartan but, none the less, again indicates that the potential benefits of losartan do not appear expensive in terms of health economics.

Substudies

A substudy on 29 patients suggested that captopril and losartan exerted equal effects on ventricular function during treatment but that the effect of captopril may persist for longer after drug withdrawal.[93]

An ECG substudy was conducted on 114 patients.[44] This showed an increase in QT dispersion on captopril but not losartan over the course of the study. This may reflect a superior effect of losartan on the substrate for arrhythmias among patients with CHF.

In another substudy, 278 patients were enrolled in a quality of life study of which 203 completed questionnaires before and after treatment (Sickness Impact Profile, Minnesota Living with Heart Failure). Trends in favour of losartan were not significant after adjustment for multiple analyses[94] but significantly fewer patients withdrew from losartan for adverse events. Patients who withdrew for adverse events were unavailable for the second questionnaire which biased this substudy against losartan.

Losartan studies meta-analysis

A meta-analysis of mortality data from the six multiple-dose heart failure studies (1154 losartan; 466 ACEI, 274 placebo) found the odds of dying in the control group significantly greater than in the losartan group (odds ratio 1.98 (95% CI 1.24–3.17).[95] Hospitalization for worsening heart failure observed with losartan was 4.9% compared to 6.2% in the control group in the six multiple-dose studies.

RESOLVD pilot

RESOLVD[47,53,54] (Table 14.5) was a randomized, double-blind trial in 768 patients evaluating three doses of candesartan alone (4, 8 and 16 mg/day) compared to enalapril alone (20 mg daily) and two doses of combination treatment (enalapril 20 mg/day plus candesartan 4 mg/day or enalapril 20 mg/day plus candesartan 8 mg/day). Exercise tolerance (6-minute walk test), ventricular function, neurohormonal parameters, NYHA class and quality of life were assessed. The age of the patients was 63 ± 11 years and they were fol-

	Enalapril	Candesartan	Enalapril and candesartan
Number	109	327	332
Mortality	4 (3.7%)	(6.1%)	(8.7%)

Table 14.5
RESOLVD pilot (follow-up 44 weeks)[54]

lowed for 43 weeks. Baseline characteristics were similar between treatment groups. Except that 23% of enalapril patients received beta-blockers versus 14% of others.

Results

No differences between groups in the 6-minute walk test, quality of life, heart rate or ejection fraction were noted. Patients treated with the combination of enalapril and candesartan had a greater reduction in blood pressure, a smaller increase in end-diastolic and systolic volumes and greater reductions in aldosterone and brain natriuretic peptide over the course of the study.[54] RESOLVD was stopped prematurely due to a higher incidence of deaths in the candesartan (6.1%) and combination groups (8.7%) than in the enalapril group (3.7%).

Comparison of ELITE and RESOLVD pilot results

There are multiple possible interpretations of the results of these studies. It is possible that losartan is superior to candesartan. Another interpretation is that enalapril could be superior to captopril. The most likely explanation is that the observed differences were due to chance, at least in their magnitude if not direction. It would be premature to conclude that ARBs are superior to ACE inhibitors (in terms of symptoms, morbidity or mortality) but this should not detract from the evidence of superiority of ARBs over placebo.

Addition of ARBs to ACE inhibitors

As outlined above there is a rationale for combining ACE inhibitors and ARBs. A series of small studies has suggested benefit. Hamroff et al[96] reported that the addition of losartan to treatment with ACE inhibitors (N = 43) was well tolerated despite reducing systolic blood pressure by 10–15 mmHg even in patients who had developed symptomatic hypotension on attempted uptitration of ACE inhibitors. Renal function and serum potassium did not change. In a double-blind placebo-controlled study of 32 patients they went on to show that losartan improved symptoms, exercise capacity and peak oxygen uptake.[97] Guazzi et al studied 15 patients in a crossover study with 8-week treatment periods comparing placebo, losartan 50 mg/day, enalapril 20 mg/day and their combination. Both agents improved peak oxygen consumption and the combination appeared to have additive benefits.[98] Tocchi et al randomized 42 patients to losartan 50 mg/day and 31 to placebo on top of conventional treatment with diuretics and ACE inhibitors and showed that losartan slightly reduced echocardiographic left ventricular volumes (3–8 ml/m^2) and improved ejection fraction at rest and during exercise by about 3–4%.[99]

However, other studies have not shown clear evidence of benefit from the addition of an ARB to an ACE inhibitor although these have generally indicated that the combination is safe and well tolerated. The RAAS pilot study showed no significant benefit of adding losartan to enalapril although the combination appeared well tolerated.[52] Houghton et al suggested that adding losartan to an ACE inhibitor improved pedometer scores in a placebo-controlled study of 20 patients.[100] However, there was no improvement in corridor walk time, treadmill exercise time, non-invasive haemodynamics, NYHA class or neuroendocrine profile. Murdoch et al randomized patients with CHF to eprosartan 400–800 mg daily ($N = 18$), or matching placebo ($N = 18$) for 8 weeks in a double-blind study.[101] Haemodynamics were measured by thermodilution catheter. The addition of the ARB to the ACE inhibitor had little effect on resting haemodynamics apart from a small reduction in SVR. In a study of 12 weeks' duration Tonkon et al[102] compared irbesartan ($N = 57$) with placebo ($N = 52$) in addition to standard treatment with diuretics and ACE inhibitors. Trends to a greater improvement in exercise capacity and left ventricular ejection fraction with irbesartan were not significant, but more patients required an increase in diuretic therapy on placebo compared to irbesartan (21% versus 12%). Finally the RESOLVD study suggested that combination therapy exerted superior effects on neuroendocrine activation and ventricular remodelling but no benefit in terms of symptoms or exercise capacity were observed. However, as noted above, the study did show trends to increased mortality with combination therapy.

In summary, a series of small studies suggest that ARBs may exert favourable effects when added to an ACE inhibitor. Whether these effects could be reproduced merely by increasing the dose of the ACE inhibitor remains uncertain.[47] These studies do suggest that combination therapy is relatively safe and in a patient who is deteriorating despite adequate conventional therapy a therapeutic trial of combination therapy appears a reasonable option.

Diastolic CHF

Diastolic CHF remains a poorly defined entity but may be common especially among elderly patients with CHF. Metzger et al[103] performed a randomized, double-blind, placebo-controlled, crossover study of 2 weeks of losartan (50 mg/day) with a 2-week washout period on 21 patients with normal LV systolic function (EF > 55%), no evidence of ischaemia, a mitral flow velocity E/A < 1, normal resting SBP (<150 mmHg), but a hypertensive response to exercise (SBP > 200 mmHg). The primary outcome measures were exercise tolerance and quality of life. After 2 weeks of losartan, peak SBP during exercise decreased by 30 mmHg ($P < 0.01$), and exercise time increased by about 60 s compared to placebo. Quality of life improved with losartan compared to baseline and placebo.

Adverse effect profile: are there advantages of ARBs over ACE inhibitors?
Cough

A persistent dry cough in undoubtedly a side-effect of ACE inhibitors, especially among women.[104] However the amount of disability it causes is unclear. Cough is reported spontaneously as an adverse effect in studies of ACE inhibitors in only about 3–4% of cases, little higher than with placebo.[49,105] Some patients have a severe cough due to ACE inhibitors but surprisingly, even if severe, do not report it spontaneously, believing the side-effect to be part of their illness. Cough can be disabling, physically tiring the patient and disrupting sleep; undoubtedly some patients 'cough themselves to death'. Cough does not appear to be a side-effect of ARBs.[5,106]

The mechanism underlying ACE inhibitor-induced cough is unclear. The most popular theory is that ACE inhibitors increase pulmonary bradykinin and that this induces cough directly or indirectly by increasing prostaglandin and thromboxane synthesis.[107,108] Nonsteroidal anti-inflammatory drugs have enjoyed mixed success for the relief of cough but are of course strongly contraindicated in patients with CHF due to their adverse renal effects.[107] Switching ACE inhibitors occasionally helps but this may have more to do with the interruption of therapy than real differences between ACE inhibitors. Anecdotally, ACE inhibitors may perpetuate cough due to a respiratory tract infection; a drug free interval may be all that is necessary to stop the cough, the patient then being able to resume the same treatment. A more recent approach is to use a mast cell stabilizer such as sodium cromoglycate.[109,110] ACE inhibitors cause angiotensin I to rise and this may be converted to angiotensin II in mast cells thereby destabilizing them. Switching patients who cough from ACE inhibitors to ARBs seems a reliable way to avoid cough and there is more evidence to show that ARBs are safe and beneficial in CHF than for other strategies for managing ACE inhibitor cough.

Angioneurotic oedema

Clinical trials of CHF have suggested that this side-effect of ACE inhibitors is rare and certainly less than 1%[49,105] The mechanisms underlying this reaction are also unclear but may be mediated by bradykinin and mast cells. Patients on renal dialysis are at greater risk of angioneurotic reactions.[111] ARBs precipitate angioneurotic reactions much less frequently than ACE inhibitors.[5,106]

Hypotension

The incidence of first-dose hypotension with ACE inhibitors has declined dramatically from the 11% recorded in the first cohort of the CONSENSUS study to around 2.2% in the SOLVD study (note that this was the combined incidence in the prevention and treatment arms, presumably the incidence would have been higher in the treatment arm as only these patients were receiving diuretics) (Table 14.6).[49,112–114] Also the data provided in the studies should be interpreted with caution because they fail to distinguish clearly between syncope, a haemodynamic crisis, and symptomless hypotension. Studies to resolve this problem are underway. Even if the incidence of first-dose syncope were 1% this would still be a major problem leading to thousands of life-threatening episodes worldwide each year.

It is not presently clear if ARBs are associated with a lower incidence of first-dose syncope. The single dose haemodynamic study discussed above noted a 3.7% (2/54) incidence of hypotension although it is not clear what proportion was symptomatic.[50] Five of 125 patients discontinued losartan due to hypotension on the first or second day of treatment in the 12-week study of losartan.[51] All of these episodes occurring with the 25- or 50-mg starting dose. No episode resulted in permanent harm. It would appear that as with ACE

Study	NYHA class	ACE inhibitor start dose	N	Symptomatic hypotension	Severe hypotension	Stroke or MI
CONSENSUS	IV	Enalapril 5 mg	34	NR	11.8% (N = 4)	NR
	IV	Enalapril 2.5 mg	219	NR	3.2% (N = 7)	NR
SOLVD	All	Enalapril 2.5 mg	7487	2.20% (N = 164)	0.50% (N = 37)	Stroke (N = 3)
	I or II	Enalapril 2.5 mg	6665*	1.83% (N = 122)	0.41% (N = 27)	Stroke (N = 2)
	III or IV	Enalapril 2.5 mg	882*	4.75% (N = 42)	1.09% (N = 10)	Stroke (N = 1)
SOLVD Hospitalized		Enalapril 2.5 mg	89	14.61% (N = 13)	2.25% (N = 2)	None
Hasford	III or IV	Enalapril 2.5 mg	1210	4.7% (N = 57)	0.5% (N = 6)	NR
Perindopril[118]	II or III	Perindopril 2 mg	513	NR	No first dose hypotension	NR
Post-infarction trials						
SAVE	I or II	Captopril 6.25 mg	2250	NR	0.84% (N = 19)	NR
AIRE	(II to III)	Ramipril 2.5 mg	1004	NR	NR	NR
TRACE	(I to II)	Trandolapril 0.5 mg	1788	NR	2.2% (N = 39)	NR
CONSENSUS-II	All MIs	Enalaprilat IV	3044	5% (placebo subtracted)	NR	NR
GISSI-3	All MIs	Lisinopril 5 mg	9435	5.3% (placebo subtracted)†	0.5% (placebo subtracted)†	No excess reported
ISIS-4	All MIs	Captopril 6.25 mg	29 028	~9% (placebo subtracted)	2.8% (placebo subtracted)	NR

*Recalculated.
†At any time over the 42 days of study.

Table 14.6
Hypotensive events associated with the initiation of ACE inhibitors

inhibitors it is wise to initiate treatment with a reduced dose of losartan and possibly monitor the patient for 3–4 hours until wider experience is gained.

Renal dysfunction

Renal dysfunction is most likely to occur when ACE inhibitors are given to very elderly patients (age >75 years), patients with severe CHF and those with pre-existing renal disease. Although the incidence of ACE inhibitor induced renal dysfunction is disputed, renal dysfunction due to ACE inhibitors is certainly perceived as a major problem by some renal physicians.[115] No differences in the effects of ACE inhibitors and ARBs on renal function in CHF have been noted so far. However, it is likely that patient selection excluded from clinical trials many patients at increased risk for renal dysfunction. Any difference between ACE inhibitors and losartan on uric acid excretion appears to be small.[90] In nondiabetic hypertensive patients losartan, like the ACE inhibitors, appears to reduce proteinuria.[116]

Study	Background ACE inhibitor?	Comparisons	Patient type	N	Primary endpoint	Recruitment	Reporting
ELITE II*[118,119]	No	Captopril 12.5–50 mg tid Losartan 12.5–50 mg/day	CHF Age >60 years NYHA II–IV EF <40%	3121	All-cause mortality	Complete June 1998	1999
ValHeFT	Yes	Placebo Valsartan 160 mg bd	CHF EF <40% LVEDD >29 mm/m²	4865	All-cause mortality	Complete December 1998	Expected Nov 2000
CHARM (1) (Systolic dysfunction)	Yes	Placebo Candesartan 4–16 mg/day	CHF EF <40%	2300	1. All-cause mortality or HF Hospitalization 2. All-cause mortality	Ongoing	Expected 2002
CHARM (2) (Normal systolic function)	No	Placebo Candesartan 4–16 mg/day	CHF EF >40%	2000	1. All-cause mortality or HF Hospitalization 2. All-cause mortality	Ongoing	Expected 2002
CHARM (3) (ACE inhibitor intolerant)	No	Placebo Candesartan 4–16 mg/day	CHF EF <40%	1700	1. All-cause mortality or HF Hospitalization 2. All-cause mortality	Ongoing	Expected 2002
OPTIMAAL	No	Captopril 12.5–50 mg tid Losartan 50 mg/day	<10 days from AMI Age >50 years Evidence of HF or major LVD	5000	All-cause mortality	Started February 1998	Expected 2001
VALIANT	Combination compared with either class alone	1. Captopril 50 mg tid 2. Valsartan 160 mg bd 3. Captopril 50 mg tid & Valsartan 80 mg bd	<10 days from AMI Evidence of HF or major LVD	14500	All-cause mortality	Ongoing	Expected 2002

*ELITE II failed to show that losartan was superior to captopril and was not powered to show if the agents were equivalent or not. Losartan was better tolerated than captopril

Table 14.7
Major ongoing studies with ARBs. ELITE II, Evaluation of Losartan in the Elderly II; Val-HeFT, Valsartan Heart Failure Trial; OPTIMAAL, Optimal Therapy in Myocardial Infarction with the Angiotensin II Antagonist Losartan; CHARM, Condesartan in Heart Failure: Assessment of Reduction in Morbidity and Mortality; VALIANT, Valsartan in the Acute Myocardial Infarction Trial.

Other side-effects

The only other important and/or frequent side-effect reported so far is headache, which appears twice as frequently with ARBs as placebo in patients with CHF, although ARBs appear to reduce the incidence of headache in hypertensive patients.[5,106] It is not likely to be a major problem for most patients and is probably similar to the frequency of headache with an ACE inhibitor.

Gout

Losartan appears to increase urinary uric acid excretion and reduce serum uric acid.[116,117] Although this effect may be welcome, the risk of precipitating acute gout and renal calculi in the chronically hyperuricaemic patients must be borne in mind. The long-term studies of ARBs have not shown a difference between ARBs and ACE inhibitors in the incidence of gout so far.

Studies in progress

A series of large outcome studies (Table 14.7) including patients with CHF or patients who have suffered large myocardial infarctions are currently underway. These should resolve many of the doubts surrounding the use of ARBs in CHF although they will not resolve whether there are clinically important differ-ences between them. The main thrust of these studies is to determine whether ARBs are superior to ACE inhibitors or whether they should be used in addition to them. There will be little more data forthcoming to show whether or not ARBs are superior to placebo.

Conclusions

ARBs are a step forward in the treatment of CHF. How big a step still remains open to question. The evidence that at least one ARB is superior to placebo in improving symptoms, morbidity and mortality appears convincing and ARBs can now be recommended for patients with CHF who are intolerant of ACE inhibitors or who have contraindications to them. In women, in whom the incidence of ACE inhibitor cough is high, and in patients with a history of multiple allergies that could predispose to angio-oedema some might con-sider ARBs as the initial treatment of choice. There is inadequate evidence to show that ARBs are superior to ACE inhibitors although their tolerability profile seems impressive. The evidence that ARBs exert benefit when added to an ACE inhibitor is encouraging but incon-clusive as yet. More evidence is required before it can be assumed that the benefits of ARBs represent a class effect. The ongoing studies of ARBs should answer most of the outstanding questions.

References

1. Messerli FH, Weber MA, Brunner HR. Angiotensin II receptor inhibition. A new therapeutic principle. *Arch Intern Med* 1996; **156**: 1957–1965.
2. Goodfriend TL, Elliot ME, Catt KJ. Angiotensin receptors and their antagonists. *N Engl J Med* 1996; **334**: 1649–1654.
3. Gradman AH, Arcuri KE, Goldberg AI et al. A randomized, placebo-controlled, double-blind, parallel study of various doses of losartan potassium compared with enalapril maleate in patients with essential hypertension. *Hypertension* 1995; **25**: 1345–1350.
4. Elmfeldt D, George M, Hubner R, Olofsson B. Candesartan cilexetil, a new generation angiotensin II antagonist, provides dose dependent antihypertensive effect. *J Hum Hypertens* 1997; **11**(suppl 2): S49–S53.
5. Belcher G, Hubner R, George M et al. Candesartan cilexetil: safety and tolerability in healthy volunteers and patients with hypertension. *J Hum Hypertens* 1997; **11**(suppl 2): S85–S89.
6. Lacourciere Y, Lefebvre J. Modulation of the renin–angiotensin–aldosterone system and cough. *Can J Cardiol* 1995; **11**: 33F–39F.
7. Pitt B, Segal R, Martinez FA et al, on behalf of the ELITE study group. Randomised trial of losartan versus captopril in patients over 65 with heart failure (Evaluation of losartan in the elderly study, ELITE). *Lancet* 1997; **349**: 747–752.
8. Zusman RM. Effects of converting-enzyme inhibitors on the renin–angiotensin–aldosterone, bradykinin, and arachidonic acid–prostaglandin systems: correlation of chemical structure and biological activity. *Am J Kidney Dis* 1987; **10**: 13–23.
9. Hornig B, Kohler C, Drexler H. Role of bradykinin in mediating vascular effects of angiotensin-converting enzyme inhibitors in humans. *Circulation* 1997; **95**: 1115–1118.
10. Cleland JGF. The renin–angiotensin system in heart failure. *Herz* 1991; **16**: 68–81.
11. Cleland JGF, Puri S. How do ACE inhibitors reduce mortality in patients with left ventricular dysfunction with and without heart failure: remodelling, resetting, or sudden death? *Br Heart J* 1994; **72**: S81–S86.
12. Cleland JGF, Kirkler D. Modification of atherosclerosis by agents that do not lower cholesterol. *Br Heart J* 1993; **69**: 54–62.
13. Lonn EM, Yusuf S, Jha P et al. Emerging role of angiotensin converting enzyme inhibitors in cardiac and vascular protection. *Circulation* 1994; **90**: 2056–2069.
14. Auch-Scwelk W, Kuchenbuch C, Claus M et al. Local regulation of vascular tone by bradykinin and angiotensin converting enzyme inhibitors. *Eur Heart J* 1993; **14**(suppl I): 154–160.
15. Cleland JGF, Bulpitt CJ, Falk RH et al. Is aspirin safe for patients with heart failure? *Br Heart J* 1995; **74**: 215–219.
16. McDonald KM, Rector T, Carlyle PF et al. Relative effects of alpha-1-adreonceptor blockade, converting enzyme inhibitor therapy and angiotensin II subtype 1 receptor blockade on ventricular remodelling in the dog. *Circulation* 1994; **90**: 3034–3046.
17. Minisi AJ, Thames MD. Distribution of left ventricular sympathetic afferents demonstrated by reflex responses to transmural myocardial ischaemia and to intracoronary and epicardial bradykinin. *Circulation* 1993; **87**: 240–246.
18. Morgan K, Wharton JM, Webb JC et al. Co-expression of renin–angiotensin system component genes in human atrial tissue. *J Hypertens* 1994; **12**(suppl): S11–S19.
19. Cleland JGF, Cowburn PJ, Morgan K. Neuroendocrine activation after myocardial infarction: causes and consequences. *Heart* 1996; **76**(suppl 3): 53–59.
20. Urata H, Healy B, Stewart RW et al. Angiotensin II-forming pathways in normal and failing human hearts. *Circ Res* 1990; **66**: 883–890.

21. Morgan K. The mechanism of ACE inhibitor actions. In: Cleland JGF, ed. *The Clinican's Guide to ACE Inhibition.* Edinburgh: Churchill Livingstone, 1993.

22. Smith RD, Timmermans C. Human angiotensin receptor subtypes. *Curr Opin Nephrol Hypertens* 1994; **3:** 112–122.

23. Haywood GA, Gullestad L, Katsuya T et al. AT-1 and AT-2 angiotensin receptor gene expression in human heart failure. *Circulation* 1997; **95:** 1201–1206.

24. Regitz-Zagrosek V, Friedel N, Heymann A et al. Regulation of the angiotensin receptor subtypes in cell cultures, animal models and human diseases. *Circulation* 1995; **91:** 1461–1471.

25. Regitz-Zagrosek V, Auch-Scwelk W, Neuss M, Fleck E. Regulation of the angiotensin subtypes in cell cultures, animal models and human diseases. *Eur Heart J* 1994; **15**(suppl D): 92–97.

26. Asano K, Dutcher DL, Port JD et al. Selective downregulation of the angiotensin II AT-1-receptor subtype in failing human ventricular myocardium. *Circulation* 1997; **95:** 1193–1200.

27. Timmermans PBM, Benfield P, Chiu AT et al. Angiotensin II receptors and functional correlates. *Am J Hypertens* 1992; **5:** 2215–2355.

28. Stoll M, Stecklings UM, Paul M et al. The angiotensin AT2-receptor mediates inhibition of cell proliferation in coronary endothelial cells. *J Clin Invest* 1995; **95:** 651–657.

29. Yamada T, Akishita M, Pollman MJ et al. Angiotensin II type 2 receptor mediates vascular smooth muscle cell apoptosis and antagonizes angiotensin II type I receptor action: an in vitro gene transfer study. *Life Sci* 1998; **63:** PL289–295.

30. McInnes GT. *Pocket Reference to Angiotensin II Antagonists.* London: Science Press, 1998; 1–47.

31. Lo MW, Goldberg MR, McCrea JB et al. Pharmacokinetics of losartan, an angiotensin II receptor antagonist, and its active metabolite EXP3174 in humans. *Clin Pharmacol Ther* 1995; **58:** 641–649.

32. Wong PC, Price WA, Chiu AT et al. Non-peptide angiotensin II receptor antagonists. XI: pharmacology of EXP 3174, an active metabolite of DuP 753, an orally active anti-hypertensive agent. *J Pharmacol Exp Ther* 1990; **255:** 211–217.

33. Christen Y, Waeber B, Nussberger J et al. Oral administration of DuP 753, a specific angiotensin II antagonist, to normal male volunteers: inhibition of pressor response to exogenous angiotensin I and II. *Circulation* 1991; **83:** 1333–1342.

34. Sweet CS, Rucinska EJ. Losartan in heart failure: preclinical experiences and initial clinical outcomes. *Eur Heart J* 1994; **15**(suppl D): 139–144.

35. Johnston CI. Angiotensin II receptor antagonists: focus on losartan. *Lancet* 1995; **346:** 1403–1407.

36. Burnier M, Waeber B, Brunner HR. The advantages of angiotensin II antagonism. *J Hypertens Suppl* 1994; **12:** S7–S15.

37. Pitt B. 'Escape' of aldosterone production in patients with left ventricular dysfunction treated with an angiotensin converting enzyme inhibitor: implications for therapy. *Cardiovasc Drugs Ther* 1995; **9:** 145–149.

38. Johnston CI, Risvanis J. Preclinical pharmacology of angiotensin II receptor antagonists. *Am J Hypertens* 1997; **10:** 306S–310S.

39. Cockcroft JR, Sciberras DG, Goldberg MR, Ritter JM. Comparison of angiotensin-coverting enzyme inhibition with angiotensin II. *Cardiovasc Pharmacol* 1993; **22:** 579–584.

40. Brown NJ, Nadeau JH, Vaughan DE. Selective stimulation of tissue-type plasminogen activator (t-PA) in vivo by infusion of bradykinin. *Thromb Haemost* 1997; **77:** 522–525.

41. Cleland JGF. Anticoagulant and antiplatelet therapy in heart failure. *Curr Opin Cardiol* 1997; **12:** 276–287.

42. Cleland JGF, Gillen G, Dargie HJ. The effects of frusemide and angiotensin-converting enzyme inhibitors and their combination on cardiac and renal haemodynamics in heart failure. *Eur Heart J* 1988; **9:** 132–141.

43. Herrlin B, Nyquist O, Sylven C. Induction of a reduction in haemoglobin concentration by enalapril in stable, moderate heart failure: a double blind study. *Br Heart J* 1991; **66:** 199–205.

44. Brooksby P, Cowley AJ, Segal R et al. Effects

of losartan and captopril on QT-dispersion in elderly patients with heart failure in the ELITE study: an initial assessment. *Eur Heart J* 1998; **19**:Abstract 858.

45. Binkley PF, Nunziata E, Leier CV. Selective AT-1 blockade with losartan does not restore autonomic balance in patients with heart failure. *J Am Coll Cardiol* 1998; **31**(suppl A): 250A.

46. Leyva F, Anker S, Swan JW et al. Serum uric acid as an index of impaired oxidative metabolism in chronic heart failure. *Eur Heart J* 1997; **18**: 858–865.

47. Richardson M, Cockburn N, Cleland JGF. Update of recent clinical trials in heart failure and myocardial infarction. *Eur J Heart Fail* 1999; **1**: 109–115.

48. Yusuf S, Nicklas JM, Timmis G et al. Effect of enalapril on mortality and the development of heart failure in asymptomatic patients with reduced left ventricular ejection fractions. *N Engl J Med* 1992; **327**: 685–691.

49. Kostis JB, Shelton B, Gosselin G et al. Adverse effects of enalapril in the Studies of Left Ventricular Dysfunction (SOLVD). *Am Heart J* 1996; **131**: 350–355.

50. Gottlieb SS, Dickstein K, Fleck E et al. Hemodynamic and neurohormonal effects of the angiotensin II antagonist losartan in patients with congestive heart failure. *Circulation* 1993; **88**: 1602–1609.

51. Crozier I, Ikram H, Awan N et al. Losartan in heart failure: hemodynamic effects and tolerability. *Circulation* 1995; **91**: 691–697.

52. Pitt B, Dickstein K, Benedict C et al. The randomized angiotensin receptor antagonist — ACE inhibitor study (RAAS) — pilot study. *Circulation* 1996; **94**(suppl): I–428 (abst).

53. Tsuyuki RT, Yusuf S, Rouleau JL et al. Combination neurohormonal blockade with ACE inhibitors, angiotensin II antagonists and beta-blockers in patients with congestive heart failure: design of the Randomized Evaluation of Strategies for Left Ventricular Dysfunction (RESOLVD) pilot study. *Can J Cardiol* 1997; **13**: 1166–1174.

54. McKelvie R, Yusuf S, Pericak D et al. Comparison of candesartan, enalapril, and their combination in congestive heart failure: a randomised evaluation of strategies for left ventricular dysfunction (RESOLVD pilot study). *Eur Heart J* 1998; Abstract suppl: Abstract 855.

55. Cleland JGF, Poole-Wilson PA. ACE inhibitors for heart failure: a question of dose. *Br Heart J* 1994; **72**: S106–S110.

56. Cleland JGF, McMurray JJF, Cowburn PJ. *Heart Failure: A Systematic Approach for Clinical Practice*. London: Science Press, 1997; 1–123.

57. The NETWORK Investigators. Clinical outcome with enalapril in symptomatic chronic heart failure; a dose comparison. *Eur Heart J* 1998; **19**: 481–489.

58. Cleland JGF, Massie BM, Packer M et al. Health economic benefits of treating patients with heart failure with high dose lisinopril versus low dose lisinopril: the Atlas Study. *Circulation* 1998; **98**: I-135.

59. Chiu AT, Roscooe WA, McCall DE, Timmermans PBMWM. Angiotensin II-1 receptors mediate both vasoconstrictor and hypertrophic responses in rat aortic smooth muscle cells. *Receptor* 1991; **1**: 133–140.

60. Kabour A, Henegar JR, Janicki JS. Angiotensin II induced myocyte necrosis: role of the angiotensin II receptor. *J Cardiovasc Pharmacol* 1994; **23**: 547–553.

61. Smits JFM, Vankrimpen C, Schoemaker RG et al. Angiotensin II receptor blockade after myocardial infarction in rats: effects on hemodynamics, myocardial DNA synthesis and interstital collagen content. *J Cardiovasc Pharmacol* 1992; **20**: 772–778.

62. Schwieler JH, Kahan T, Nussberger J, Hjemdahl P. Converting enzyme inhibition modulates sympathetic neurotransmission in vivo via multiple mechanisms. *Am J Physiol Endocrinol Metab* 1993; **264**: E631–E637.

63 Koepke JP, Bovy PR, McMahon EG et al. Central and peripheral actions of a nonpeptidic angiotensin II receptor antagonist. *Hypertension* 1991; **15**: 841–847.

64. Chua CC, Chua BHL, Diglio CA, Siu BB. Induction of endothelin-1 transcripts by angiotensin II in rat heart endothelial cells. *FASEB J* 1992; **6**: A1636.

65. Raya TE, Fonken SJ, Lee RW et al. Hemodynamic effects of direct angiotensin II blockade compared to converting enzyme inhibition in

rat model of heart failure. *Am J Hypertens* 1991; **4**: 334S–340S.

66. Fitzpatrick MA, Pademaker MT, Charles CJ et al. Angiotensin II receptor antagonism in ovine heart failure: acute hemodynamic, hormonal and renal effects. *Am J Physiol* 1992; **263**: H250–H256.

67. Deck CC, Gaballa MA, Raya TE. Renal function in rats with experimental heart failure: angiotensin II blockade versus ACE inhibition. *Circulation* 1993; **88**(suppl): I-514.

68. Qing G, Garcia R. Chronic captopril and losartan (Dup 735) administration in rats with high output heart failure. *Am J Physiol* 1992; **263**: 833H–840H.

69. Tanaka A, Matusumori A, Wang W, Sasayama S. An angiotensin II receptor antagonist reduces myocardial damage in an animal model of myocarditis. *Circulation* 1994; **90**: 2051–2055.

70. Tanimura M, Sabbah HN, Shimoyama H et al. Effects of valsartan, an angiotensin-II AT1 receptor antagonist, on left ventricular function and remodelling in dogs with heart failure. *Circulation* 1997; **96**(suppl): 2933 (abst).

71. Schieffer B, Wirger A, Meybrunn M et al. Comparative effects of chronic angiotensin converting enzyme inhibition and angiotensin II type 1 receptor blockade on cardiac remodelling after myocardial infarction in the rat. *Circulation* 1994; **89**: 2273–2282.

72. Smits JFM, Passiier PCJJ, Daemen MJAP. ACE inhibition and AT receptor inhibition following myocardial infarction: structural and functional consequences. *Can J Cardiol* 1994; **10**(suppl A): 59A (abst).

73. Linz W, Henning R, Scholkenns BA, Becker RHA. ACE inhibition and angiotensin II receptor antagonism on development and regression of cardiac hypertrophy in rats. In: *Current Advances in ACE inhibition* Vol. 2. New York: Union of Physiological Sciences and American Physiological Societies 1991; 118–190.

74. Himmelmann A, Svensson A, Bergbrant A, Hansson L. Long term effects of losartan on blood pressure and left ventricular structure in essential hypertension. *J Hum Hypertens* 1996; **10**: 729–734.

75. Lip GYH. Do angiotensin II receptor antago-nists regress left ventricular hypertrophy? *J Hum Hypertens* 1996; **10**: 725–727.

76. Cheung B. Increased left-ventricular mass after losartan treatment. *Lancet* 1997; **349**: 1743–1744.

77. Shen YT, Wiedmann RT, Greenland JJ et al. Combined effects of angiotensin converting enzyme inhibition and angiotensin II receptor antagonism in conscious pigs with congestive heart failure. *Cardiovasc Res* 1998; **39**: 413–422.

78. Krombach RS, Clair MJ, Hendrick JW et al. Angiotensin converting enzyme inhibition, AT1 receptor inhibition, and combination therapy with pacing induced heart failure: effects on left ventricular performance and regional blood flow patterns. *Cardiovasc Res* 1998; **38**: 631–645.

79. Lambert C, Bastien NR, Legault M, Juneau A. Comparative study of converting enzyme inhibition and angiotensin II receptor antagonism on survival from chronic heart failure in cardiomyopathic hamsters. *Eur Heart J* 1998; Abstract suppl: Abstract 854.

80. Araki M, Kanda T, Imai S et al. Comparative effects of losartan, captopril and enalapril on murine acute myocarditits due to encephalomyocarditis virus. *J Cardiovasc Pharmacol* 1995; **26**: 61–65.

81. LeJemtel T, Awan N, Liang C et al. Irbesartan: a new angiotensin II antagonist: acute hemodynamic effects in patients with heart failure. *Circulation* 1996; **94**(suppl): 3646 (abst).

82. Havranek EP, Thomas I, Smith WB et al for the Irbesartan Heart Failure Group. Dose-related beneficial long-term hemodynamic and clinical efficacy of Irbesartan in heart failure. *J Am Coll Cardiol* 1999; **33**: 1174–1181.

83. Mazayev VP, Fomina IG, Kazakov EN et al. Efficacy and tolerability after chronic AT1 angiotensin II receptor blockade with valsartan in heart failure patients previously untreated with an ACE inhibitor. *Eur Heart J* 1997; **18**(suppl): 403 (abst).

84. Klinge R, Polis A, Dickstein K, Hall C. Effects of angiotensin II receptor blockade on N-terminal proatrial natriuretic factor plasma levels in chronic heart failure. *J Cardiac Fail* 1997; **3**: 75–81.

85. Dickstein K, Chang P, Willenheimer R et al. Comparison of the effects of losartan and enalapril on clinical status and exercise performance in patients with moderate or severe chronic heart failure. *J Am Coll Cardiol* 1995; **26**: 438–445.

86. Guazzi M, Melzi G, Agostini P. Comparison of changes in respiratory function and exercise oxygen uptake with losartan versus enalapril in congestive heart failure secondary to ischaemic or idiopathic dilated cardiomyopathy. *Am J Cardiol* 1997; **80**: 1572–1576.

87. Klinger G, Jaramillo N, Ikram H et al. Effects of losartan on exercise capacity, morbidity and mortality in patients with symptomatic heart failure. *J Am Coll Cardiol* 1997; **29**: 205A (abst).

88. Riegger GAJ, George M, Arens H. Improvement in exercise tolerance and symptoms with candesartan cilexetil in patients with congestive heart failure. *Eur Heart J* 1998; Abstract 857.

89. Granger C, Ertl G, Kuch J et al. A randomized trial evaluating tolerability of candesartan cilexetil for patients with congestive heart failure and intolerance to angiotensin converting enzyme inhibitors. *Eur Heart J* 1998; Abstract 856.

90. Lang RM, Elkayam U, Yellen LG et al, on behalf of the Losartan Pilot Exercise Study Investigators. Comparative effects of losartan and enalapril on exercise capacity and clinical status in patients with heart failure. *J Am Coll Cardiol* 1997; **30**: 983–991.

91. Vijay N, Alhaddad IA, Denny MD et al. Irbesartan compared with lisinopril in patients with mild to moderate heart failure. *J Am Coll Cardiol* 1998; **31**: 68A (abst).

92. Dasbach EJ, Gerth WC, Segal R et al. The cost-effectiveness of losartan versus captopril in patients with symptomatic heart failure within and beyond trial. *Eur Heart J* 1998; Abstract suppl: Abstract 3058.

93. Konstam MA, Thomas I, Ramahi TM et al. Effects of losartan and captopril on left ventricular volumes in elderly patients with heart failure: results of the ELITE ventricular function substudy. *Circulation* 1997; **96**(suppl): I–452 (abst).

94. Cowley AJ, Wiens BL, Segal R et al. Quality of life in elderly patients with symptomatic heart failure: losartan versus captopril. *Eur Heart J* 1998; Abstract 859.

95. Segal R, Klinger GH, Sharma D. Losartan in patients with heart failure — overall safety and tolerability. *Circulation* 1998; **98**:I-301.

96. Hamroff G, Blaufarb I, Mancini D et al. Angiotensin II receptor blockade further reduces afterload safely in patients maximally treated with ACE inhibitors for heart failure. *J Cardiovasc Pharmacol* 1997; **30**: 533–536.

97. Hamroff G, Katz S, Mancini D et al. Addition of angiotensin II receptor blockade to maximal angiotensin-converting enzyme inhibition improves exercise capacity in patients with severe congestive heart failure. *Circulation* 1999; **99**: 990–992.

98. Guazzi M, Agostoni P, Pontone G et al. AT1 receptor blockade, angiotensin converting enzyme inhibition and their combination in chronic heart failure. A comparative evaluation by cardiopulmonary exercise test. *Circulation* 1998; **98**: I-156 (Abstract).

99. Tocchi M, Rosanio S, Anzuini A et al. Angiotensin II receptor blockade combined to ACE-inhibition improves left ventricular dilation and exercise ejection fraction in congestive heart failure. *J Am Coll Cardiol* 1998; **31**: 188A (abst).

100. Houghton AR, Harrison M, Perry AJ et al. Combined treatment with losartan and an angiotensin converting enzyme inhibitor in chronic heart failure: a randomised, double-blind, placebo-controlled trial. *Eur Heart J* 1998; Abstract 1702.

101. Murdoch DR, McDonagh TA, Morton JJ et al. Haemodynamic effects of the addition of eprosartan, a specific AT1 receptor antagonist, to ACE inhibitor treatment in chronic heart failure. *Eur Heart J* 1998; Abstract.

102. Tonkon M, Awan N, Niazi I et al, for the Irbesartan Heart Failure group. Irbesartan combined with conventional therapy, including angiotensin converting enzyme inhibitors, in heart failure. *J Am Coll Cardiol* 1998; **31**: 188A (abst).

103. Metzger DC, Warner JG, Kitzman DW et al. Losartan improves exercise tolerance and quality of life in patients with diastolic dysfunction. *Circulation* 1998; Abstract.

104. Os I, Bratland B, Dahlof B et al. Female sex as an important determinant of lisinopril-induced cough. *Lancet* 1992; **339**: 303–310.
105. Yusuf S. Effect of enalapril on survival in patients with reduced left ventricular ejection fractions and congestive heart failure. *N Engl J Med* 1991; **325**: 293–302.
106. Weber M. Clinical safety and tolerability of losartan. *Clin Ther* 1997; **19**: 604–616.
107. Malini PL, Strocchi E, Zanardi M et al. Thromboxane antagonism and cough induced by angiotensin-converting enzyme inhibitor. *Lancet* 1997; **350**: 15–18.
108. Israili ZH, Hall WD. Cough and angioneurotic edema associated with angiotensin-converting enzyme inhibitor therapy. A review of the literature and pathophysiology. *Ann Intern Med* 1992; **117**: 234–242.
109. Hargreaves M. Sodium cromoglycate: a remedy for ACE inhibitor-induced cough. *Br J Clin Pract* 1993; **47**: 319–320.
110. Cleland JGF. Lack of effect of nedocromil sodium in ACE inhibitor-induced cough. *Lancet* 1995; **345**: 394.
111. Schulman G, Hakim R, Arias R et al. Bradykinin generation by dialysis membranes: possible role in anaphylactic reaction. *J Am Soc Nephrol* 1993; **3**: 1563–1569.
112. Hood WB, Youngblood M, Ghali JK et al. Initial blood pressure response to enalapril in hospitalized patients (studies of left ventricular dysfunction (SOLVD)). *Am J Cardiol* 1991; **68**: 1465–1468.
113. Kostis JB, Shelton BJ, Yusuf S et al. Tolerability of enalapril initiation by patients with left ventricular dysfunction: results of the medication challenge phase of the studies of left ventricular dysfunction. *Am Heart J* 1994; **128**: 358–364.
114. Cleland JGF. ACE inhibitors and heart failure. *Lancet* 1992; **339**: 687–688.
115. Czapla K, Ahmed E, McMillan MA. Renal artery stenosis and congestive heart failure. *Lancet* 1993; **342**: 302 (letter).
116. Fuavel JP, Velon S, Berra N et al. Effects of losartan on renal function in patients with essential hypertension. *J Cardiovasc Pharmacol* 1996; **28**: 259–263.
117. Nakashima M, Uematsu T, Kosuge K, Kanamaru M. Pilot study of the uricosuric effect of DuP-753, a new angiotensin II receptor antagonist in healthy subjects. *Eur J Clin Pharmacol* 1992; **42**: 333–335.
118. Pitt B, Poole Wilson PA, Segal R et al. Effect of losartan compared with captopril on mortality in patients with symptomatic heart failure: randomised trial – the Losartan Heart Failure Survival Study ELITE II. *Lancet* 2000; **355**: 1582–1587
119. Witte K, Thackray S, Banerjee T, Clark AL, Cleland JGF. Update of ELITE II, BEST, CHAMP and IMPRESS clinical trials in heart failure. *Eur J Heart Failure* 2000; **2**: 107–112.

15

Digitalis: the curtain comes down?
Inder S Anand and Y Chandrashekhar

Introduction

Digitalis has been used in the treatment of heart failure for thousands of years. Ancient Indian Ayurvedic tests[1] and ancient roman physicians[2] referred to its utility in oedematous patients. The Ayurvedic texts also mention that 'This medicine either cures patients or kills them' suggesting that they recognized its narrow therapeutic window. Despite these ancient origins, there has been a persistent debate about its utility in heart failure. Some of the recent trials,[3,4] especially the National Institutes of Health (NIH)-sponsored Digitalis Investigation Group (DIG) study[5] have clarified its role in heart failure to a large extent. None the less, some questions remain unresolved and it is unlikely that there would be another major trial to decide these remaining issues. It is therefore important to critically review the available data to establish guidelines for its use in heart failure.

Historical background of digitalis use before the advent of major clinical trials

Clinicians have always agreed that digitalis has a definite role in the management of patients with heart failure complicated by supraventricular tachyarrhythmias such as atrial fibrillation or flutter, where it acts mainly by slowing heart rate.[6,7] However, the role of digitalis in the management of chronic heart failure in patients with sinus rhythm has been seriously questioned from time to time. This controversy started at the turn of the century when Sir James Mackenzie, on the basis of his considerable clinical experience in Britain, advocated the use of digoxin only in patients with heart failure in atrial fibrillation.[8] However, his equally experienced counterpart in the United States, Thomas Christian held the view that digoxin was effective in heart failure irrespective of the rhythm.[9] The views of these stalwarts prevailed in their respective countries for years. With the introduction of cardiac catheterization, studies from both sides of the Atlantic, in the early 1940s, showed that digoxin improved haemodynamics of patients with chronic heart failure even in sinus rhythm[10,11] Later, it was confirmed that the acute positive inotropic effects of digoxin[12] persist chronically without tachyphylaxis.[13] Yet the clinical efficacy of chronic digoxin therapy remained less clear. During the 1970s a number of reports showed that discontinuation or withdrawal of digoxin from patients with chronic heart failure and sinus rhythm did not produce any adverse effects.[14–20] While most of these studies were small, uncontrolled and had serious flaws, they led to the development of several randomized controlled trials. Physicians also recognized that digoxin had a narrow therapeutic to toxic window and questioned the utility of adding this potentially toxic drug to optimally treated patients. This question became more important with the introduction of angiotensin-converting enzyme (ACE) inhibitors which are not only effective in the treatment of chronic heart failure but also prevent the development and progression of heart failure and improve survival.[21-23] In contrast, all the inotropic agents tested until that time increased mortality[24-27] and raised the possibility that digitalis, an inotropic agent, may have adverse effects on mortality. These thoughts led to a critical evaluation of the role of digitalis in heart failure.

Digitalis and potential issues in the treatment of heart failure

A proper reassessment of the role of digoxin must take into account the present day objectives in the management of heart failure, that is to:

1. Prevent the occurrence of heart failure following the initial myocardial injury
2. Delay progression of the disease
3. Alleviate signs, symptoms and improve quality of life
4. Prolong survival.

There is no evidence that digoxin, unlike the ACE inhibitors, has any effect on ventricular remodelling following myocardial infarction[28] — a process that leads to the development of heart failure. On the other hand, there are studies that have shown digoxin to be harmful in the year following myocardial infarction.[29-31] Thus the main issues with the use of digitalis centre on the extent of clinical benefit and effect on mortality. The following presentation analyses all the randomized trials that have used a double-blind, placebo-controlled design in patients with well-defined chronic heart failure, systolic dysfunction and sinus rhythm. A special effort will be made to see whether the largest and most recent trial, the DIG study, is able to end the digoxin controversy and to redefine its role for the next century.

The early randomized placebo-controlled trials

Before the publication of the DIG trial, there were at least eight small single-centre and seven large multicentre randomized, double-blind, placebo-controlled trials of digoxin in chronic heart failure (Table 15.1). These trials enrolled patients with mild to moderate heart failure with systolic dysfunction and sinus rhythm. Most patients tested were being treated with diuretics, some were receiving vasodilators (ACE inhibitors in only one study) but many had received digoxin before being randomized. Therefore, most of these are drug withdrawal studies.

Small single-centre trials

A number of smaller studies have looked at the role of digitalis in patients with heart failure and sinus rhythm.[32-40] These studies are mentioned here mainly for their historical significance. They helped generate the debate associated with digitalis but did not contribute significantly to define its role in present day clinical practice.

One of the more influential studies was reported by Lee et al[33] who studied 25 patients using a crossover design. These patients were stable and adequately treated with diuretics. However, ACE inhibitors were not used. Using a scoring system that evaluated symptoms, signs, cardiac dimension on chest X-ray and echocardiogram, they showed that 14 of the 19 patients with ejection fractions less

Trials	No. of patients	Design	Duration (weeks)	NYHA class	EF (%)	Digoxin level (ng/ml)	Diuretics	Vasodilators	ACE inhibitors	Exercise capacity	% Change in EF from baseline	Placebo	Digoxin	Comments overall clinical benefit yes/no
							Concomitant therapy (% patients)					Worsening HF (%)		
Small single centre trials														
Dobbs et al 1977[38]	46	CO/DW	6	NA	Not done	0.9	60	0	0	Not done	Not done	34	0*	Yes but flawed study
Lee et al 1982[39]	25	CO/DW	9	II–III	29	1.15	88	24	0	Not done	No change	56	24*	Yes in selected patients
Fleg et al 1982[40]	30	CO/DW	12	I–III	23(FS)	1.4	76	16	0	No change	↓9% (V_{cf}) placebo*	10	10	No
Taggart et al 1983[51]	22	CO/DW	12	I–II	Not done	1.2	95	35	0	Not done	↓5%(STI) placebo*	18	10	No
Guyatt et al 1988[42]	20	CO/DW	7	I–III	19 (FS)	1.75	90	55	0	↑5% digoxin*	↓19% (FS) placebo*	35	0*	Yes
Pugh et al 1989[43]	44	CO/DW	8	NA	28(FS)	0.8	75	9	0	Not done	↓(STI) placebo*	25	11*	Yes
Fleg et al 1991[45]	10	CO/DW	4	II–III	33	1.4	100	41	0	No change	↓16% placebo* on exercise	0	0	No
Haerer et al 1988[46]	28	PA/DI	3	II–III	25 (FS)	1.8	0	0	0	Not done	↓(FS) digoxin*	—	—	Not evaluated
Large multicentre trials														
Captopril–Digoxin 1988[47]	196	PA/DW	24	II–III	25	0.7	84	0	0	No change	↑16% digoxin*	29	15*	Yes
Xamoterol 1988[48]	213	PA	12	II–III	Not done	0.9	25	10	0	No change	Not done	6	4	No
DiBianco et al 1989[49]	111	PA/DW	12	II–III	25	1.1	100	48	0	↑14% digoxin*	↑3.4% digoxin*	47	15*	Yes but flawed study
Just et al 1993[50]	133	PA	52	II	50	NA	0	0	0	No change	Not done	NA	NA	Yes even with good EF
DIMT 1993[51]	108	PA	26	II–III	28	0.9	0	0	0	↓12% placebo*	Not done	4	0	No
PROVED 1993[36]	88	PA/DW	12	II–III	27	1.2	100	0	0	↓18% placebo*	↓10% placebo*	39	19*	Yes
RADIANCE 1993[37]	178	PA/DW	12	II–III	26	1.2	100	0	100	↓7.5% placebo*	↓13% placebo*	25	5*	Yes

CO, crossover; DW, digoxin withdrawal; NA, not available; PA, parallel design; DI, digoxin introduction; FS, fraction shortening by echocardiography; V_{cf}, velocity of circumferential fibre shortening; STI, systolic time intervals; ex, exercise; HF, heart failure; * $P < 0.05$ placebo versus digoxin.

Table 15.1
Randomized, double-blind, placebo-controlled trials of digoxin in heart failure

than 50% improved with digoxin therapy. All 14 patients who improved had a third heart sound compared with only one of the 11 patients who did not improve. Digoxin did not improve the ejection fraction but decreased the cardiac size on chest X-ray and reduced left ventricular diastolic dimension on echocardiography. The authors concluded that while digoxin was useful, only those patients who have a third heart sound or raised pulmonary wedge pressures respond to it. This study was instrumental in encouraging the use of digitalis in patients with a large heart and severe dysfunction.

A number of other studies done around the same time provided conflicting results. Some showed that digoxin withdrawal did not significantly worsen exercise capacity and had minimal effects on left ventricular (LV) size and function in mild to moderate heart failure.[34,35,39] Other studies showed that digoxin withdrawal did result in clinical deterioration, reduced functional capacity and worse echocardiographic indices of LV function.[32,33,36,37] Interestingly diuretics reversed some of the clinical deterioration suggesting that these patients were suboptimally treated. One of these studies suggested that changes in the number of digoxin binding sites on red blood cells might identify patients likely to deteriorate after digoxin withdrawal.[37,38]

Large multicentre trials

Seven large multicentre randomized placebo-controlled digoxin trials were performed between 1988 and 1992 (Table 15.1). These were better designed than the single-centre studies and showed that digoxin improved clinical symptoms, increased the ejection fraction and exercise capacity and reduced the number of hospitalizations in heart failure patients.[3,4,41–45] These studies, however, did not completely resolve the controversy associated with the use of digitalis in clinical practice. The captopril-digoxin trial[41] compared captopril, digoxin and placebo in 300 patients, 84% of whom were on diuretics and 65% had been on long-term digoxin. Digoxin increased ejection fraction (4.4 percentage points), but had no effect on exercise capacity or New York Heart Association (NYHA) class. Worsening heart failure (hospitalization, emergency room visits, or increased diuretic requirement) occurred more often in the placebo-treated patients (29%) compared to the digoxin group (15%, $P < 0.05$). In the German–Austrian Xamoterol trial[42] 433 patients with mild to moderate symptoms of heart failure (without any objective documentation of left ventricular systolic dysfunction), were randomized to digoxin, xamoterol or placebo. After 3 months, compared to placebo, patients on digoxin therapy had improvement in some symptoms and signs of heart failure (using the Likert scale) but not exercise capacity. The study was seriously flawed because the extent of left ventricular dysfunction was not defined, 25% of patients were NYHA class I, and an equal number were not taking diuretics.

DiBianco et al[43] reported the results of the Milrinone Multicenter trial in 1989. In this trial, 230 patients with an average ejection fraction of 25% were stabilized on diuretics and digitalis for 4–8 weeks and then randomized to digoxin, placebo, milrinone alone, or digoxin and milrinone combination. Digoxin improved ejection fraction and reduced treatment failures compared with the placebo group. There was an unexpected increase in ejection fraction and exercise capacity in the group continued on digoxin. This increase occurred despite no change in therapy and is difficult to explain.

The Captopril and Digoxin Study (CADS)[44] evaluated the effects of captopril (25 mg twice a day), digoxin (0.25 mg/day) and placebo in

222 patients in a multicentre double-blind placebo-controlled trial. This study included patients, at least 2 months following myocardial infarction, who had regional wall motion abnormalities but well preserved global ejection fraction (~50%). They had symptoms of mild heart failure (NYHA IIA and B), only when taken off all medication. Patients were randomized to digoxin, captopril or placebo after all drugs had been discontinued for a 14 day run-in period. After 1 year, digoxin improved the NYHA class in 45% of the patients compared with 25% of patients with placebo. The symptoms and quality of life also improved with digoxin compared with placebo ($P < 0.05$) but exercise tolerance did not change in either group.

In the Dutch Ibopamine Multicenter Trial (DIMT),[45] 161 patients with mild to moderate heart failure, treated with diuretics alone, were randomized to digoxin, ibopamine (dopamine agonist), or placebo. After 6 months, the exercise capacity in the digoxin group was significantly higher than placebo only by intention-to-treat analysis. The incidence of worsening heart failure was not different from the placebo group.

Although many of the above trials were well performed, there were wide variations in study design. Many were of short duration, small sample size, lacked objective criteria of left ventricular systolic dysfunction, and lacked optimization of medical therapy before randomization especially with ACE inhibitors. The failings have left doubts about the role of digitalis in the present day management of patients with chronic heart failure. Nevertheless, the data from these withdrawal studies make it clear that digitalis has long-term inotropic effects. The noninvasive indices of contractility were better in digoxin compared with placebo groups in all studies where these were measured. However, clear beneficial clinical effects of positive inotropy were seen in only half the studies. Moreover, these effects appeared to be small and were seen in only a selected group of patients, particularly those who had cardiomegaly, third heart sound, signs of fluid retention, that is probably those not optimally treated with diuretics. A convincing increase in exercise capacity was seen in only three of eight trials where it was measured.

PROVED and RADIANCE trials

The PROVED and RADIANCE (Tables 15.2 and 15.3) trials addressed the above-mentioned deficiencies and evaluated whether digoxin confers an additional benefit in patients optimally treated with diuretics and ACE inhibitors. These companion trials had an identical design, except that in the PROVED trial[4] the effect of digoxin withdrawal was tested on patients receiving a background therapy with diuretics alone whereas, in the RADIANCE trial[3] patients received optimal treatment with both diuretics and ACE inhibitors. Both trials were randomized, double-blind, placebo-controlled, withdrawal studies in patients with chronic heart failure (NYHA class II and III). Only patients with systolic dysfunction in sinus rhythm with ejection fraction less than 35%, echocardiographic left ventricular end-diastolic dimension greater than 60 mm, and reduced exercise capacity on treadmill test were randomized (Table 15.2). Eligible patients underwent an 8-week single-blind phase during which digoxin dose was adjusted to achieve serum digoxin levels of 0.9–2.0 ng/ml. Patients were required to remain stable on their medication for at least 4 weeks before randomization. After 8 weeks of single-blind phase, patients were randomized to continue digoxin (digoxin

	PROVED		RADIANCE	
	Placebo (N = 46)	Digoxin (N = 42)	Placebo (N = 93)	Digoxin (N = 85)
Age (years)	64 ± 2	64 ± 2	59 ± 1	61 ± 1
Sex (males %)	77	90	81	70
Aetiology (ICM/non-ICM, %)	67/33	60/40	56/44	65/35
Duration of heart failure (years)	3.1 ± 0.5	3.6 ± 0.5	—	—
NYHA class II/III (%)	83/17	83/17	75/25	71/29
Heart rate (beats/min)	73 ± 1	73 ± 2	78 ± 1	77 ± 1
JVD (% patients)	22	45	—	
CTR (%)	50 ± 0.01	50 ± 0.01	53 ± 0.01	54 ± 0.01
LVEF (%)	29 ± 2	27 ± 1	28 ± 1	26 ± 1
LVEDD (mm)	67 ± 1	67 ± 1	67 ± 1	69 ± 1
Median treadmill time (sec)	540	494	571	510
Average digoxin dose (mg)	0.375	0.375	0.4	0.37
Digoxin level (ng/ml)	1.1 ± 0.05	1.2 ± 0.05	1.1 ± 0.03	1.2 ± 0.03
Average daily captopril dose (mg)	—	—	73	77
Average daily enalapril dose (mg)	—	—	134	17

ICM, ischaemic cardiomyopathy; non-ICM, dilated cardiomyopathy, hypertension and end-stage valve disease; JVD, jugular venous distension; CTR, cardiothoracic ratio; LVEF, left ventricular ejection fraction; LVEDD, left ventricular dimension in diastole.

Table 15.2
Comparison of patient characteristics in PROVED and RADIANCE trials

group) or to discontinue digoxin (placebo group). All patients in the PROVED trial were maintained on constant doses of diuretics whereas patients in the RADIANCE trial were on a constant dose of diuretic and ACE inhibitors. Treatment lasted 12 weeks and patients were seen every 2 weeks. Primary endpoints for both studies were:

1. Incidence of treatment failure (increase or change in medical therapy, emergency room visits, hospitalization for heart failure or death)
2. Time to treatment failure
3. Maximal treadmill exercise time
4. Distance covered in the 6-minute walk test.

Secondary endpoints included change in signs and symptoms, response to the quality of life questionnaire, heart failure score, evaluation of progress by the patient, left ventricular ejection fraction and dimensions, heart rate, blood pressure and body weight (Table 15.3).

The PROVED trial was stopped prematurely after only 88 patients were randomized, because of difficulty in finding patients who were not taking ACE inhibitors. There were 46 and 42 patients in the placebo and digoxin groups, respectively. The RADIANCE trial randomized 178 patients, 93 in the placebo and 85 in the digoxin group. The demographic variables of patients in both trials are shown in Table 15.2. While pretreatment characteristics in the placebo and digoxin groups were well matched in the RADIANCE trial, there

	PROVED		RADIANCE	
	Placebo (N = 46)	Digoxin (N = 42)	Placebo (N = 93)	Digoxin (N = 85)
Primary endpoints				
Treadmill time	↓ 18%	↑ 1%‡	↓ 7.5%	No change†
6-min walk distance		No difference	↓ 11%	No change*
Incidence of treatment failure	39%	19%†	25%	5%*
Time to treatment failure	Significantly less in placebo			Significantly less in placebo
Secondary endpoints				
Increase in signs and symptoms of CHF		No difference	38%	18%†
Quality of life		No difference	↓ 48%, ↑ 33%	↓41%, ↑47%†
CHF score (increase in NYHA class)		No difference	27%	10%†
Global evaluation (assessed by patient)		No difference	↓ 31%	↓ 9%*
LVEF	↓ 10%	↑ 7%†	↓13%	↓4.0%*
LVEDD	No change	No change	↑ 3%	↓1.5%†
Heart rate	↑ 15%	No change‡	↑ 9%	No change*
Body weight	↑ 0.6%	↓1%†	↑ 1%	↓1%*

LVEF, left ventricular ejection fraction; LVEDD, left ventricular dimension in diastole. For placebo versus digoxin group:
* $P < 0.001$; † $P < 0.01$; ‡ $P < 0.05$.

Table 15.3
Comparison of primary and secondary endpoints in PROVED and RADIANCE Trials

was a higher incidence of jugular venous distension in the digoxin (45%) compared to the placebo group (22%, $P = 0.02$) in the PROVED trial. Although a statistical comparison of patient characteristics between the two trials cannot be made, they appear to be fairly similar except perhaps for a greater percentage of NYHA class III patients in the RADIANCE trial. The RADIANCE patients, as shown in Table 15.2, were on adequate doses of ACE inhibitors. Unfortunately, the dose of diuretics used was not reported in either trial, making it difficult to assess whether PROVED patients had to be stabilized on higher doses of diuretics than the RADIANCE patients.

In the RADIANCE trial significant deterioration in all four primary endpoints was seen more in the placebo than the digoxin group (Table 15.3). The most striking difference was in the incidence of treatment failure (placebo 25% versus digoxin 5%). Deterioration of NYHA class, quality of life, chronic heart failure score and patient's own evaluation of progress was also significantly worse in the placebo group. In addition, left ventricular ejection fraction decreased more and left ventricular dimensions, heart rate and body weight increased by a greater extent in the placebo group. In the PROVED trial, all four primary endpoints except for the 6-minute walk test showed significant differences between placebo and digoxin. There was also a significant decrease in ejection fraction, increase in heart rate, and increase in body weight in placebo compared to digoxin. However, no significant differences were seen in the NYHA class, quality of life, chronic heart failure score or patient's own evaluation of progress. There was only one episode of digoxin toxicity in the RADIANCE and none in the PROVED trial, despite use of relatively high doses of digoxin (0.375 mg/day in PROVED and 0.370 mg/day in RADIANCE).

It is interesting to compare the results of these two trials in an attempt to better define the role of digoxin during background treatment with ACE inhibitors (Table 15.3). Although the incidence of treatment failure was significantly higher in placebo compared to digoxin for both trials, a far greater number of patients in both the placebo and digoxin groups had treatment failure in the PROVED trial (39 and 19%) compared to the RADIANCE trial (25 and 5%). It is likely that this difference was due to the additional beneficial effect of ACE inhibitors in the RADIANCE patients. The fact that significant clinical deterioration in heart failure occurred on withdrawal of digoxin in the RADIANCE trial, suggests that ACE inhibitor therapy, in moderate doses, is unable to prevent worsening heart failure when digoxin is withdrawn. On the other hand, it could be argued that these patients were not treated with optimal doses of ACE inhibitors and diuretics. Another interesting observation in these trials was that the curves relating the incidence of treatment failure continued to diverge throughout the 12-week study period. The reason for this is not clear since tissue stores of digoxin are known to clear from the body much earlier than the duration of this study.[46] This finding also underscores the importance of performing trials with a long duration of follow-up because trials of shorter duration may miss clinical deterioration seen with withdrawal of digoxin.

In summary, these two well-designed com-panion trials were able to overcome many of the problems of previous studies. They demonstrate that patients with mild to moderate chronic heart failure due to left ventricular systolic dysfunction who are clinically stable on either maintenance therapy of digoxin and diuretics (PROVED) or with additional background therapy with ACE inhibitors (RADIANCE), are at considerable risk for clinical deterioration if digoxin is withdrawn. The problem remains, however, that because these were withdrawal studies, they did not answer the important clinical question of whether initiation of digitalis therapy in patients optimally treated with maximally tolerated doses of diuretics and ACE inhibitors further improves clinical state, functional capacity and survival.

Problems with withdrawal trials

A major concern, common to most trials discussed in this chapter, is the problem inherent in the interpretation of withdrawal studies.[47] Such studies address only the question of whether a drug once started should or should not be stopped, and do not answer the question of whether adding a drug to the treatment in the first place confers additional advantage to the patient. In this context it is important to remember that unlike digoxin trials, all other studies that have tested new inotropic agents have used drug introduction protocols in patients who have never received that experimental drug previously.[26,42,43] These studies have shown that although most inotropic drugs have short-term beneficial clinical effects, their prolonged use increases mortality.[24–27] Even more interesting is the observation that some patients develop marked clinical deterioration when inotropic drugs like amrinone[48] are withdrawn. One explanation of these findings might be that prolonged administration of these drugs somehow damages the myocardium but that their inotropic effects are sufficiently efficacious to conceal any clinical deterioration while the patient receives the drug. Clinical deterioration seen after cessation may, under such circumstances, provide a measure of the harm caused by the drug. A number of inotropic drugs have been shown to hasten myocyte death.[49–51] It is, therefore, entirely possible that deterioration after digoxin withdrawal has a similar mechanism. Another limitation of withdrawal studies is the inherent bias in patient selection. These patients are at least known to tolerate the drug and are, therefore, more likely not only to have a low incidence of adverse reaction but also more likely to benefit.

Comparison of digoxin with ACE inhibitors

ACE inhibitors are clearly indicated in the treatment of all stages of chronic heart failure but it is worthwhile to compare the extent of clinical benefits of digoxin versus ACE inhibitors (Table 15.4). Six randomized trials have compared digoxin with an ACE inhibitor using either a placebo or nonplacebo protocol. Taken together these trials showed that both digoxin and ACE inhibitors confer comparable symptomatic benefit in patients with mild to moderate chronic heart failure and mildly reduced ejection fraction. While captopril increased exercise capacity in all except the CADS trial (patients with ejection fraction ~50%), digoxin increased exercise capacity in only three of the seven trials. However, digoxin improved ejection fraction in two of the three trials and captopril increased it in only one.

Neurohormonal effects of digoxin

There is increasing evidence that neurohormonal activation seen in congestive heart failure is an important mechanism for progression of the disease.[52] Therefore, agents that reduce neurohormones may be beneficial in heart failure. The high- and low-pressure baroreceptors modulate sympathetic and neurohormonal activity and help to maintain arterial blood pressure. Whenever systemic blood pressure falls, baroreceptor nerve activity decreases and this leads to reflex increase in sympathetic activity. The result is an increase in the release of renin and arginine vasopressin and a decrease in parasympathetic activity. In chronic heart failure, baroreceptor activity is attenuated because of resetting of baroreceptors and this contributes to the increase in sympathetic and neurohormonal activation seen in patients with chronic heart failure.[53] It was believed that the inotropic effects of digoxin improve the haemodynamics of patients with heart failure leading to reflex reduction in sympathetic activity. However, recent evidence from direct recording of baroreceptor and sympathetic neural activity has shown that digitalis can directly stimulate baroreceptor endings, restoring a more normal sympathetic tone.[54]

It is possible that digitalis may have both haemodynamic and direct autonomic modulating effects. Which of these effects is more important in clinical congestive heart failure is under active investigation (Table 15.5). At least three studies have recently shown that digitalis decreases the levels of neurohormones in patients with congestive heart failure. Alicandri et al[55] were the first to show that long-term digoxin treatment decreased plasma norepinephrine in patients with mild to moderate chronic heart failure. In the Dutch

Trials	No. of patients	Design	Duration (weeks)	NYHA class	Baseline EF (%)	% Patients with improvement in heart failure		% Patients with worsening heart failure		% increase in exercise capacity from baseline		Increase in EF from baseline (percentage points)	
						Digoxin	ACE I	Digoxin	ACE I	Digoxin	ACE I	Digoxin	ACE I
Allicandri et al 1987[54]	16	CO/DW	4	II–III	NM	—	—	—	—	27*	36*	↑(STI)*	↑(STI)*
Captopril-Digoxin 1988[47]	200	PA/DW	24	II–III	25	31	41	16	16	9.6	14.3*	4.4*†	1.8
Beaune 1989[55]	142	PA/DW	8	II–IV	NM	28*	35*	—	—	9.4	8.4*	NM	NM
Kromer et al 1990[56]	19	CO‡	6	II	24(FS)	NM	NM	NM	NM	3.8	6.3*	1(FS)	1(FS)
Davies et al 1991[57]	145	PA‡	14	II–III	30	19	18	30	13	12*	8*	5(FS)*	5(FS)*
Herlitz 1992[76]	217	PA¶	12	II–III	<45	16	17	2	5	6.2	11.4*	NM	NM
CADS 1993[50]	129	PA	52	II	50	—	—	NA	NA	3.7	4.1	NM	NM

EF, ejection fraction; ACE I, angiotensin-converting enzyme inhibitors; CO, crossover; DW, digoxin withdrawal; PA parallel design; NM, not measured; STI, systolic time intervals; FS, fraction shortening by echocardiography. * $P < 0.05$ from baseline; † $P < 0.05$ digoxin versus ACE I; ‡ digoxin withdrawn before randomization in those using it. ¶ digoxin-naive patients.

Table 15.4
Randomized trials comparing ACE inhibitors with digoxin in heart failure

Trials	No. of patients	Change in plasma norepinephrine (pg/ml)	
		Placebo	Digoxin
Allicandri et al 1987[54]	16	—	↓ 113*
Kromer et al 1990[56]	19	—	↑ 50
DIMT 1993[51]	84	↑ 62	↓ 106*
Gheorghiade et al 1992[65]	16	—	↓ 36
Gheorghiade et al 1993[66]	20	↑ 127	↓ 209
Krum et al 1995[64]	27	—	↓ 162*

* $P < 0.05$ digoxin versus placebo or baseline.

Table 15.5
Effect of digoxin on plasma norepinephrine

Ibopamine Multicenter Trial[45] digoxin caused a marginal increase in exercise duration at 6 months follow-up and this was associated with decreased plasma norepinephrine and renin activity. Digoxin also increased heart rate variability at 3 months in these patients, suggesting an improvement in autonomic function.[56] More recently, Krum et al[57] measured plasma norepinephrine and parasympathetic activity from heart rate variability in 27 patients with mild to moderate chronic heart failure before and after 4 to 8 weeks of digoxin therapy. Digoxin caused a significant decrease in plasma norepinephrine and substantial improvement in parasympathetic activity. However, an equal number of studies have not confirmed these findings. Kromer et al[58] found that plasma norepinephrine did not change significantly after treatment with digoxin. Gheorghiade et al[59] found that in optimally treated patients, when the dose of digoxin was increased from 0.2 to 0.4 mg per day, digoxin levels (0.7–1.2 ng/ml) and ejection fraction increased significantly after 6 weeks but there was no effect on any of the

neurohormones. Similarly, digoxin withdrawal did not increase neurohormones significantly in a subset of 11 patients in the RADIANCE trial despite a significant decrease in the ejection fraction.[60] Therefore, firm conclusions about potential direct neurohormonal modulating effects of digoxin cannot be drawn from these studies and further research in this area is clearly required.

Conclusions from the trials performed prior to the DIG study

The randomized, double-blind, placebo-controlled trials of digoxin in patients with chronic heart failure and sinus rhythm lead to some important conclusions. These showed that digoxin improves haemodynamics at rest and exercise, consistently improves signs and symptoms, increases exercise capacity and ejection fraction, and enhances quality of life. Studies on digoxin withdrawal proved beyond doubt that withdrawing digoxin in patients with both mild or mild to moderate heart failure worsens haemodynamics, exercise capacity and quality of life. This occurred in the presence of adequate treatment with either diuretics[4] or diuretics and ACE inhibitors.[3] These trials also showed that the clinical effects of digoxin are not dramatic. Withdrawal of digoxin causes clinical deterioration in only about a quarter of the patients who have been clinically stable on digoxin and diuretics with or without ACE inhibitors. Patients with more severe heart failure and with evidence of fluid overload fare worse.[33,61] A number of key questions remained unanswered despite all the above trials: the most important question was whether treatment with digoxin affected survival in patients with heart failure. It is clear from PROVED, RADIANCE and other trials that treatment failure on placebo could easily be managed by increasing diuretic therapy. A more aggressive diuretic and ACE inhibitor regimen could achieve the same results as digoxin. Addition of a potentially toxic drug like digoxin to therapy in chronic heart failure would, therefore, make sense only if it were also to prolong survival. Secondly, the available trials were of short duration and did not address the role of digitalis over the long term. Finally they did not evaluate the role of digitalis in the treatment of patients with diastolic dysfunction.

The DIG trial

Since the publication of this chapter in the 1st edition of this book, the main results of the DIG trial, have been published.[5] This important study was sponsored by the US National Heart Lung and Blood Institute (NHLBI) and the Veterans Affairs Cooperative studies program. It is the largest heart failure trial performed so far; it enrolled 9789 patients and was carried out in over 300 centres in the US and Canada. Although there have been some criticisms of this study and it may not be able to resolve all the outstanding issues, this trial is likely to be the last large scale study on the clinical use of digoxin. This study, therefore, deserves very close examination. This main purpose of the study was to investigate whether cardiac glycosides influenced all mortality and the number of hospitalizations in patients with chronic heart failure who were in normal sinus rhythm. This randomized double-blind trial had two components, the main trial involving patients with an ejection fraction less than 45% and an ancillary trial in patients with heart failure and an ejection fraction greater than 45%. In the main trial, patients treated with conventional therapy (diuretics in about 80% of patients and ACE inhibitors in 94% of patients) were randomized to digoxin ($N = 3397$ patients) or placebo ($N = 3403$ patients) and were followed for 37 months. The average dose of digoxin was 0.25 mg/day (in 70% of patients) and the mean digoxin level was 0.86 ng/ml and 0.80 ng/ml at 1 and 12 months into the trial. Most patients (average age 63 years, 22% of the patients were females) had heart failure due to an ischaemic aetiology (70%), with an average ejection fraction of 28%. Less than half of the patients ($N = 3365$, 44%) were already on digoxin at the start of the trial and they were randomized without any washout period. Digoxin had an overall neutral effect on all-cause mortality (risk ratio 0.99, 95% CI 0.91–1.07, $P = 0.8$) but tended to decrease the risk of death due to worsening heart failure (risk ratio 0.88, 95% CI 0.77–1.01, $P = 0.06$). The combined endpoint of death due to worsening heart failure or hospitalizations for that cause was significantly reduced with digoxin (risk ratio 0.75, 95% CI 0.69–1.82, $P < 0.001$). Digoxin caused 6% fewer total hospitalizations ($P = 0.01$), and fewer patients were hospitalized for worsening heart failure (26.8 versus 34.7%, risk ratio 0.72, 95% CI 0.66–0.79, $P < 0.001$), but did not affect hospitalizations due to arrhythmia or cardiac arrest. Greater benefit was seen in patients with more severe heart failure (lowest ejection fraction, larger hearts, NYHA III–IV) and this was evident very soon after randomization. The benefit of digoxin on the combined endpoint of death or hospitalizations due to worsening heart failure was similar in patients with ischaemic or nonischaemic aetiology. Digoxin toxicity was uncommon and was suspected in 11.9% patients on digoxin and in 7.9% in the placebo group. However, only 2.0% of patients on digoxin needed hospitalization for digitalis toxicity compared to 0.9% in the placebo group. In the ancillary trial ejection fraction >0.45), 492 patients were randomly assigned to digoxin and 496 to placebo. There was no benefit in terms of mortality but surprisingly, digoxin helped improve functional capacity and reduced hospitalizations.

Risk–cost–benefit analysis

There have been a number of economic analyses of digitalis use in heart failure before and after publication of the DIG trial. Many trials, both large and small, have shown that the drug is cheap and safe when used appropriately. The major cost of treating patients with heart failure is due to repeated hospital admissions necessitated by worsening heart failure.[62,63] In the DIG trial, digitalis had a significant effect on reducing first and subsequent hospitalizations. This would have important economic implications. An initial analysis[64] erroneously suggested that 1000 patients would need to be treated for 1 year to prevent nine hospitalizations. Subsequent analysis showed this to be an underestimate and it appears that seven to eight patients

needed to be treated for 3 years to prevent one hospital admission.[65,66] A more recent analysis with detailed data[67] showed that treating 1000 patients for 1 year reduced the number of hospitalizations by 53. It is interesting that the risk reduction for hospitalizations with digitalis in the DIG study is as impressive as that seen with ACE inhibition in the SOLVD study in a comparable population (30% with digitalis compared to 32% with ACE inhibitors in patients with an ejection fraction <0.35%). This is even more remarkable since the benefit of digitalis in the DIG trial was seen in patients who were already receiving ACE inhibitor therapy. The benefit of digoxin in reducing hospitalizations in the initial 6 months was even greater (52%). This impressive reduction in hospitalizations was achieved with very minimal increase in digitalis toxicity. Another analysis, from a different data set, showed that use of digoxin could reduce health care costs by US$400 million.[68] These are therefore compelling reasons to use digitalis in most patients with heart failure.

How does the DIG trial influence the use of digitalis in heart failure?

Because digitalis had a neutral effect on all-cause mortality in the DIG trial, one major controversy surrounding digoxin can finally be laid to rest. Therefore, in future, its use in patients with heart failure must be determined by its clinical efficacy and its effects in decreasing the progression of heart failure. When and how should digitalis be used in heart failure?

Mild versus moderate to severe heart failure

The conventional wisdom has been that digitalis is most useful in patients with severe heart failure, large hearts and those with significant symptoms of fluid retention.[33] The Agency for Health Care Policy Research (AHCPR) and European guidelines recommend the use of digitalis in patients who do not respond to diuretic and ACE inhibitor therapy.[62] Some data suggest that digitalis may not be useful in patients with mild heart failure, especially in patients with coronary artery disease.[19,34,39] However, more recent data suggest that digitalis may have a role in patients with even mild heart failure. Subanalysis of the PROVED and RADIANCE studies show that while patients with severe heart failure worsen most often, patients with mild heart failure also deteriorate when digoxin is withdrawn from their therapeutic regimen.[63] The DIG trial data confirmed that the benefit of digitalis is seen in all patients with heart failure, including those with normal ejection fraction.[5,67]

Effects in heart failure with preserved LV function

Traditionally digitalis has been considered to be most useful in patients with systolic dysfunction. However the ancillary trial of the DIG study showed that digitalis is equally beneficial in patients with heart failure with ejection fraction greater than 0.45%. These findings therefore imply a therapeutic role for digitalis in patients with diastolic dysfunction. The reason for this is unclear. Digitalis has not been shown to improve diastolic dysfunction[69,70] except in occasional reports.[71] There is, however, evidence that digitalis may reduce LV hypertrophy[72] and decrease interstitial collagen.[73] These effects of digoxin might influence LV diastolic function and relieve pulmonary congestion. There is very little data on the effect of digitalis on ventricular remodelling. The only study that examined this issue did not show any benefit.[28] It is possible that the benefits in the group with normal LV function could be due to 'nonhaemodynamic' effects of digitalis (like actions on neurohormones or the autonomic system). However, it is possible that the patients randomized into the ancillary trial of the DIG study may have a number of diverse clinical conditions other than heart failure. The entry criteria for this trial did not allow for careful exclusion of patients with noncardiac causes of dyspnea. The use of digitalis in patients with diastolic dysfunction should therefore await further data.

Role in patients with asymptomatic heart failure

Digitalis decreased the progression of heart failure in the DIG trial (at least in terms of hospitalizations for worsening heart failure). Therefore, a case could be made for its use in patients with asymptomatic LV dysfunction. If the neurohormonal hypothesis of the progression of heart failure is correct,[52] then the favourable neurohormonal effects of digitalis might help to retard the development of symptomatic heart failure in patients with asymptomatic LV dysfunction. This needs to be evaluated in the future.

Optimum dose of digitalis

The optimal serum concentration of digoxin and need to titrate the dose of digoxin in patients with chronic heart failure has never been adequately addressed. Limited clinical evidence suggests that digitalis might augment myocardial contractility in a dose-dependent manner. However, there is little additional therapeutic benefit and a dramatic increase in toxic effects, when digoxin levels are increased beyond 1.5–2.0 ng/ml.[74] Hence serum digoxin concentration of 1.0–2.0 ng/ml have generally been considered optimal.[46]

A number of clinical trials including the RADIANCE and PROVED studies used a large dose (median 0.375 mg/day and mean 0.380 mg/day, respectively) with an aim to reach higher serum levels (0.9 to 2 ng/ml; final mean level achieved 1.2 ng/ml). These high doses were not associated with an unacceptable incidence of digitalis toxicity. It must be remembered, however, that most of the patients randomized in these trials were relatively young and had normal renal function. The incidence of drug toxicity might have been higher if the study had enrolled older patients and those with impaired renal function.[75] An international survey of digoxin dosing showed that physicians in France prescribed very high doses (with higher toxicity) than those in the US. Physicians in the UK and especially those in Italy use a much lower dose.[76] In fact, before the publication of the DIG trial, there was some concern that the dose used in the UK and Italy may be subtherapeutic.[77]

There may be a case for using a lower dose of digitalis, however. The dose of digitalis used currently evolved from studies which suggested that digitalis had dose-dependent inotropic effects.[59] Some of the other studies have not been able to demonstrate this phenomenon.[78] For example, Slatton et al used load-independent indices to study the dose response relationship of digitalis in heart failure.[79] They found that low dose (0.125 mg/day) digoxin significantly improved ventricular performance and this effect was not enhanced by higher doses (0.25 mg/day). Similarly, a low dose had maximal autonomic effects and reduced norepinephrine levels as much as that with higher doses. A recent retrospective analysis of the PROVED and RADIANCE trials, did not find any significant difference in exercise duration between patients with low (0.5–0.9 ng/ml) or high

(>1.2 ng/ml) serum digoxin concentration.[80] The DIG trial showed that digitalis was effective at a dose much lower than that used in the PROVED and RADIANCE trials. In fact, about 70% of patients were on 0.25 mg/day or less and the serum levels were less than 1.0 ng/ml. This dose was associated with a very low incidence of toxicity. A preliminary analysis from the DIG study and number of other data[81–83] suggests that there is a trend towards increased adverse events with increasing dose of digitalis. We can therefore conclude that digitalis is effective at low doses and that higher doses are associated with very little additional advantage but significantly increase toxicity. Thus, given the modest benefits of digitalis, there is no reason to push the dose of digitalis. A reasonable goal might be to attain a steady state serum level of 0.8–1 ng/ml. This might be more relevant in the elderly patients and other similar groups prone to digitalis toxicity.

The possible role of digitalis in the next century

Based on all of the above-mentioned data it appears that digitalis will continue to be used in patients with heart failure and normal sinus rhythm, in the foreseeable future. It will be used mainly for its effects in ameliorating symptoms and in reducing repeated hospitalizations for heart failure. All patients with symptomatic heart failure will now be candidates for this drug, unlike previous recommendations which limited it to sicker patients. Its role in pure diastolic dysfunction needs to be evaluated further. Unlike ACE inhibitors, digoxin has no proven role in patients with asymptomatic LV dysfunction.

Low dose digitalis (0.125–0.25 mg/day), aiming for a target serum level of 0.8–1.0 ng/ml, has the most optimal risk–

benefit ratio. The era for major clinical trials concerning the role of digitalis in heart failure is probably over, given the results of the DIG trial. Its place in the future will be determined by the existing data. With improvements in the medical management of heart failure, it is likely to play an increasingly lesser role in future. Until that time digitalis is still a player in the medical management of heart failure.

Reality is an illusion; albeit a very persistent one (Albert Einstein).

References

1. Sharma JN. Cardiovascular system and its diseases in the ancient Indian literature. *Indian J Dis* 1986; **9**: 32.

2. Moore DA. William Withering and digitalis. *BMJ* 1985; **290**: 324.

3. Packer M, Gheorghiade M, Young JB et al for the RADIANCE Study. Withdrawal of digoxin from patients with chronic heart failure treated with angiotensin-converting enzyme inhibitors. *N Engl J Med* 1993; **329**: 1–7.

4. Uretsky BF, Young JB, Shahidi FE et al on behalf of the PROVED Investigative Group. Randomized study assessing the effect of digoxin withdrawal in patients with mild to moderate chronic congestive heart failure: results of the PROVED trial. *J Am Coll Cardiol* 1993; **22**: 955–962.

5. The DIG Investigation Group. The effect of digoxin on mortality and morbidity in patients with heart failure. The Digitalis Investigation Group. *N Engl J Med* 1997; **336**: 525–533 (comments).

6. Shapiro W. Digitalis update. *Arch Intern Med* 1981; **141**: 17–18.

7. Anon. A reappraisal of digoxin usage. *Drug Ther Bull* 1979; **13**: 49–51.

8. MacKenzie J. *Diseases of the Heart*, 3rd edn London: Oxford University Press, 1913.

9. Christian HA. Digitalis effects in chronic cardiac cases with regular rhythm in contrast to auricular fibrillation. *Med Clin North Am* 1922; **5**: 1173–1190.

10. Harvey RM, Ferrer MI, Cathcart RT et al. Some effects of digoxin upon the heart and circulation in man: digoxin in left ventricular failure. *Am J Med* 1949; 7: 439–453.

11. McMichael J, Sharpey-Schafer EP. The action of intravenous digoxin in man. *Q J Med* 1944; **13**: 123–135.

12. Gheorghiade M, Hall V, Lekier J et al. Comparative hemodynamic and neurohormonal effects of intravenous captopril and digoxin and their combinations in patients with severe heart failure. *J Am Coll Cardiol* 1989; **13**: 134–142.

13. Arnold SB, Bird RC, Meister W et al. Long-term digitalis therapy improves left ventricular function in heart failure. *N Engl J Med* 1980; **303**: 1443–1448.

14. Starr I, Luchi RJ. Blind study of the action of digitoxin on elderly women. *Am Heart J* 1969; **78**: 740–751.

15. Johnston GC, McDevitt DG. Is maintenance digoxin necessary in patients with sinus rhythm? *Lancet* 1979; **i**: 567–570.

16. Dall JLC. Maintenance digoxin in elderly patients. *BMJ* 1970; **ii**: 705–706.

17. Krakauer R, Petersen B. The effects of discontinuing maintenance digoxin therapy. *Dan Med Bull* 1979; **26**: 10–13.

18. Hull SM, Mackintosh A. Discontinuation of maintenance digoxin therapy in general practice. *Lancet* 1977; **ii**: 1054–1055.

19. Gheorghiade M, Beller G. Effects of discontinuing maintenance digoxin therapy in patients with ischemic heart disease and congestive heart failure in sinus rhythm. *Am J Cardiol* 1983; **51**: 1243–1250.

20. McHaffie D, Purcell H, Mitchell-Hegs P et al. The clinical value of digoxin in patients with heart failure and sinus rhythm. *Q J Med* 1978; **47**: 401–419.

21. The CONSENSUS Trial Study Group. Effect of enalapril on mortality in severe congestive heart failure: results of the Cooperative North Scandinavian Enalapril Survival Study (CONSENSUS). *N Engl J Med* 1987; **316**: 1429–1435.

22. The SOLVD Investigators. Effect of enalapril on survival in patients with reduced left ventricular ejection fractions and congestive heart failure. *N Engl J Med* 1991; **325**: 293–302.

23. Pfeffer MA, Braunwald E, Moye LA et al. Effect of captopril on mortality and morbidity in patients with left ventricular dysfunction after myocardial infarction. Results of the survival and ventricular enlargement trial. The SAVE Investigators. *N Engl J Med* 1992; **327**:

669–677.

24. Krell MJ, Kline EM, Bates ER et al. Intermittent, ambulatory dobutamine infusions in patients with severe congestive heart failure. *Am Heart J* 1986; **112**: 787–791.

25. Dies F, Krell MJ, Whitlow P et al. Intermittent doubtamine in ambulatory outpatients with chronic cardiac failure. *Circulation* 1986; 74: II-38 (abstr).

26. Packer M, Carver JR, Rodeheffer RJ et al. Effect of oral milrinone on mortality in severe chronic heart failure. *N Engl J Med* 1991; **325**: 1468–1475.

27. Curfman GD. Inotropic therapy for heart failure — an unfulfilled promise. *N Engl J Med* 1991; **325**: 1509–1510.

28. Sabbah HN, Shimoyama H, Kono T et al. Effects of long-term monotherapy with enalapril, metoprolol, and digoxin on the progression of left ventricular dysfunction and dilation in dogs with reduced ejection fraction. *Circulation* 1994; **89**: 2852–2859.

29. Bigger JT, Fleiss JL, Rolnitzky LM et al. Effect of digitalis treatment on survival after acute myocardial infarction? *Am J Cardiol* 1985; **55**: 623–630.

30. Moss AJ, Davis HT, Conrad DL et al. Digitalis-associated cardiac mortality after myocardial infarction. *Circulation* 1981; **64**: 1150–1156.

31. The Digitalis Subcommittee of the Multicenter Post-infarction Research Group. The mortality risk associated with digitalis treatment after myocardial infarction. *Cardiovasc Drugs Ther* 1987; **1**: 125–132.

32. Dobbs SM, Kenyon WI, Dobbs RJ. Maintenance digoxin after an episode of heart failure: Placebo-controlled trial in outpatients. *BMJ* 1977; **i**: 749–752.

33. Lee DCS, Johnson RA, Bingham JB et al. Heart failure in outpatients: a randomized trial of digoxin versus placebo. *N Engl J Med* 1982; **306**: 699–705.

34. Fleg L, Gottlieb SH, Lakalta EG. Is digoxin really important in compensated heart failure? *Am J Med* 1982; **73**: 244–250.

35. Taggart AJ, Johnston GD, McDevitt DG. Digoxin withdrawal after cardiac failure in patients with sinus rhythm. *J Cardiovasc Pharmacol* 1983; **5**: 229–234.

36. Guyatt GH, Sullivan MJJ, Fallen EF et al. A controlled trial of digoxin in congestive heart failure. *Am J Cardiol* 1988; **61**: 371–375.

37. Pugh SE, White NJ, Aronson JK et al. Clinical, hemodynamic, and pharmacological effects of withdrawal and reintroduction of digoxin in patients with heart failure in sinus rhythm after long-term treatment. *Br Heart J* 1989; **61**: 529–539.

38. Ford AR, Aronson JK, Grahame-Smith DG, Carver JG. The acute changes seen in cardiac glycoside receptor sites, [86]rubidium uptake and intracellular sodium concentrations during early phases of digoxin therapy and after chronic therapy. *Br J Clin Pharmacol* 1979; **8**: 135–142.

39. Fleg JL, Rothfeld B, Gottlieb SH. Effect of maintenance digoxin therapy on aerobic performance and exercise left ventricular function in mild to moderate heart failure due to coronary artery disease: a randomized placebo-controlled crossover trial. *J Am Coll Cardiol* 1991; **17**: 743–751.

40. Haerer W, Bauer U, Hetzel M, Fehske J. Long-term effects of digoxin and diuretics in congestive heart failure. Results of a placebo-controlled randomized double blind study. *Circulation* 1988; **78**: 53.

41. The Captopril-Digoxin Multicenter Research Group. Comparative effects of therapy with captopril and digoxin in patients with mild to moderate heart failure. *JAMA* 1988; **259**: 539–544.

42. German and Austrian Xamoterol Study Group. Double-blind placebo-controlled comparison of digoxin and xamoterol in chronic heart failure. *Lancet* 1988; **i**: 489–493.

43. DiBianco R, Shabetai R, Kostuk W et al for the Milrinone Multicenter Trial Group. A comparison of oral milrinone, digoxin, and their combination in the treatment of patients with chronic heart failure. *N Engl J Med* 1989; **320**: 677–683.

44. Just H, Drexler H, Taylor SH et al. Captopril versus digoxin in patients with coronary artery disease and mild heart failure. A prospective, double-blind, placebo-controlled multicenter study. The CADS Study Group. *Herz* 1993; **18** (Suppl 1): 436–443.

45. Van Veldhuisen DJ, Man in 't Veld AJ, Dunsel-

man PH et al. Double-blind placebo-controlled study of ibopamine and digoxin in patients with mild to moderate heart failure: results of the Dutch Ibopamine Multicenter Trial (DIMT). *J Am Coll Cardiol* 1993; **22**: 1564–1573.

46. Lewis RP. Clinical use of serum digoxin concentrations. *Am J Cardiol* 1992; **69**: 97G–106G.

47. Poole-Wilson PA. Digoxin withdrawal in patients with heart failure. *J Am Coll Cardiol* 1994; **24**: 578–579 (letter).

48. Packer M, Medina N, Yushak M. Hemodynamic and clinical limitations of long-term inotropic therapy with amrinone in patients with severe chronic heart failure. *Circulation* 1984; **70**: 1038–1047.

49. Rona G. Catecholamine cardiotoxicity. *J Mol Cell Cardiol* 1985; **17**: 291–306.

50. Tan LB, Jalil JE, Pick R et al. Cardiac myocyte necrosis induced by angiotensin II. *Circ Res* 1991; **69**: 1185–1195.

51. Mann DL, Kent RL, Parsons B, Cooper G. Adrenergic effects on the biology of the adult mammalian cardiocytes. *Circulation* 1992; **85**: 790–804.

52. Packer M. The neurohormonal hypothesis: a theory to explain the mechanism of disease progression in heart failure. *J Am Coll Cardiol* 1992; **20**: 248–254.

53. Eckberg DL, Drabinsky M, Braunwald E. Defective cardiac parasympathetic control in patients with heart disease. *N Engl J Med* 1971; **285**: 877–883.

54. Ferguson DW, Berg WJ, Sanders JS et al. Sympathoinhibitory responses to digitalis in heart failure patients. Direct evidence from sympathetic neural recordings. *Circulation* 1989; **80**: 65–77.

55. Alicandri C, Fariello R, Boni E et al. Captopril versus digoxin in mild-moderate chronic heart failure: a crossover study. *J Cardiovasc Pharmacol* 1987; **9**: S61–S67.

56. Brouwer J, van Veldhuisen DJ, Man in 't Veld AJ et al for the DIMT Study Group. Relation between heart rate variability and neurohumoral status in patients with heart failure. Effects of neurohumoral modulation by digoxin and ibopamine. *Circulation* 1993; **88**: I-108.

57. Krum H, Bigger JT Jr, Goldsmith RL, Packer M. Effect of long-term digoxin therapy on autonomic function in patients with chronic heart failure. *J Am Coll Cardiol* 1995; **25**: 289–294.

58. Kromer EP, Elsner D, Riegger GAJ. Digoxin, converting-enzyme inhibition (quinapril), and the combination in patients with congestive heart failure functional class II and sinus rhythm. *J Cardiovasc Pharmacol* 1990; **16**: 9–14.

59. Gheorghiade M, Hall VB, Jacobson G et al. The effects of increasing maintainance dose of digoxin on left ventricular function and neurohormones in patients with chronic heart failure treated with diuretics and angiotensin converting enzyme inhibitors. *Circulation* 1995; **92**: 1801–1807.

60. Gheorghiade M, Hall VB, Fenn NM et al. Chronic effects of digoxin withdrawal on neurohormones in patients with stable heart failure treated with converting-enzyme inhibitors. *Eur Heart J* 1993; **14**: 131.

61. Gheorghiade M, Young JB, Uretsky B et al on behalf of the PROVED and RADIANCE Investigators. Predicting clinical deterioration after digoxin withdrawal in heart failure. *Circulation* 1993; **88**: I-604.

62. Task Force of the Working Group on Heart Failure of the European Society of Cardiology. Treatment of heart failure. *Eur Heart J* 1997; **18**: 736–753.

63. Adams KF Jr, Gheorghiade M, Uretsky BF et al. Clinical predictors of worsening heart failure during withdrawal from digoxin therapy. *Am Heart J* 1998; **135**: 389–397.

64. Packer M. End of the oldest controversy in medicine. Are we ready to conclude the debate on digitalis?. *N Engl J Med* 1997; **336**: 575–576 (edit; comment).

65. McMurray J, Davie AP. Digoxin for patients with heart failure in sinus rhythm. *Lancet* 1997; **350**: 519 (letter; comment).

66. Cleland JGF, Swedberg K, Poole-Wilson PA. Successes and failures of current treatment of heart failure. *Lancet* 1998; **352** (Suppl): 19–28.

67. Yusuf S. Digoxin in heart failure: results of the recent Digoxin Investigation Group trial in the context of other treatments for heart failure. *Eur Heart J* 1997; **18**: 1685–1688 (edit).

68. Ward RE, Gheorghiade M, Young JB, Uretsky B. Economic outcomes of withdrawal of digoxin therapy in adult patients with stable congestive heart failure. *J Am Coll Cardiol* 1995; **26**: 93–101.

69. Weiss JL, Frederiksen JW, Weisfeldt ML. Hemodynamic determinants of the time course of fall in canine left ventricular pressure. *J Clin Invest* 1976; **58**: 751–760.

70. Little WC, Rassi A Jr, Freeman GL. Comparison of the effects of dobutamine and ouabain on left ventricular contraction and relaxation in closed chest dogs. *J Clin Invest* 1987; **80**: 613–620.

71. Eichhorn EJ, Alvarez LG, Willard JE, Grayburn PA. Digitalis improves myocardial relaxation in patients with heart failure. *J Am Coll Cardiol* 1992; **19**: 254A.

72. Turto H, Lindy S. Digitoxin treatment of experimental cardiac hypertrophy in the rat. *Cardiovasc Res* 1973; **7**: 482–489.

73. Turto H. Collagen metabolism in experimental cardiac hypertrophy and the effect of digitoxin treatment. *Cardiovasc Res* 1977; **11**: 358–366.

74. Lewis RP. Digitalis. In: Leier CV (ed) *Cardiotonic Drugs: A Clinical Survey*. New York: Marcel Dekker, 1986; 85–150.

75. Warren JL, McBean AM, Hass SL, Babish JD. Hospitalizations with adverse events caused by digitalis therapy among elderly Medicare beneficiaries. *Arch Intern Med* 1994; **154**: 1482–1487.

76. Saunders KB, Amerasinghe AK, Saunders KL. Dose of digoxin prescribed in the UK compared with France and the USA. *Lancet* 1997; **349**: 833–836 (comments).

77. Zuccala G, Pedone C, Carosella L et al. Optimum dose of digoxin. *Lancet* 1997; **349**: 1845 (letter; comment).

78. Ware JA, Snow E, Luchi JM, Luchi RJ. Effect of digoxin on ejection fraction in elderly patients with congestive heart failure. *J Am Geriatr Soc* 1984; **32**: 631–635.

79. Slatton ML, Irani WN, Hall SA et al. Does digoxin provide additional hemodynamic and autonomic benefit at higher doses in patients with mild to moderate heart failure and normal sinus rhythm? *J Am Coll Cardiol* 1997; **29**: 1206–1213.

80. Young JB, Gheorghiade M, Packer M et al on behalf of the PROVED and RADIANCE Investigators. Are low serum levels of digoxin effective in chronic heart failure? Evidence challenging the accepted guidelines for a therapeutic serum level of the drug. *J Am Coll Cardiol* 1993; **21**: 378A.

81. Mancini DM, Benotti JR, Elkayam U et al and the PROMISE Investigators. Antiarrythmic drug use and high serum levels of digoxin are independent adverse prognostic factors in patients with chronic heart failure. *Circulation* 1991; **84** (Suppl II): II-243.

82. Packer M. The development of positive inotropic agents for chronic heart failure: how have we gone astray. *J Am Coll Cardiol* 1993; **22** (Suppl A): 119A–126A.

83. Leor J, Goldbourt U, Rabinowitz B et al. Digoxin and increased mortality among patients recovering from acute myocardial infarction: importance of digoxin dose. *Cardiovasc Drugs Ther* 1995; **9**: 723–729.

16

Beta-blockers in heart failure: help, hope or hype?

Robert Neil Doughty and Norman Sharpe

Introduction

Chronic heart failure is a major public health problem in most Western countries. In the United States, about 3 million people (2% of the adult population) have heart failure and about 400 000 patients are admitted to hospital each year with this diagnosis.[1] In recent decades there have been considerable advances in medical therapy for patients with heart failure. Most notably the angiotensin-converting enzyme (ACE) inhibitors have been shown to reduce morbidity and mortality in a broad spectrum of patients with heart failure[2,3] or asymptomatic left ventricular dysfunction.[4] However, despite these advances morbidity and mortality remain unacceptably high and there remains a need for further therapies which may improve the outlook for such patients. One group of drugs which may provide further benefit are the beta-adrenergic antagonists.

Beta-blockers were first used in heart failure in Sweden in the mid-1970s.[5,6] These early studies, although uncontrolled, showed beneficial effects on haemodynamics and symptoms in patients with severe chronic heart failure due to idiopathic dilated cardiomyopathy. Despite traditional teaching that beta-blockers are contraindicated in patients with heart failure, these early studies suggesting clinical improvement led the way for the development of a strong rationale for using beta-blockers in heart failure.[7] Since the early studies there have been a number of randomized controlled trials assessing the effects of beta-blockade on symptoms, exercise, left ventricular function and mortality.[8–31] This chapter reviews the data from these trials and discusses the current place of beta-blockers in the treatment of patients with heart failure. Several large-scale randomized, controlled trials currently underway will provide reliable data on the benefits and risks of the use of such therapy in all patients with heart failure.

Rationale for the use of beta-blockers in heart failure

The rationale for the use of beta-blockers in the treatment of heart failure is now well established.[7] Several neurohormonal systems are activated in heart failure, including the renin–angiotensin–aldosterone and sympathetic nervous systems. In acute heart failure these systems provide support for the heart and circulation and activation may be considered compensatory. However, in chronic heart failure, activation of these systems continues, contributing to the vasoconstriction, volume expansion and progressive left ventricular dysfunction which is characteristic of chronic heart failure. This 'neurohormonal hypothesis' of heart failure progression[32] is central to the rationale for the use of beta-blockers in treatment.

Blockade of the activated renin-angiotensin

system with the ACE inhibitors now has an established place in the treatment of heart failure.[2,3] However, the sympathetic nervous system is often activated earlier and to a greater degree than the renin-angiotensin system. Prolonged and excessive activation of the sympathetic nervous system, especially central cardiac sympathetic activity, has many potential adverse effects including direct toxic effects on the myocardium,[33] decreased coronary blood flow,[34] and tissue anoxia from vasoconstriction[35] which may be linked with the genesis of ventricular arrhythmias in heart failure.[34] Consequently, the excessive sympathetic activity in heart failure appears as important as that of the renin–angiotensin– aldosterone system and contributes to the progression of the disease process and associated poor prognosis. Consequently, blockade of the sympathetic nervous system may provide clinical benefits which are complementary to the effects of ACE inhibitors.

Clinical trials of beta-blockers in patients with heart failure

Traditionally the use of beta-blockers in heart failure has been considered contraindicated because of their acute negative inotropic effect. The first reports of the application of beta-blockers in patients with heart failure were from a Swedish group in the mid 1970s.[5,36] These reports described patients with severe idiopathic dilated cardiomyopathy who had a favourable clinical response to metoprolol. Subsequent reports from the same group suggested that survival was improved in this situation,[6] although comparison was with historical controls. Since then there have been 24 randomized, controlled trials of the effects of beta-blockade in patients with heart failure (Table 16.1).[8–27,37] These trials have involved

3141 patients, approximately half of whom had ischaemic heart disease as the underlying cause of heart failure with most of the remainder having idiopathic dilated cardiomyopathy. In general, these patients were in New York Heart Association (NYHA) functional class II or III and were clinically stable at entry to the trials. The results of these trials are summarized below.

Effects of beta-blockade on symptoms

The randomized trials of beta-blockers in patients with heart failure have shown disparate effects on symptoms. Several trials have reported lessening on symptoms and improved NYHA functional class,[10–22,24–26] although others have not confirmed these findings.[8,9,27] The Australia–New Zealand (ANZ) carvedilol trial,[27] in patients with chronic stable heart failure due to ischaemic heart disease, showed a trend to worsening of symptom status after 6 months of treatment,[38] but no overall effect on symptoms after 12 months of treatment.[27] This study involved a significant proportion of patients in NYHA functional class I at entry to the study and this may partly account for this apparent slight worsening of symptoms early during treatment.

The US Carvedilol Trial Programme involved a series of four studies run concurrently. Entry to each of the four studies[28–31] in the programme was on the basis of the distance covered in a 6-minute walk test prior to randomization. Each trial had different randomization protocols and primary end-points. Two of these trials reported improvements in NYHA functional class and a global assessment of progress, one involving patients with moderate to severe[29] and the other mild,[31] heart failure. However, neither trial demonstrated improvement in quality of life, as assessed by the Minnesota Living with

Trial	N	Beta-blocker	Follow-up (months)	Endpoints
Ikram and Fitzpatrick[*8]	17	Acebutolol	1	LV function, exercise
Currie et al[*9]	10	Metoprolol	1	LV function, exercise, symptoms
Anderson et al[*10]	50	Metoprolol	19	Mortality
Engelmeier et al[*11]	25	Metoprolol	12	LV function, exercise
Sano et al[12]	22	Metoprolol	12	LV function, exercise
Leung et al[*13]	12	Labetalol	2	LV function, exercise, symptoms
Pollock et al[14]	20	Bucindolol	3	Exercise, symptoms
Gilbert et al[†15]	23	Bucindolol	3	LV function, exercise, symptoms
Woodley et al[†16]	50	Bucindolol	3	LV function, exercise, symptoms
Paolisso et al[*17]	10	Metoprolol	3	Metabolic and LV function, symptoms
MDC[18]	383	Metoprolol	18	Need for transplantation and mortality
Wisenbaugh et al[19]	29	Nebivolol	3	LV function
Fisher et al[20]	50	Metoprolol	6	LV function, exercise, symptoms
Bristow et al[21]	139	Bucindolol	3	Dose titration study
Eichhorn et al[22]	25	Metoprolol	3	LV function
Metra et al[24]	40	Carvedilol	6	LV function, exercise, symptoms
CIBIS[23]	641	Bisoprolol	23	Mortality
Olsen et al[25]	60	Carvedilol	4	LV function, exercise, symptoms
Krum et al[26]	49	Carvedilol	3.5	LV function, exercise, symptoms
ANZ[27]	415	Carvedilol	19	LV function, exercise, symptoms
US 'MOCHA'[28]	345	Carvedilol	6.5	LV function, exercise, QOL
US 'PRECISE'[29]	278	Carvedilol	6	LV function, exercise, symptoms
US 'Severe'[30]	105	Carvedilol	3.5	LV function, QOL
US 'Mild'[31]	366	Carvedilol	6	Disease progression
TOTAL	**3141**		**12.9**	

*Cross-over trial; †23 patients appear in both totals from these two trial reports (but are included only once in the column total); ‡overall treatment effect in these trials represents the change between active and control groups by the intention to treat principle; ANZ, Australia–New Zealand Heart Failure Research Collaborative Group; CIBIS, Cardiac Insufficiency Bisoprolol Study; IHD, ischaemic heart disease; MDC, metoprolol in dilated cardiomyopathy; N, number of patients; NYHA, New York Heart Association functional class; QOL, quality of life.

Table 16.1
Randomized, controlled trials of beta-blocker in patients with heart failure.

Heart Failure Questionnaire. The trial which included patients with severe heart failure was stopped early when the trial programme was curtailed due to the finding of a large survival benefit with carvedilol (see below). Thus, few data are available related to the effects of carvedilol on symptoms in patients with severe heart failure.

Effects of beta-blockade on exercise tolerance

The effects of beta-blockade on exercise performance in heart failure have been variable, as with symptomatic effects. Some studies have reported improvement in maximum exercise duration[11,13,14,17,18,20] while others have shown no effect[9,15,16,19,24–27] or even a decrease in exercise performance.[8,21] Long-term beta-blockade attenuates maximum oxygen consumption,[39] consequently, maximal exercise testing may not be the most appropriate method for assessing improvement in functional capacity. Submaximal exercise may better reflect limitations in regular daily physical activities in patients with heart failure.[40] Some studies have shown that submaximal exercise improved with beta-blocker therapy[19,25,26] although this too has not been a consistent finding.[27,28,31]

In general, these results suggest that improvement in symptoms or exercise performance should not be a primary aim or expectation of treatment when using beta-blockers in patients with heart failure. However, there may be important effects on the natural progression of the disease process, perhaps mediated through sustained improvements in left ventricular remodelling.

Effects of beta-blockade on left ventricular function

A pooled analysis of the earlier beta-blocker trials showed that left ventricular ejection frac-

tion was increased by about 5 absolute percentage points over 3–6 months with beta-blocker therapy.[7] Similar effects were also shown in the recent ANZ carvedilol trial,[38] where patients with heart failure due to ischaemic heart disease showed an improvement in ejection fraction of about 5.5% after 6 months of treatment which was maintained

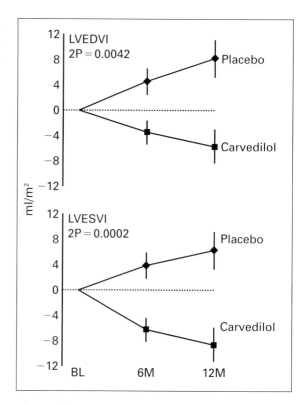

Figure 16.1
Changes in left ventricular end-diastolic and end-systolic volume index from baseline (BL) to 6 and 12 months. LVEDVI, left ventricular end-diastolic volume index; LVESVI, left ventricular end-systolic volume index. Values represent mean ± SE. P values comparing carvedilol and placebo are for repeated measures multivariate analysis of variance (MANOVA) over 12 months of treatment. (From Doughty et al[41] with permission.)

at 12 months. Consistent improvements in left ventricular (LV) ejection fraction were also observed in the US carvedilol trials.[28,29,31] However, in one trial there was a dose–response relationship with carvedilol, with an increase of approximately 5, 6 and 7.5 absolute percentage points with 6.25 mg bid, 12.5 mg bid and 25 mg bid respectively.

Such improvements in LV ejection fraction have recently been shown to be associated with reductions in left ventricular end-diastolic and end-systolic volumes (Figure 16.1).[41] These data, with an improvement in LV ejection fraction with reductions in both end-diastolic and end-systolic volumes, suggest that beta-blockade results in intrinsic improvement in LV function. These beneficial effects on LV function occur in patients already on optimal standard treatment for heart failure, including ACE inhibitor therapy, and may, at least in part, mediate the improvement in the natural history of the condition (see below).

Effects of beta-blockade on survival and hospitalizations

A recent systematic overview has provided data on total mortality among all of the 24 completed randomized, controlled trials of beta-blocker therapy in patients with heart failure.[42] There were a total of 135 deaths among the 1775 patients allocated to treatment with a beta-blocker compared with 162 deaths among the 1366 patients allocated to control during an average follow-up of approximately 1 year (Figure 16.2). This represents a 31% reduction in total mortality (odds ratio 0.69, 95% confidence interval 0.54–0.89 $2P = 0.0035$), and a reduction in mean annual mortality rate from 9.7 to 7.5%. The effect on mortality of vasodilating beta-blockers (47% reduction, SD 15) was non-significantly greater ($2P = 0.09$) than those of

standard agents (18% reduction, SD 15). Vasodilating beta-blockers were given to 61% of the patients assigned beta-blocker therapy. This was principally carvedilol (53%), with bucindolol, nebivolol and labetalol comprising the others.

As carvedilol was more frequently used than other beta-blockers and appeared to have a more pronounced effect on mortality it is worth examining the carvedilol trials in more detail. In March 1995 the carvedilol trial programme in the United States[37] involving patients with heart failure of mixed aetiology was terminated early by the trial Data and Safety Monitoring Board. Each trial[28-31] had different randomization protocols and primary endpoints but total mortality was a prespecified endpoint for the four trials combined. There was a total of 53 deaths among 1094 patients enrolled in these four trials during an average of only 6-months follow-up and a 65% reduction in total mortality with carvedilol. Such a large mortality benefit has not been seen with any heart failure treatment before although none of the previous trials had been adequately powered to detect significant effects on survival. Indeed the primary reason for combining the four US carvedilol trials was to rule out an adverse effect of carvedilol on survival. While it appears likely that beta-blockade does indeed have a significant mortality benefit in patients with heart failure, it is likely that this result was an extreme effect from analysis of a relatively small data set with short-term follow-up. Plausibly the actual effect is likely to be more moderate. In the ANZ carvedilol trial[27] there was a 26% reduction in the combined endpoint of death or hospital readmission ($2P = 0.02$). However, for death alone there was no significant difference between the groups despite a similar number of deaths (46) to that occurring in the US trials (53).

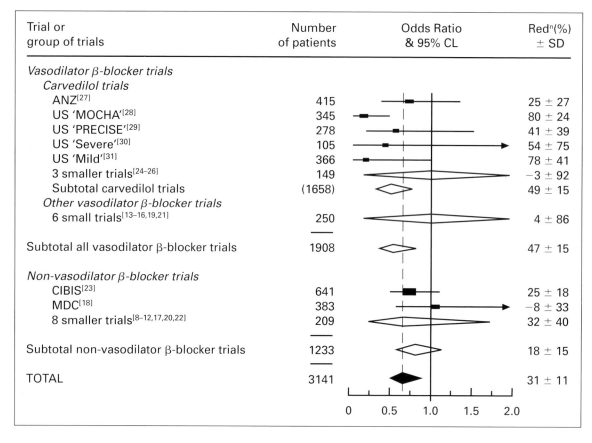

Trial or group of trials	Number of patients	Odds Ratio & 95% CL	Red^n(%) ± SD
Vasodilator β-blocker trials			
Carvedilol trials			
ANZ[27]	415		25 ± 27
US 'MOCHA'[28]	345		80 ± 24
US 'PRECISE'[29]	278		41 ± 39
US 'Severe'[30]	105		54 ± 75
US 'Mild'[31]	366		78 ± 41
3 smaller trials[24–26]	149		−3 ± 92
Subtotal carvedilol trials	(1658)		49 ± 15
Other vasodilator β-blocker trials			
6 small trials[13–16,19,21]	250		4 ± 86
Subtotal all vasodilator β-blocker trials	1908		47 ± 15
Non-vasodilator β-blocker trials			
CIBIS[23]	641		25 ± 18
MDC[18]	383		−8 ± 33
8 smaller trials[8–12,17,20,22]	209		32 ± 40
Subtotal non-vasodilator β-blocker trials	1233		18 ± 15
TOTAL	3141		31 ± 11

0   0.5   1.0   1.5   2.0

Figure 16.2
Total mortality for all trials of beta-blocker therapy in patients with heart failure. N, number of patients; OR, odds ratio; CL, confidence limits; SD, standard deviation; Red^n, reduction; ◇ represents the odds ratio and 95% confidence interval. (From Doughty et al[42] with permission.)

Among the larger trials a consistent reduction in hospitalizations has been reported. The US carvedilol trials reported a 27% reduction in hospitalization for cardiovascular causes (19.6 versus 14.1% for placebo and carvedilol respectively). Similar reductions have been reported in the ANZ carvedilol,[27] MDC[18] and CIBIS I[23] trials.

Clinical use of beta-blockers in patients with heart failure

As summarized above a consistent effect of beta-blocker therapy in patients with heart failure appears to be improvement of left ventricular size and function with long-term treatment. This effect probably mediates in part the improvements in long-term outcomes with reduction in hospital admissions and improvements in survival reported with beta-blockade. Symptoms and exercise capacity are not a consistent effect of beta-blocker treatment and these effects should not be a primary expectation with beta-blocker use. It should also be noted that the patients entered into these trials were often carefully selected, and only started on the study treatment when clinically stable. Following entry into the trials, there was usually a slow titration period from low to higher dose with careful clinical monitoring in specialized heart failure units. There is potential for an increase in symptoms and signs of congestion early during treatment which can be managed with an increase in the dose of diuretic with continuation of beta-blockade. Such deterioration early during treatment does not directly imply lack of possible long-term clinical benefit. Consequently, beta-blocker therapy may not be easy to initiate in patients with heart failure and may, at least at present, require specialist review early during treatment.

Despite these reports of favourable long-term outcomes with beta-blockers in patients with heart failure it is important to consider whether the current data are sufficient to support the widespread use of beta-blockers in all patients with heart failure. Following publication of the results from the US carvedilol trials,[37] opinion has been expressed both for[43] and against[44] accepting the current data as sufficient to warrant widespread use of carvedilol in all patients with heart failure. Several aspects need to be considered in such decisions. First, the current data set is relatively small: by way of comparison, the total number of deaths observed in the beta-blocker trials represents less than one-quarter of the total number of deaths observed in the major randomized controlled trials of ACE inhibitors in patients with heart failure.[45] This smaller data

set limits the generalizability of the results. For example, only approximately 100 patients with NYHA functional class IV symptoms have been involved in these randomized trials, thus limiting recommendations for use in these patients. As mentioned above, most patients in these trials had heart failure due to ischaemic heart disease or idiopathic dilated cardiomyopathy, consequently, there is little experience in patients with other causes of heart failure. Finally, the total number of deaths was relatively small and thus the relative contributions of reduction in death due to worsening heart failure, myocardial infarction or sudden death cannot be reliably determined.

Overall, the results from these trials of beta-blockade do suggest a worthwhile benefit, particularly increased survival, the magnitude of which may be considerable and in addition to that seen with ACE inhibitors. However, additional reliable clinical data such as the effects on cause-specific mortality, effects in more severe heart failure and outcome in other major subgroups of heart failure are still required. Finally, the observed effects of the vasodilating beta-blockers, mainly carvedilol, may be somewhat larger than other agents, principally metoprolol. However, the number of events in each subgroup is relatively small and does not exclude the possibility that such differences were observed by chance alone. Before beta-blocker therapy can be recommended for widespread use in all patients with heart failure these questions need to be answered by appropriately powered clinical trials. Many such trials are currently underway and will report over the next few years (Table 17.2). These trials will provide reliable data to address many of the questions posed above and allow clear recommendations to be made for the many thousands of patients with heart failure who may be eligible for beta-blocker therapy. Just as this chapter is going

Trial	N	Beta-blocker	Patients	NYHA	LVEF
COPERNICUS	1800	Carvedilol	Severe HF	IIIb–IV	<0.25
BEST[46]	2800	Bucindolol	Moderate–severe HF	III–IV	≤0.35
CIBIS II[47]	2500	Bisoprolol	Moderate–severe HF	III–IV	≤0.35
MERIT-HF	3000	Metoprolol	Mild–moderate–severe HF	II–IV	≤0.40
CAPRICORN	2600	Carvedilol	Post-MI LV dysfunction ± HF	I–IV	<0.40
COMET	3000	Carvedilol versus metoprolol	Moderate–severe HF	II–IV	≤5:0.35

N, number of patients; HF, heart failure; LVEF, left ventricular ejection fraction; NYHA, New York Heart Association functional Class.

Table 16.2
Ongoing mortality trials of beta-blockers in patients with heart failure.

to press, the results of CIBIS II[47] have been published, and MERIT-HF[48] presented. These two studies, with bisoprolol and metoprolol respectively, show identical results with a 34% reduction in mortality, exactly in agreement with the point estimate from the meta-analysis above. These data altogether provide sufficient evidence to allow clinical recommendations for beta-blocker use in chronic stable heart failure

Conclusions

The present role of beta-blockers in heart failure treatment appears to be as an addition to standard treatment in patients with chronic stable heart failure, carefully selected and monitored. The aims of treatment are to provide long-term improvement in left ventricular function and in the natural history of the condition, with improved survival and reduced hospital admissions. Beta-blockers are, however, not as easy to initiate as ACE inhibitors and clinical trial experience is still relatively limited in patients with more severe symptoms and also in the elderly (who represent a large part of the heart failure population).

References

1. Smith WM. Epidemiology of congestive heart failure. *Am J Cardiol* 1985; **55**: 3A–8A.
2. The CONSENSUS Trial Study Group. Effects of enalapril on mortality in severe congestive heart failure. Results of the Cooperative North Scandinavian Enalapril Survival Study (CONSENSUS). *N Engl J Med* 1987; **316**: 1429–1435.
3. The SOLVD Investigators. Effect of enalapril on survival in patients with reduced left ventricular ejection fractions and congestive heart failure. *N Engl J Med* 1991; **325**: 293–302.
4. Pfeffer MA, Braunwald E, Moye LA et al on behalf of the SAVE Investigators. Effect of captopril on mortality and morbidity in patients with left ventricular dysfunction after myocardial infarction. Results of the Survival and Ventricular Enlargement Trial. *N Engl J Med* 1992; **327**: 669–677.
5. Waagstein F, Hjalmarson A, Varnauskas E, Wallentin I. Effect of chronic beta-adrenergic receptor blockade in congestive cardiomyopathy. *Br Heart J* 1975; **37**: 1022–1036.
6. Swedberg K, Hjalmarson A, Waagstein F, Wallentin I. Prolongation of survival in congestive cardiomyopathy by beta-receptor blockade. *Lancet* 1979; **i**: 1374–1376.
7. Doughty RN, MacMahon S, Sharpe N. Beta-blockers in heart failure: promising or proved? *J Am Coll Cardiol* 1994; **23**: 814–821.
8. Ikram H, Fitzpatrick D. Double-blind trial of chronic oral beta-blockade in congestive cardiomyopathy. *Lancet* 1981; **ii**: 490–493.
9. Currie PJ, Kelly MJ, McKenzie A et al. Oral beta-adrenergic blockade with metoprolol in chronic severe dilated cardiomyopathy. *J Am Coll Cardiol* 1984; **3**: 203–209.
10. Anderson JL, Lutz JR, Gilbert EM et al. A randomized trial of low-dose beta-blockade therapy for idiopathic dilated cardiomyopathy. *Am J Cardiol* 1985; **55**: 471–475.
11. Engelmeier RS, O'Connell JB, Walsh R et al. Improvement in symptoms and exercise tolerance by metoprolol in patients with dilated cardiomyopathy: a double-blind, randomized, placebo-controlled trial. *Circulation* 1985; **72**: 536–546.
12. Sano H, Kawabata N, Yonezawa K et al. Metoprolol was more effective than captopril for dilated cardiomyopathy in Japanese patients. *Circulation* 1989; **80** (Suppl II): II-118 (abstract).
13. Leung WH, Lau CP, Wong CK et al. Improvement in exercise performance and haemodynamics by labetalol in patients with idiopathic dilated cardiomyopathy. *Am Heart J* 1990; **119**: 884–890.
14. Pollock SG, Lystash J, Tedesco C et al. Usefulness of bucindolol in congestive heart failure. *Am J Cardiol* 1990; **66**: 603–607.
15. Gilbert EM, Anderson JL, Deitchman D et al. Long-term beta-blocker vasodilator therapy improves cardiac function in idiopathic dilated cardiomyopathy: a double-blind, randomized study of bucindolol versus placebo. *Am J Med* 1990; **88**: 223–229.
16. Woodley SL, Gilbert EM, Anderson JL et al. Beta-blockade with bucindolol in heart failure caused by ischemic versus idiopathic dilated cardiomyopathy. *Circulation* 1991; **84**: 2426–2441.
17. Paolisso G, Gambardella A, Marrazzo G et al. Metabolic and cardiovascular benefits deriving from beta-adrenergic blockade in chronic congestive heart failure. *Am Heart J* 1992; **123**: 103–110.
18. Waagstein F, Bristow MR, Swedberg K et al for the Metoprolol in Dilated Cardiomyopathy (MDC) Trial Study Group. Beneficial effects of metoprolol in idiopathic dilated cardiomyopathy. *Lancet* 1993; **342**: 1441–1446.
19. Wisenbaugh T, Katz I, Davis J et al. Long-term (3 month) effects of a new beta-blocker (nebivolol) on cardiac performance in dilated cardiomyopathy. *J Am Coll Cardiol* 1993; **21**: 1094–1100.
20. Fisher ML, Gottlieb SS, Plotnick GD et al. Beneficial effects of metoprolol in heart failure

associated with coronary artery disease: a randomized trial. *J Am Coll Cardiol* 1994; **23**: 943–950.

21. Bristow MR, O'Connell JB, Gilbert EM et al for the Bucindolol Investigators. Dose-response of chronic beta-blocker treatment in heart failure from either idiopathic dilated cardiomyopathy or ischemic cardiomyopathy. *Circulation* 1994; **89**: 1632–1642.

22. Eichhorn EJ, Heesch CM, Barnett JH et al. Effect of metoprolol on myocardial function and energetics in patients with non-ischemic dilated cardiomyopathy: a randomized, double-blind, placebo-controlled study. *J Am Coll Cardiol* 1994; **24**: 1310–1320.

23. CIBIS Investigators and Committees. A randomized trial of beta-blockade in heart failure. The Cardiac Insufficiency Bisoprolol Study (CIBIS). *Circulation* 1994; **90**: 1765–1773.

24. Metra M, Nardi M, Giubbini R. Effects of short- and long-term carvedilol administration on rest and exercise hemodynamic variables, exercise capacity and clinical conditions in patients with idiopathic dilated cardiomyopathy. *J Am Coll Cardiol* 1994; **24**: 1678–1687.

25. Olsen SL, Gilbert EM, Renlund DG et al. Carvedilol improves left ventricular function and symptoms in chronic heart failure: a double-blind randomized study. *J Am Coll Cardiol* 1995; **25**: 1225–1231.

26. Krum H, Sackner-Bernstein JD, Goldsmith RL et al. Double-blind, placebo-controlled study of the long-term efficacy of carvedilol in patients with severe chronic heart failure. *Circulation* 1995; **92**: 1499–1506.

27. Australia–New Zealand Heart Failure Research Collaborative Group. Effects of carvedilol in patients with congestive heart failure due to ischemic heart disease: final results from the Australia–New Zealand Heart Failure Research Collaborative Group trial. *Lancet* 1997; **349**: 375–380.

28. Bristow MR, Gilbert EM, Abraham WT et al for the MOCHA Investigators. Carvedilol produces does-related improvements in left ventricular function and survival in subjects with chronic heart failure. *Circulation* 1996; **94**: 2807–2816.

29. Packer M, Colucci WS, Sackner-Bernstein JD et al for the PRECISE Study Group. Double-blind, placebo-controlled study of the effects of carvedilol in patients with moderate to severe heart failure. The PRECISE Trial. *Circulation* 1996; **94**: 2793–2799.

30. Cohn JN, Fowler MB, Bristow MA et al for the Carvedilol Study Group. Effect of carvedilol in severe chronic heart failure. *J Am Coll Cardiol* 1996; **27** (Suppl A): 169A (abstract).

31. Colucci WS, Packer M, Bristow MR et al for the US Carvedilol Heart Failure Study Group. Carvedilol inhibits clinical progression in patients with mild symptoms of heart failure. *Circulation* 1996; **94**: 2800–2806.

32. Packer M. The neurohormonal hypothesis: a theory to explain the mechanisms of disease progression in heart failure. *J Am Coll Cardiol* 1992; **20**: 248–254.

33. Szakacs JE, Cannon A. I-Norepinephrine myocarditis. *Am J Clin Pathol* 1958; **30**: 425–435.

34. Bigger JT. Why patients with congestive heart failure die: arrhythmias and sudden cardiac death. *Circulation* 1987; **75** (Suppl IV): IV-28–IV-35.

35. Mancia G. Sympathetic activation in congestive heart failure. *Eur Heart J* 1990; **11** (Suppl A): 3–11.

36. Swedberg K, Hjalmarson A, Waagstein F, Wallentin I. Beneficial effects of long-term beta-blockade in congestive cardiomyopathy. *Br Heart J* 1980; **44**: 117–133.

37. Packer M, Bristow MR, Cohn JN et al for the US Carvedilol Study Group. The effect of carvedilol on morbidity and mortality in patients with chronic heart failure. *N Engl J Med* 1996; **334**: 1349–1355.

38. Australia–New Zealand Heart Failure Research Collaborative Group. Effects of carvedilol, a vasodilator-beta-blocker in patients with congestive heart failure due to ischemic heart disease. *Circulation* 1995; **92**: 212–218.

39. Sweeney ME, Fletcher BJ, Fletcher GF. Exercise testing and training with beta-adrenergic blockade: role of drug washout period in 'unmasking' a training effect. *Am Heart J* 1989; **118**: 941–946.

40. Lipkin DP, Scriven AJ, Crake T. Six minute walk test for assessing exercise capacity in

chronic heart failure. *BMJ* 1986; **292:** 653–655.

41. Doughty RN, Whalley GA, Gamble G on behalf of the Australia–New Zealand Heart Failure Research Collaborative Group. Left ventricular remodelling with carvedilol in patients with congestive heart failure due to ischemic heart disease. *J Am Coll Cardiol* 1997; **29:** 1060–1066.

42. Doughty RN, Rodgers A, Sharpe N, MacMahon S. Effects of beta-blocker therapy on mortality in patients with heart failure. A systematic overview of randomized controlled trials. *Eur Heart J* 1997; **18:** 560–565.

43. Cleland JGF, Swedberg K. Carvedilol for heart failure, with care. *Lancet* 1996; **347:** 1199–1200.

44. Pfeffer MA, Stevenson LW. Beta-adrenergic blockers and survival in heart failure. *N Engl J Med* 1996; **334:** 1396–1397.

45. Garg R, Yusuf S for the Collaborative Group on ACE Inhibitor Trials. Overview of randomized trials of angiotensin-converting enzyme inhibitors on mortality and morbidity in patients with heart failure. *JAMA* 1995; **273:** 1450–1456.

46. The BEST Steering Committee. Design of the Beta-Blocker Evaluation Survival trial (BEST). *Am J Cardiol* 1995; **75:** 1220–1223.

47. CIBIS II Investigators. The Cardiac Insufficiency Bisoprolol Study II (CIBIS II): a randomised trial. *Lancet* 1999; **353:** 9–13.

48. Hjalmarson A. MERIT-HF. Metoprolol Randomised Intervention Trial in Heart Failure. Presentation ACC Scientific Meetings, New Orleans, March 1999.

17

Arrhythmia and sudden death in heart failure: is there light on the horizon?

Andrew C Rankin and Stuart M Cobbe

Introduction

Cardiac arrhythmias are common in patients with heart failure. Ventricular premature beats are virtually universal and are usually asymptomatic.[1] Atrial fibrillation occurs in between 15 and 20% of patients with heart failure[2] and may provoke haemodynamic decompensation. Most seriously, patients with heart failure are at risk from ventricular tachycardia or fibrillation and resultant sudden death.[3] Arrhythmic death remains a major contributor to total mortality in patients with heart failure.[4,5] Identification of those at high risk is of increasing importance because of advances in the treatments for life-threatening arrhythmia.[6] However, in addition to improved arrhythmia management, there are indicators that other improvements in the management of heart failure may reduce not only total mortality but also sudden death.[7]

Sudden death and heart failure

Cardiac failure is a lethal condition. Death may be due to progressive haemodynamic deterioration secondary to pump failure or may be sudden, without a prior increase in symptoms. The Framingham study reported the development of heart failure in 461 patients during a 30-year follow-up of over 5000 patients.[4] Within 4 years of diagnosis of heart failure, 55% of men and 24% of women had died. Approximately 50% of these deaths were sudden. Analysis of the mechanism of 568 deaths in the Vasodilator-Heart Failure Trials (V-HeFT I and II) reported 40% were sudden deaths and 31.5% were due to progressive heart failure.[5] A further 15% of deaths were sudden, but in the context of worsening symptoms (Figure 17.1). Mortality rises markedly with increasing severity of heart failure but the proportion of sudden deaths decreases. Annual mortality rates increase from 10 to 15% in class I and II to over 60% in class IV, whereas sudden death accounts for over 50% of deaths in class I and II and less than 30% in class IV.[8] Similarly, increasing severity of left ventricular dysfunction is associated with increased mortality, but a lower proportion of sudden deaths (Figure 17.2).[9]

Sudden death, often defined as within 1 hour of the onset of symptoms in patients who were clinically stable, is often caused by ventricular arrhythmia.[10] However, sudden death may be due to mechanisms other than ventricular fibrillation, such as asystole. Of patients with out-of-hospital cardiac arrest, the presenting rhythms are shockable ventricular tachyarrhythmia in about two-thirds.[10,11] Most of these patients, however, have their cardiac arrest in the context of acute myocardial infarction or ischaemia

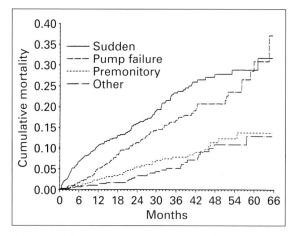

Figure 17.1
Mechanisms of death in heart failure. Cumulative mortality by cause of death in the Vasodilator-Heart Failure Trial I. During follow-up, 283 of 642 patients died. (From Goldman et al[5] with permission.)

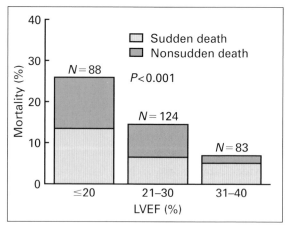

Figure 17.2
Relation between left ventricular ejection fraction and subsequent mortality rate. The average follow-up period was 16 months. (From Gradman et al[9] with permission.)

and not heart failure. In a review of 157 patients, mostly without cardiac failure, who died suddenly while undergoing ambulatory rhythm recording, the cause of death was malignant ventricular arrhythmias in 84% of cases and bradyarrhythmia in 16%.[12] By contrast, in 20 patients with severe heart failure the mechanism of unexpected cardiac arrest was severe bradycardia or electromechanical dissociation in 62% and ventricular tachyarrhythmia in only 38%.[13]

Despite the reported occurrence of sudden death, the exact incidence of fatal ventricular arrhythmia in heart failure is unknown. As discussed, sudden death may be due to causes other than ventricular arrhythmia but, conversely, arrhythmic deaths may not fall within the definition of sudden death.[14,15] The classification of deaths as arrhythmic or nonarrhythmic after myocardial infarction has been found to be particularly difficult in patients

with long-standing symptoms of chronic heart failure.[15] The problem of differentiating arrhythmic death from death due to pump failure is illustrated by those patients with heart failure who have shown clear evidence of haemodynamic deterioration requiring hospital admission but in whom the immediate mechanism of death is arrhythmia.[5] This raises the possibility that patients may be more prone to lethal arrhythmia during periods of haemodynamic decompensation, and contributes to the dilemma of the classification of mode of death.

Arrhythmic deaths preceded by cardiac decompensation have been classified as sudden or nonsudden in different studies, which may account for apparently conflicting results, for example from trials with angiotensin-converting enzyme inhibitors.[16] Narang et al reviewed 27 studies that reported 50 or more deaths among patients with heart failure and found a marked lack of consistency in definitions of mode of death.[17] The definition of sudden death ranged from unexpected death, to instantaneous death in the absence of cardiac deterioration, to death within a specified time period from onset of symptoms, ranging from 15 minutes to 24 hours. A total of 3909 deaths occurred in the 27 studies, of which 27–39% were classified as sudden deaths, and 35–67% as heart failure deaths. Most studies did not provide data about arrhythmic death in the context of worsening heart failure. The problems of defining mode of death in these patients is illustrated by a study of 109 deaths in 834 patients who had received an implantable cardioverter defibrillator (ICD).[18] Only seven of 17 'sudden deaths' had evidence of ventricular arrhythmias, while nine of 51 patients classified as nonsudden deaths had evidence of ventricular arrhythmia in the 6 hours prior to death. Autopsy information provided nonarrhythmic diagnoses in seven 'sudden death' cases, including myocardial infarction, pulmonary embolism, cerebral infarction and ruptured aortic aneurysm. However, despite these problems with identifying arrhythmic death, the evidence points to a substantial proportion of the mortality in heart failure being due to primary ventricular arrhythmia,[19] with risk of arrhythmic death even in patients with mild to moderate heart failure.[9]

Arrhythmogenic mechanisms in heart failure

A number of different mechanisms of cardiac arrhythmia induction have been identified[20] and there are arrhythmogenic factors associated with heart failure that may predispose to each (Table 17.1).[21,22] Re-entrant mechanisms are believed to underlie many sustained tachyarrhythmias, including ventricular tachycardia and fibrillation. This is particularly the case in patients with coronary artery disease

and prior myocardial infarction where regions of abnormal slow conduction at the border zone of the scar provide the substrate for re-entry circuits. Many patients with heart failure secondary to myocardial infarction, therefore, have the potential for re-entrant arrhythmia. A second mechanism for arrhythmia is triggered activity, where after-depolarizations are triggered by the preceding beat. These may be delayed after-depolarizations, occurring after repolarization of the action potential and caused by intracellular calcium overloading. These abnormalities may underlie the generation of arrhythmia in heart failure.[23] A second form of triggered activity, early after-depolarizations, occurs prior to repolarization of the action potential, and may result from abnormalities of repolarization in heart failure.[24] These may be induced by the effects of mechanically induced changes in electrophysiology.[25] Other factors that predispose to arrhythmia include electrolyte abnormalities, such as diuretic-induced hypokalaemia or hypomagnesaemia,[26] and increased catecholamines.[27]

Identification of risk of arrhythmia

Treatment strategies to prevent arrhythmia or sudden death would be best applied to those patients at highest risk and efforts have been directed at their identification.[28]

Prior cardiac arrest

Patients with left ventricular dysfunction who have previously survived an episode of ventricular tachycardia or fibrillation are at high risk of recurrent malignant ventricular arrhythmia.[29] Heart failure increases the risk of further arrhythmia. Cobbe et al reported the survival of 1476 patients initially resuscitated from out-of-hospital cardiac arrest, of

Mechanisms of arrhythmia	Arrythmogenic factors
Re-entry	Scarring and fibrosis
	Regions of slow conduction
	Myocardial ischaemia
Triggered activity	
(i) Delayed after-depolarizations	Calcium overload
	Digoxin toxicity
	Myocardial ischaemia
(ii) Early after-depolarizations	Prolonged repolarization
	Increased catecholamines
	Hypokalaemia
	Hypomagnesaemia
Increased automaticity	Increased catecholamines

Table 17.1
Mechanisms of arrhythmias and arrhythmogenic factors in heart failure.

which 680 survived to be discharged from hospital.[30] During follow-up there was 176 deaths of which 81 were sudden cardiac deaths. Treatment for heart failure was identified as an independent predictor of recurrent cardiac arrest.

In patients with severe heart failure, the prognostic impact of prior cardiac arrest has been reported in 458 patients, of whom 53 patients (12%) had survived cardiac arrest.[31] Twenty-two patients had cardiac arrest secondary to an identifiable cause (acute heart failure in 11, drug-induced torsades de pointes in 10, and hypokalaemia in one patient). Despite treatment of these underlying causes, the 1-year sudden death risk was 39%, and the 1-year total mortality was 54%. In the 31 patients with primary cardiac arrest, with no identified cause, who received antiarrhythmic treatments (amiodarone in 17, class I antiarrhythmic drugs in eight and an implantable cardioverter defibrillator in five patients), the 1-year sudden death risk was 17% and total

mortality rate was 24%. These risks were similar to those patients without prior cardiac arrest (17% sudden death and 30% mortality). With available treatments, therefore, patients with primary cardiac arrest had a prognosis similar to those without prior cardiac arrest, but secondary arrest was indicative of high risk despite attempts to control the precipitating factors.

Left ventricular dysfunction

The severity of heart failure, whether assessed by symptoms, functional capacity or measures of left ventricular dysfunction, is a major predictor of total mortality and also of sudden death.[5,9] The prognostic importance of left ventricular dysfunction and symptomatic heart failure has been demonstrated both in patients who have had,[32] and who have not yet had,[33] an arrhythmic event.

Ventricular arrhythmia

Spontaneous chronic ventricular arrhythmia

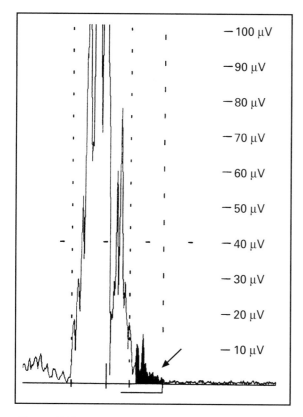

Figure 17.3

Signal-averaged electrocardiogram. The high amplitude deflection corresponds to the QRS complex, with the last 40 ms shaded in black. There is a low amplitude 'late potential' (arrow). The standard QRS duration was 85 ms, the total QRS (filtered 40–250 Hz) was 135 ms, the duration under 40 µV was 62 ms and the RMS voltages in the last 40 ms were 5.5 µV. Criteria for late potentials include a total filtered QRS of >114 ms, a duration of low amplitude signal (less than 40 µV) of >38 ms and terminal (last 40 ms) voltages of <25 µV.

of ventricular arrhythmia increases with increasing severity of heart failure and high-grade ventricular arrhythmias are associated with a worse overall prognosis, but not specifically with the risk of sudden death.[8,34] The frequency of nonsustained ventricular tachycardia is independently associated with both total mortality and sudden death.[9] A study of 515 patients with severe heart failure confirmed that nonsustained ventricular tachycardia was associated with severity of ventricular dysfunction and was an independent marker of increased mortality, especially sudden death.[35] Particularly, absence of nonsustained ventricular tachycardia indicated a low probability of sudden death.

Late potentials

The signal-averaged electrocardiogram (SAECG) is a technique that allows the identification of low amplitude late potentials occurring after the standard QRS complex on a surface ECG (Figure 17.3).[36] Late potentials indicate the presence of areas of slow conduction in the diseased myocardium, which may represent potential substrates for re-entrant arrhythmia.[37] In patients with left ventricular dysfunction secondary to coronary artery disease, the presence of late potentials has a weak positive predictive accuracy for arrhythmic events. However, their absence is a strong negative predictor, with very low likelihood of arrhythmia in patients with normal signal-averaged ECG, even in the presence of ventricular dysfunction.[38] In patients with nonischaemic cardiomyopathy, the presence of an abnormal SAECG was a marker for past and future arrhythmic events and was an independent predictor of outcome.[39] The 1-year survival was 95% in patients with normal SAECG and only 39% in 20 patients with an abnormal SAECG. However, in patients with advanced heart failure, late potentials are poor

detected during ambulatory monitoring might be considered to be evidence of likelihood of more serious arrhythmia, either as manifestations of an arrhythmic focus or as triggers for re-entrant tachyarrhythmias. The prevalence predictors of sudden, or nonsudden, death possibly due to the heterogeneity of causes of sudden death.[40] In a study of 151 patients with heart failure, including 57 with bundle branch block, the SAECG improved the risk stratification for sustained ventricular tachycardia (18% in the presence, and 2% in the absence, of late potentials) but failed to identify patients at high risk of sudden death.[41]

Heart rate variability

If the SAECG is an indication of arrhythmia substrate, and ventricular premature beats may be the triggers which initiate sustained arrhythmia, then autonomic tone may be the environment which allows their interaction. Heart rate variability can be measured from Holter recordings and is a measure of autonomic tone.[42] Reduced heart rate variability has been shown to be associated with adverse outcome following myocardial infarction.[43,44] Patients with idiopathic dilated cardiomyopathy, even those without heart failure, had reduced heart rate variability that was related to left ventricular dysfunction and not to ventricular arrhythmia.[45] In chronic heart failure, the decrease in heart rate variability has been shown to be a marker of sympatho-excitation, as assessed by muscle sympathetic nerve activity and plasma noradrenaline.[46] Such autonomic influences may be important in the initiation of sustained arrhythmia.[47] However, a prospective study of mortality in chronic heart failure identified reduction in heart rate variability as a powerful predictor of death due to progressive heart failure but not sudden death.[48]

QT dispersion

The QT interval on the surface electrocardiogram is an indicator of ventricular repolarization and variations in the duration of the QT interval may reflect inhomogeneity of repolar-

ization, which may predispose to arrhythmia.[49] The assessment of QT dispersion as a method of stratifying risk in heart failure has produced conflicting results, with some finding it to be predictive of sudden death[50–52] but others did not.[53,54] A study of 108 patients awaiting heart transplant found increased QT dispersion to be predictive of mortality.[51] Repolarization dispersion has been reported to be the most important predictor of sudden death and ventricular tachyarrhythmia in 163 patients with impaired left ventricular function.[52] By contrast, a study of 107 patients with dilated cardiomyopathy found QT dispersion to be of limited clinical usefulness due to the large overlap among patients with and without arrhythmic events.[53] Similarly, QT dispersion did not predict arrhythmia or death in 135 patients with heart failure secondary to dilated cardiomyopathy.[54] The application of QT dispersion assessment was limited by the presence of atrial fibrillation or bundle branch block. The discrepancies in results may reflect problems of methodology[55,56] and the future role of QT dispersion in the risk assessment of patients with heart failure remains to be clarified.

Induction of tachyarrhythmia

Sustained ventricular arrhythmia can be induced by electrical stimulation of the ventricles during invasive electrophysiological studies. The majority of patients who have had spontaneous monomorphic ventricular tachycardia will have a similar tachycardia induced by stimulation studies, especially patients with prior myocardial infarction and scar-related re-entrant tachycardias. The response of induced arrhythmia at electrophysiology study is of value in guiding selection of therapy in patients with prior ventricular tachycardia or fibrillation.[29] In patients with recent myocardial infarction who have never had spontaneous arrhythmia, induction of sustained ventricular tachycardia is predictive of subsequent arrhythmic events.[57] In these patients the negative predictive accuracy was high (98%), with a lower positive predictive accuracy (30%). This may not be the case in patients with heart failure. In a study of 72 patients with severe heart failure, ventricular tachycardia was inducible in nine (13%) patients of whom one died suddenly. However, 13 of 63 patients in whom arrhythmias were noninducible died suddenly, and the actuarial risk of sudden death in noninducible patients was 30% at 6 months.[58] Similarly, survivors of out-of-hospital cardiac arrest who do not have inducible ventricular tachycardia are still at risk of recurrent arrhythmia, particularly patients with left ventricular dysfunction and dilated cardiomyopathy.[59] Inducible arrhythmias were of predictive value in patients with severe heart failure awaiting cardiac transplantation in whom sustained ventricular tachyarrhythmias were induced in 13 of 37 patients (35%).[60] The positive predictive value for sudden death or nonfatal ventricular arrhythmia of induced tachyarrhythmia was 38% and increased to 50% when combined with an abnormal SAECG. Induction of ventricular arrhythmia, therefore, is an indicator of risk but lacks sensitivity, particularly in patients with dilated cardiomyopathy.[61]

Treatment of heart failure and arrhythmias

Vasodilator therapy and risk of arrhythmia

Medical treatment may improve some of the arrhythmogenic factors in heart failure, such as raised filling pressures and increased wall tension. If this were to reduce the likelihood of arrhythmia it might alter the markers of arrhythmia risk. Ventricular late potentials, however, are unaltered by ventricular pressure reduction in heart failure. Despite marked reduction in pulmonary capillary wedge pressure, and increase in cardiac output, in response to intravenous nitroprusside and diuretics, there was no significant change in the SAECG in 27 patients with heart failure (mean left ventricular ejection fraction 20%).[62] Changes in haemodynamic state also have little acute effect on cardiac electrophysiology and arrhythmia induction. In 12 patients with left ventricular dysfunction secondary to coronary artery disease, acute haemodynamic improvement due to nitroprusside, with a reduction in left ventricular size, did not affect induction of ventricular tachycardia.[63] Similarly, neither captopril nor hydralazine combined with nitrate altered arrhythmia induction in eight patients with left ventricular dysfunction due to prior myocardial infarction and inducible ventricular tachycardia.[64] Similarly, acute haemodynamic decompensation in nine patients with dilated cardiomyopathy did not predispose to arrhythmia induction.[65] Despite lack of inducible tachycardia in this study, there were three sudden deaths during follow-up, confirming the lack of predictive value of ventricular stimulation in dilated cardiomyopathy.[61] These observations would be consistent with the lack of reduction in sudden death, despite improved total mortality, produced by vasodilator therapy in V-HeFT I using hydralazine-isosorbide combination.[5]

Angiotensin-converting enzyme inhibitors and arrhythmias

The beneficial effects of angiotensin-converting enzyme (ACE) inhibitors on mortality in patients with heart failure are now well established,[66–68] but the mechanisms are still debated.[16] Despite the lack of effect of

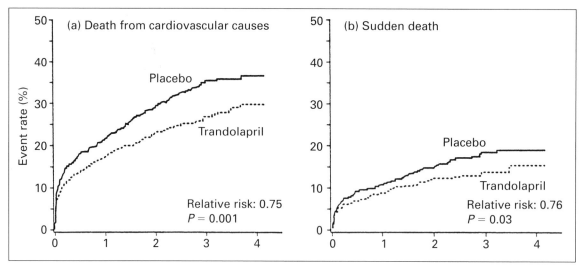

Figure 17.4
Reduction in mortality with trandolapril in patients with left ventricular dysfunction after myocardial infarction. Event rates for the secondary end-points of (a) death from cardiovascular causes and (b) sudden death. (From Køber et al[76] with permission.)

captopril on ventricular tachycardia induction, it prolongs ventricular refractoriness and repolarization, which are potentially beneficial electrophysiological effects.[64] The frequency of ventricular premature beats, couplets and non-sustained ventricular tachycardia in patients with heart failure is reduced by captopril[69] or enalapril.[70,71] Early studies with small numbers of patients indicated a reduction in sudden death compared to placebo.[72,73] Larger controlled studies, however, have shown no significant reductions in sudden death with enalapril in moderate[67] or severe[66] heart failure, or with captopril in patients with left ventricular dysfunction after myocardial infarction.[74]

The apparent lack of benefit of ACE inhibitors in preventing sudden death in the presence of asymptomatic left ventricular dysfunction[74] or moderate heart failure[67] may be partially attributable to the definitions of sudden death in these studies. Arrhythmic deaths occurring during periods of haemodynamic decompensation were regarded as 'haemodynamic' rather than 'arrhythmic' in origin. This problem of the definition of the mode of death is further illustrated by the AIRE study, in which ramipril produced a 30% reduction in sudden death in patients with heart failure following acute myocardial infarction.[75] However, 45% of those who died suddenly had severe or worsening heart failure prior to death and only 39% of sudden deaths were considered to be due to arrhythmia. Ramipril did not appear to reduce the proportion of deaths due to any specific arrhythmia. However, support for an effect of ACE inhibitors on arrhythmic death came from the TRACE study of trandolapril in patients with left ventricular dysfunction after myocardial infarction, with or without, heart failure.[76] There were significantly fewer sudden deaths in the trandolapril group (Figure 17.4) and, in addition, there were fewer episodes of documented ventricular fibrillation (2.9 versus 4.8%, $P = 0.03$).

Reduction in sudden deaths in patients treated with captopril and enalapril have been observed in studies in which they were compared to hydralazine-isosorbide combinations.[68,77] The Hy-C study showed a reduction in sudden death in 117 patients with advanced heart failure evaluated for cardiac transplantation in whom the drugs were titrated to produce equivalent haemodynamic improvements.[77] The actuarial incidence of sudden death at 1 year was 5% in the captopril-treated group and 37% in the hydralazine-treated patients. In the V-HeFT II trial of 804 men with moderate heart failure the improved survival with enalapril compared to hydralazine-isosorbide was due to a lower incidence of sudden death with or without premonitory worsening.[68] Much of this benefit was seen in the patients with relatively preserved left ventricular function.[5] In patients with left ventricular ejection fraction less than 0.35 treated with enalapril there were 37 sudden deaths without, and 12 with, premonitory symptoms compared to 46 and 22, respectively, with hydralazine-isosorbide combination. In those with better left ventricular function (ejection fraction >0.35) there were fewer sudden deaths, but proportionally greater benefit (in enalapril group, three sudden deaths without and one with premonitory symptoms; in hydralazine-isosorbide group, 13 sudden deaths without and five with premonitory symptoms). Thus, it would appear that there is a real benefit from ACE inhibitors with respect to sudden death, although this is only one aspect of their actions. A further certainty is that the problem of sudden death in heart failure persists despite ACE inhibition, accounting for between 11% of deaths in CONSENSUS (where the majority of deaths were nonsudden or due to pump failure) and 37% in V-HeFT II.

There is the possibility that other advances in drug therapy may make further impact on sudden death. The Evaluation of Losartan in the Elderly (ELITE) study showed that losartan, an angiotensin II receptor antagonist, was associated with an unexpected lower mortality than that found with captopril.[78] This reduction in mortality was mainly due to fewer sudden deaths on losartan (1.4 versus 3.8%). It has been suggested that the additional mortality benefit may be related to the more complete blockade of angiotensin II by losartan compared to ACE inhibition, but this was a relatively small study and confirmation of this benefit is required.

Beta-blockers and arrhythmias

Beta-adrenergic receptor blockade is increasingly accepted as having an established role in the treatment of heart failure.[79] Improvements in cardiac function and clinical outcome have been reported with beta-blockers in heart failure. Some of the mortality benefit may be related to a reduction in arrhythmic death.[80] Raised catecholamine levels have been considered to be arrhythmogenic in heart failure.[22] Beta-blockade may be beneficial, therefore, and has been reported to be associated with prognostic benefit in patients with ventricular tachycardia and left ventricular dysfunction,[81] and survivors of cardiac arrest.[82]

In patients with heart failure, β-blockers may exacerbate failure, but if used with caution may paradoxically result in improvement.[83] Initial randomized studies using selective $β_1$-receptor antagonists (metoprolol, bisoprolol) in patients with heart failure, secondary to a variety of causes including ischaemic heart disease and cardiomyopathy, showed haemodynamic benefit but no clear mortality benefit.[84,85] In particular, no reduction in sudden death was demonstrated.[85] However, the larger, randomized trial of bisoprolol, CIBIS-II, showed a significant reduction in sudden death.[80] In 2647 symptomatic patients with heart failure, treated with diuretics and ACE inhibitors, there was a 34% reduction in all-cause mortality, from 17.3% with placebo to 11.8% on bisoprolol. There was a 44% reduction in sudden deaths, with 48 sudden deaths (3.6%) in patients taking bisoprolol compared to 83 (6.3%) in the placebo group. Treatment effects were independent of severity or cause of heart failure.

There had been previous indications that beta-blockade may reduce sudden death in heart failure from smaller studies with carvedilol, a non-selective β_1-, β_2- and α_1-receptor antagonist, which also has vasodilating properties. These had shown reduction in total mortality and sudden death.[86,87] A meta-analysis of 18 double-blind controlled trials of beta-blockers in heart failure showed that they reduced the risk of death by 32%.[88] Another overview of 24 randomized trials of β-blockers in over 3000 patients with heart failure showed a 31% reduction in the odds of death.[89] Benefit appeared greatest with vasodilating non-selective β-blockers, in particular carvedilol, but these meta-analyses did not include CIBIS-II, which has shown clear benefit with selective β_1-antagonism, including reduction in sudden death. Results of further on-going studies may further clarify the benefits of β-blockers in heart failure.[90]

Inotropic agents and arrhythmias

Other drug treatments for heart failure, in particular inotropic agents, are not promising agents for the reduction in sudden death.[91] Vesnarinone, an oral inotropic agent, produced a 50% risk reduction in death with improvements in sudden and cardiac mortality, but was associated with neutropenia and had a narrow therapeutic window with increased mortality with a higher dose.[92] Other inotropic drugs, for example milrinone, a phosphodiesterase inhibitor, have also been associated with increased mortality of unknown cause, but proarrhythmia has been suspected.[93]

Antiarrhythmic drugs and heart failure
Adverse actions of class I antiarrhythmic drugs

Ventricular arrhythmias in patients with heart failure are associated with sudden death[9,35] and antiarrhythmic drug treatment may reduce the frequency of ventricular ectopy but will this improve mortality? There are reasons to believe that this may not be the case with most antiarrhythmic drugs, particularly those with class I actions (sodium channel blockade). In patients with sustained ventricular tachycardia or ventricular fibrillation, antiarrhythmic drugs are less effective in patients with severe left ventricular dysfunction, both with respect to inducible sustained arrhythmia during short-term assessment[94,95] and recurrent arrhythmia during long-term follow-up.[96,97] Many antiarrhythmic drugs have negative inotropic effects[98] and heart failure may be caused or exacerbated by their use.[99,100] There is additional concern that, in patients with heart failure, class I drugs are not only relatively ineffective at suppressing ventricular arrhythmia but may be causing harm by increasing the susceptibility to fatal arrhythmia. This was most powerfully demonstrated by the Cardiac Arrhythmia Suppression Trial (CAST) in which mortality was increased by the class I drugs encainide and flecainide compared to placebo (8.5 versus 4%) in over 1000 patients with left ventricular dysfunction and asymptomatic ventricular arrhythmia following myocardial infarction.[101] There was a greater absolute increase in the risk of death or cardiac arrest associated with antiarrhythmic therapy in the subgroup of patients with

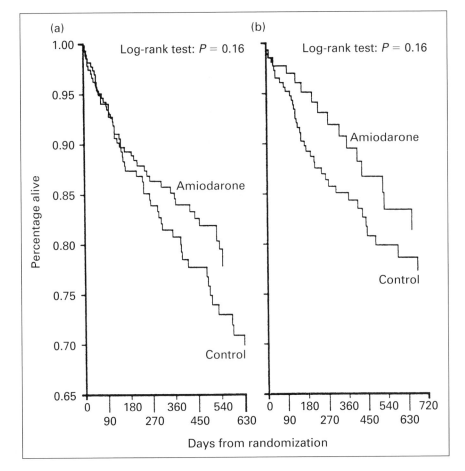

Figure 17.5
Improved survival with amiodarone in heart failure (GESICA). Survival curves of 256 patients with heart failure in the control group and 260 patients in the amiodarone group. (a) Death from progressive heart failure; (b) sudden death. (From Doval et al[110] with permission.)

radionuclide left ventricular ejection fractions less than 0.30. Heart failure or ischaemic event rates were not increased but the risk of death associated with such events was increased fourfold for heart failure,[102] and greater for ischaemic events.[103] Concern regarding the safety of class I agents is supported by the observation that patients with heart failure treated with antiarrhythmic drugs, not for ventricular arrhythmia, but for atrial fibrillation, had increased mortality.[104] Drugs with class I antiarrhythmic action, therefore, are of little value and likely to be harmful in heart failure.[105]

Amiodarone in heart failure

Amiodarone, a drug with a class III effect (prolongation of refractoriness) has few detrimental haemodynamic actions[106] and is generally tolerated by patients with heart failure. It reduces the incidence of ventricular premature beats and nonsustained ventricular tachycardia in patients with heart failure.[107] Initial studies had pointed to beneficial effects of amiodarone in heart failure, with arrhythmia reduction but no clear benefit on mortality.[107–109] The study from Argentina (GESICA)

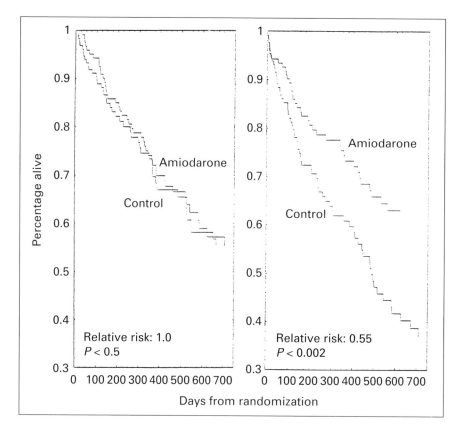

Figure 17.6
Heart rate and mortality. Survival differences between amiodarone-treated and control patients according to (a) baseline heart rate <90 beats/min and (b) baseline heart rate >90 beats/min. (From Nul et al[111] with permission.)

of 516 patients with severe heart failure, with or without documented arrhythmia, showed a 28% risk reduction in mortality with amiodarone, 300 mg daily.[110] The benefit was due to an early (30-day) decrease in sudden death and a late reduction in mortality from progressive heart failure (Figure 17.5). The beneficial effect of amiodarone was equal in patients with or without nonsustained ventricular tachycardia at baseline. Subsequent analysis has shown that the survival benefit was seen only in patients with severe heart failure with baseline heart rates greater than 90 beats per minute (Figure 17.6).[111]

In contrast to the encouraging results of the

GESICA study, the Veterans Administration study (CHF STAT) of amiodarone, 300 mg, in 633 patients with heart failure and greater than 10 ventricular ectopic beats per hour on ambulatory monitoring failed to demonstrate any significant reduction in mortality despite suppression of ventricular arrhythmia.[112] One contributory factor to these discrepant results may be the different proportions of underlying aetiologies, with the majority of patients having coronary artery disease in CHF-STAT (70%) compared to the minority (39%) in GESICA. There was a trend towards a reduction in mortality among patients with nonischaemic cardiomyopathy in CHF-STAT,[113] in

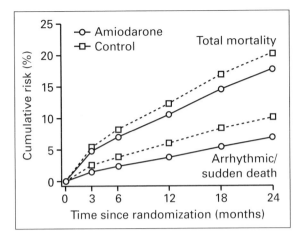

Figure 17.7
Effect of prophylactic amiodarone on mortality after acute myocardial infarction and in congestive heart failure. Cumulative risk of death from a meta-analysis of individual data from 6500 patients in randomized trials. (From Amiodarone Trials Meta-analysis Investigators[33] with permission.)

larger studies have failed to find significant mortality benefit from amiodarone. The Canadian Myocardial Infarction Amiodarone Trial (CAMIAT) of 1202 survivors of myocardial infarction found a significant reduction in ventricular fibrillation or arrhythmic death (3.3 versus 6.0%) but only trends towards reduction in cardiac death and all-cause mortality.[116] The absolute-risk reductions were greatest among patients with heart failure or previous myocardial infarction. The European Myocardial Infarct Amiodarone Trial (EMIAT) of 1486 patients after myocardial infarction with left ventricular dysfunction found no benefit of amiodarone on total mortality, although there was a 35% risk reduction in arrhythmic deaths.[117] This was offset by an increase in nonarrhythmic and noncardiac deaths. A retrospective analysis identified patients most likely to benefit from amiodarone as those with reduced left ventricular ejection fraction (<30%), with arrhythmia on Holter, a high initial heart rate (>80 beats per minute) and those on β-blocker treatment.[118]

The effects of amiodarone on mortality after acute myocardial infarction and in chronic heart failure has been reassessed by a meta-analysis of individual data from 6500 patients from 13 randomized trials.[33] There were eight post-MI and five heart failure trials. Individually, only three of the 13 studies had shown a significant reduction in all-cause mortality. None was sufficiently large to detect reliably reduction of mortality of 10–29%. The meta-analysis showed a reduction of total mortality of 13%, essentially due to reduction in sudden or arrhythmic deaths (Figure 17.7). The risk of sudden or arrhythmic death was higher in heart failure than in post-MI studies (10.7 versus 4.1%) and was reduced by amiodarone in both conditions. The best single predictor of risk of sudden death was symptomatic heart failure, which carried a

whom there was significant reduction in the combined end-point of cardiac death plus hospitalization for heart failure. The relevance of heart rate was also confirmed with relation to improved ventricular function. There was a substantial increase (33%) in the mean left ventricular ejection fraction, with the greatest improvement in those patients who showed the most reduction in heart rate.

Benefit from amiodarone in patients with myocardial infarction, with or without heart failure, has been reported, but results have also been conflicting. Benefit was confined to patients with preserved left ventricular function in the Basel Antiarrhythmic Study of Infarct Survival (BASIS),[114] but reduced mortality has also been reported in patients with left ventricular dysfunction.[115] More recent

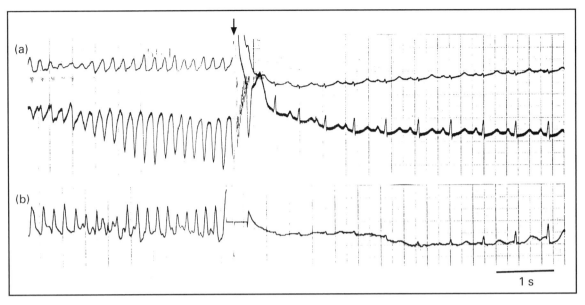

Figure 17.8
Defibrillation from ventricular fibrillation by an implanted cardioverter defibrillator (ICD). A shock of 20 joules delivered via a transvenous endocardial lead restored sinus rhythm. The upper tracings (a) show surface electrograms, I and aVf, during a test of the device which detected induced ventricular fibrillation and delivered a shock (arrow). The lower trace (b) shows intracardiac electrograms of the same event retrieved from the memory of the device.

12.2% annual risk of sudden death compared to 5.0% for those without symptoms. Amiodarone was discontinued at 2 years by 41% of patients, compared to 27% of control patients, indicating approximately a 14% rate of adverse effects with amiodarone, the most common being hypothyroidism. The excess risk of pulmonary toxicity was 1% per year. Another meta-analysis of 15 trials of amiodarone confirmed reductions in total mortality (19%) and sudden death (30%).[119] The apparent inconsistencies among trial results appeared to be due mainly to differences in trial design and methods, rather than the patient populations enrolled, in particular the small sample sizes and the types of control group used. For example, trials with placebo controls (like CHF-STAT) had less striking risk reductions than trials using usual-care controls (like GESICA). Limiting evidence to that from placebo-controlled trials indicated that the risk reduction was only 10%, compared to risk reduction of 42% with usual-care controls.

These studies show that amiodarone has a small beneficial effect on total mortality in heart failure, of greatest likely benefit in those with nonischaemic aetiology with relatively high heart rates. They support the role of amiodarone as the antiarrhythmic drug of choice for symptomatic arrhythmia in heart failure. There are indications that amiodarone may exert beneficial actions independent of its class III antiarrhythmic actions. For comparison, *d*-sotalol, a class III agent with minimal β-blocking activity, was found to increase mortality in patients with impaired left ventricular function or cardiac failure after previous myocardial infarction.[120] Amiodarone may improve ventricular function, associated with heart rate reduction, and its noncompetitive α- and β-adrenoceptor antagonist properties may be of importance.

Implantable cardioverter defibrillators and heart failure

The recognition of the limitation of antiarrhythmic drug treatment for patients with ventricular arrhythmia and survivors of cardiac arrest has been paralleled by the development of nonpharmacological therapy, in particular the implantable cardioverter-defibrillator (ICD). This device monitors cardiac rhythm and responds to rapid ventricular tachyarrhythmias by delivering a direct current shock to the heart (Figure 17.8). ICDs have been highly successful at preventing sudden death in high-risk patients.[121,122] The original systems used intrathoracic patches around the heart to deliver the shocks, and implantation, which required thoracotomy, was associated with a perioperative mortality of 3–5%. The development of nonthoracotomy systems using transvenous leads has reduced the perioperative mortality to less than 1% and therefore increased the potential use of such therapy even in high-risk patients with severe cardiac disease.[123,124]

In patients who have survived episodes of life-threatening ventricular arrhythmia the implantation of an ICD virtually eliminated sudden death[121,122,124] but the effect on total mortality has been less certain. The first decade of experience with the ICD was characterized by a complete absence of randomized controlled trials. From uncontrolled studies, there were indications of improved total mortality, even in patients with left ventricular dysfunction, based on historical[125] or matched controls,[126] or on projected mortality based on device shocks indicating potential sudden death.[127] However, the main determinant of prognosis in patients with ICD therapy was the severity of left ventricular dysfunction.[125,126–130] Even in reports of improved outcome with ICD therapy the absolute improvement in total mortality during long-term follow-up was modest.[126,127] Particularly in patients with left ventricular dysfunction there is a continuing substantial cardiac mortality rate due to the underlying cardiac disease, in addition to arrhythmia-related but nonsudden deaths.[128] However, there is evidence of potential benefit from the ICD in patients with heart failure. Interrogation of modern devices allows accurate documentation of arrhythmia recurrence and thus an estimate of the hypothetical death rate (recurrence of fast ventricular arrhythmia, >240 beats per minute), which would probably have been fatal without treatment. Hypothetical death rate was significantly greater than overall mortality in 603 ICD patients, with and without heart failure.[131] In the 175 patients in NYHA class III at the time of ICD implantation, the total mortality rate at 3 years was 28.6% compared to a hypothetical death rate of 50.5%. There were indications that the initial benefit from the ICD was greatest in patients with more severe heart failure but that increased benefit out to 5 years was greatest in those without, or with mild, heart failure. In patients with heart failure of sufficient severity to be evaluated for cardiac transplantation and with ventricular arrhythmia, ICD therapy reduced sudden death rates but did not improve total mortality when compared to patients treated with antiarrhythmic drugs or with no history of arrhythmia.[132]

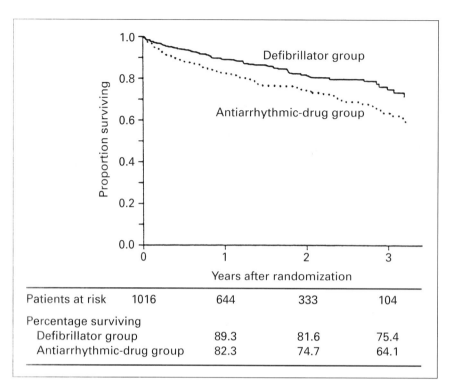

Figure 17.9
Improved survival with the implantable cardioverter-defibrillator compared to antiarrhythmic drugs in patients resuscitated from near-fatal ventricular arrhythmia. (From the AVID Investigators[135] with permission.)

Years after randomization	0	1	2	3
Patients at risk	1016	644	333	104
Percentage surviving				
Defibrillator group		89.3	81.6	75.4
Antiarrhythmic-drug group		82.3	74.7	64.1

Long-awaited results from randomized trials in ICD therapy have now become available. The Multicenter Automatic Defibrillator Implantation trial (MADIT) was a primary prevention study which enrolled 196 patients with prior myocardial infarction, left ventricular dysfunction (LV ejection fraction <35%), asymptomatic nonsustained ventricular tachycardia and inducible, nonsuppressible ventricular tachyarrhythmia.[133] They were randomized to ICD or 'conventional' therapy, which included antiarrhythmic drugs in the majority. The ICD was associated with improved survival (84 versus 61%). Half of the patients required treatment for heart failure. This study can be criticized for the relatively small patient numbers, their highly selected nature and for the use of class I

antiarrhythmic drugs, which may be hazardous in patients with coronary disease, in over 10% of patients. The Coronary Artery Bypass Graft (CABG) Patch trial was another primary prevention study, which randomized 900 patients to receive an ICD or not.[134] The patients had left ventricular dysfunction and an abnormal signal-averaged electrocardiogram, and participated in a study that was as close to 'placebo-controlled' as will be possible with the ICD, all patients underwent surgery. Again, half of the patients required treatment for heart failure. The result was different from MADIT, however, with no evidence of improved survival with the ICD, despite a similar incidence of shocks from the devices (50% at 1 year). It is not known whether it was the benefits of the surgical revascularization or a lower risk of ventricular arrhythmia, spontaneous or induced, which altered the efficacy of the ICD.

Evidence of benefit of the ICD in patients with spontaneous arrhythmia, when compared with antiarrhythmic treatment, has come from the Antiarrhythmic Versus Implantable Defibrillator (AVID) study.[135] Over 1000 survivors of life-threatening ventricular arrhythmia, about half with heart failure, were randomized to ICD or antiarrhythmic therapy (mainly amiodarone). The ICD conferred a reduction in mortality of approximately 30%, which persisted for up to 3 years of follow-up (Figure 17.9). A potentially confounding factor in the AVID trial was the imbalance in the use of β-blockers which were prescribed to 42% of the ICD group but only 16.5% of those on amiodarone. Results from two other studies of ICD compared to drug treatment in patients who have had ventricular arrhythmia have been reported. The mortality benefit of 20% from the ICD in the Canadian Internal Defibrillator study, CIDS, did not reach significance ($P = 0.07$). The smaller Cardiac Arrest Study of Hamburg, CASH, reported a 37% reduction in 2-year mortality with the ICD compared to amiodarone and metoprolol ($P = 0.047$). The results of ongoing studies, including a placebo-controlled study of the ICD and amiodarone in patients with heart failure, may clarify the role of device therapy, particularly in patients who have not yet had life-threatening arrhythmia.[136]

ICD therapy is expensive and the cost–benefit ratio depends on the level of risk of arrhythmic death. The estimated cost for each additional year of survival conferred by the defibrillator was $27 000 for the high-risk patients in MADIT, but was more expensive ($127 000) in the less selective AVID study.[137] However, there would be additional cost in identifying the highest-risk patients for primary prevention, and the optimal methods for this are still uncertain. For patients with controlled heart failure who have survived life-threatening ventricular arrhythmia there is increasing evidence the ICD confers survival benefit, in addition to avoiding the risks of drug-induced adverse effects. Such patients should be fully assessed for available therapies, which may include surgical revascularization and/or an ICD.

Conclusion

Cardiac arrhythmias contribute to the high mortality in patients with cardiac failure. It is clear that antiarrhythmic drug treatment can be detrimental, because of deterioration in cardiac function and proarrhythmia. Conversely, there is evidence that amiodarone may improve survival in patients with heart failure, by reducing both sudden death and death due to pump failure. The contribution of arrhythmias to mortality remains uncertain, because of the difficulties in separating arrhythmic death from death due to progressive heart failure, and because arrhythmia may be secondary to pump failure. Progress in the medical management of heart failure may indirectly reduce the incidence of arrhythmia. Optimal medical treatment of heart failure, including ACE inhibition β-blockers and avoidance of class I antiarrhythmic therapy, has improved mortality and this benefit may be in part due to reduction in sudden death.[7] Increasing use of beta-blockers in heart failure will further improve outcome, in part by reducing sudden death. Finally, patients with heart failure who have survived a cardiac arrest should be considered for ICD implantation. Device therapy will reduce mortality from recurrent cardiac arrest but the long-term outcome will be determined by the severity of heart disease.

References

1. Chakko CS, Gheorghiade M. Ventricular arrhythmias in severe heart failure: incidence, significance, and effectiveness of antiarrhythmic therapy. *Am Heart J* 1985; **109:** 497–504.

2. Carson PE, Johnson GR, Dunkman WB et al. The influence of atrial fibrillation on prognosis in mild to moderate heart failure. The V-HeFT studies. *Circulation* 1993; 87(Suppl IV): 102–110.

3. Kottkamp H, Budde T, Lamp B et al. Clinical significance and management of ventricular arrhythmias in heart failure. *Eur Heart J* 1994; **15**(Suppl D): 155–163.

4. Kannel WB, Plehn JF, Cupples LA. Cardiac failure and sudden death in the Framingham study. *Am Heart J* 1988; **115:** 869–875.

5. Goldman S, Johnson G, Cohn JN et al. Mechanisms of death in heart failure. The Vasodilator-Heart Failure Trials. *Circulation* 1993; 87(Suppl VI): 24–31.

6. Domanski MJ, Zipes DP, Schron E. Treatment of sudden cardiac death. Current understandings from randomized trials and future research directions. *Circulation* 1997; **95:** 2694–2699.

7. Stevenson WG, Stevenson LW, Middlekauff HR et al. Improving survival for patients with advanced heart failure. *J Am Coll Cardiol* 1995; **26:** 1417–1423.

8. Kjekshus J. Arrhythmias and mortality in congestive heart failure. *Am J Cardiol* 1990; **65:** 42I–48I.

9. Gradman A, Deedwania P, Cody R et al. Predictors of total mortality and sudden death in mild to moderate heart failure. *J Am Coll Cardiol* 1989; **14:** 564–570.

10. Demirovic J, Myerburg RJ. Epidemiology of sudden coronary death: an overview. *Prog Cardiovasc Dis* 1994; **37:** 39–48.

11. Sedgwick ML, Dalziel K, Watson J et al. Performance of an established system of first responder out-of-hospital defibrillation. The results of the second year of the Heartstart Scotland Project in the 'Utstein Style'. *Resuscitation* 1993; **26:** 75–88.

12. De Luna AB, Coumel P, Leclerq JF. Ambulatory sudden cardiac death: mechanisms of production of fatal arrhythmia on the basis of data from 157 cases. *Am Heart J* 1989; **117:** 151–159.

13. Luu M, Stevenson WG, Stevenson LW et al. Diverse mechanisms of unexpected cardiac arrest in advanced heart failure. *Circulation* 1989; **80:** 1675–1680.

14. Goldstein S, Friedman L, Hutchinson R et al. Timing, mechanism and clinical setting of witnessed deaths in postmyocardial infarction patients. *J Am Coll Cardiol* 1984; **3:** 1111–1117.

15. Greene HL, Richardson DW, Barker AH et al. Classification of deaths after myocardial infarction as arrhythmic or nonarrhythmic (the Cardiac Arrhythmia Pilot Study). *Am J Cardiol* 1989; **63:** 1–6.

16. Cleland JGF, Puri S. How do ACE inhibitors reduce mortality in patients with left ventricular dysfunction with and without heart failure: remodeling, resetting, or sudden death? *Br Heart J* 1994; **72**(Suppl): 81–86.

17. Narang R, Cleland JGF, Erhardt L et al. Mode of death in chronic heart failure. A request and proposition for more accurate classification. *Eur Heart J* 1996; **17:** 1390–1403.

18. Pratt CM, Greenway PS, Schoenfeld MH. Exploration of the precision of classifying sudden cardiac death. Implications for the interpretation of clinical trials. *Circulation* 1996; **93:** 519–524.

19. Stevenson WG, Stevenson LG, Middlekauff HR, Saxon LA. Sudden death prevention in patients with advanced ventricular dysfunction. *Circulation* 1993; **88:** 2953–2961.

20. The Task Force of the Working Group on Arrhythmias of the European Society of Cardiology. The 'Sicilian Gambit'. A new approach to the classification of antiarrhyth-

mic drugs based on their actions and arrhythmogenic mechanisms. *Circulation* 1991; **84:** 1831–1851.

21. Pyre MP, Cobbe SM. Mechanisms of ventricular arrhythmias in cardiac failure and hypertrophy. *Cardiovasc Res* 1992; **26:** 740–750.

22. Campbell RWF. Electrophysiological disturbances in heart failure. *Br Heart J* 1994; **72**(Suppl): S31–S35.

23. Pogwizd SM, Corr PB. Biochemical and electrophysiological alterations underlying ventricular arrhythmias in the failing heart. *Eur Heart J* 1994; **15**(Suppl D): 145–154.

24. Tomaselli GF, Beuckelmann DJ, Calkins HG et al. Sudden cardiac death in heart failure. The role of abnormal repolarisation. *Circulation* 1994; **90:** 2534–2539.

25. Dean JW, Lab MJ. Arrhythmia in heart failure: role of mechanically induced changes in electrophysiology. *Lancet* 1989; **i:** 1309–1312.

26. Storstein L. Electrophysiological impact of diuretics in heart failure. *Br Heart J* 1994; **72**(Suppl): 54–46.

27. Francis GS. Neuroendocrine manifestations of congestive heart failure. *Am J Cardiol* 1988; **62:** 9A–13A.

28. Cowburn PJ, Cleland JGF, Coats AJS, Komajda M. Risk stratification in chronic heart failure. *Eur Heart J* 1998; **19:** 696–710.

29. Wilber DJ, Garan H, Finkelstein D et al. Out-of-hospital cardiac arrest: use of electrophysiologic testing in the prediction of long-term outcome. *N Engl J Med* 1988; **318:** 19–24.

30. Cobbe SM, Dalziel K, Ford I, Marsden AK. Survival of 1476 patients initially resuscitated from out of hospital cardiac arrest. *BMJ* 1996; **312:** 1633–1637.

31. Stevenson WG, Middlekauf HR, Stevenson LW et al. Significance of aborted cardiac arrest and sustained ventricular tachycardia in patients referred for treatment therapy of advanced heart failure. *Am Heart J* 1992; **124:** 123–130.

32. Caruso AC, Marcus FI, Hahn EA et al and the ESVEM Investigators. Predictors of arrhythmic death and cardiac arrest in the ESVEM trial. *Circulation* 1997; **96:** 1888–1892.

33. Amiodarone Trials Meta-Analysis Investigators. Effect of prophylactic amiodarone on mortality after acute myocardial infarction and in congestive heart failure: meta-analysis of individual data from 6500 patients in randomised trials. *Lancet* 1997; **350:** 1417–1424.

34. Cleland JGF, Dargie HJ, Ford I. Mortality in heart failure: clinical variables of prognostic value. *Br Heart J* 1987; **58:** 572–582.

35. Doval HC, Nul DR, Grancelli HO et al. Nonsustained ventricular tachycardia in severe heart failure. Independent marker of increased marker due to sudden death. *Circulation* 1996; **94:** 3198–3203.

36. Vester EG, Strauer BE. Ventricular late potentials: state of the art and future perspectives. *Eur Heart J* 1994; **15**(Suppl C): 34–48.

37. Hood MA, Pogwizd SM, Peirick J, Cain ME. Contribution of myocardium responsible for ventricular tachycardia to abnormalities detected by analysis of signal-averaged ECGs. *Circulation* 1992; **86:** 1888–1901.

38. Kuchar DL, Thorburn CW, Sammel NL. Prediction of serious arrhythmic events after myocardial infarction: signal-averaged electrocardiogram, holter monitoring and radionuclide ventriculography. *J Am Coll Cardiol* 1987; **9:** 531–538.

39. Mancini DM, Wong KL, Simson MB. Prognostic value of an abnormal signal-averaged electrocardiogram in patients with nonischemic congestive cardiomyopathy. *Circulation* 1993; **87:** 1083–1092.

40. Middlekauff HP, Stevenson WG, Woo MA et al. Comparison of frequency of late potentials in idiopathic dilated cardiomyopathy and ischemic cardiomyopathy with advanced congestive heart failure and their usefulness in predicting sudden death. *Am J Cardiol* 1990; **66:** 1113–1117.

41. Galinier M, Albenque J-P, Afchar N et al. Prognostic value of late potentials in patients with congestive heart failure. *Eur Heart J* 1996; **17:** 262–271.

42. Task Force of the European Society of Cardiology and the North American Society of Pacing and Electrophysiology. Heart rate variability: standards of measurements, physiological interpretation and clinical use. *Circulation* 1996; **93:** 1043–1065.

43. Kleiger RE, Miller JP, Bigger JT et al. Decreased heart rate variability and its association with increased mortality after acute myocardial infarction. *Am J Cardiol* 1987; **59**: 256–262.

44. Cripps TR, Malik M, Farrell TG, Camm AJ. Prognostic value of reduced heart rate variability after myocardial infarction: clinical evaluation of an new analysis method. *Br Heart J* 1991; **65**: 14–19.

45. Fauchier L, Babuty D, Cosnay P et al. Heart rate variability in idiopathic dilated cardiomyopathy: characteristics and prognostic value. *J Am Coll Cardiol* 1997; **30**: 1009–1014.

46. Kienzle MG, Ferguson DW, Birkett CL et al. Clinical, hemodynamic and sympathetic neural correlates of heart rate variability in congestive heart failure. *Am J Cardiol* 1992; **69**: 761–767.

47. Coumel P, Leenhardt A, Leclerq J-F. Autonomic influences on ventricular arrhythmias in myocardial hypertrophy and heart failure. *Circulation* 1993; **87**(Suppl VII): 84–91.

48. Nolan J, Batin PD, Andrews R et al. Prospective study of heart rate variability and mortality in chronic heart failure. Results of the United Kingdom Heart Failure Evaluation and Assessment of Risk Trial (UK-Heart). *Circulation* 1998; **98**: 1510–1516.

49. Day CP, McComb JM, Campbell RW. QT dispersion: an indication of arrhythmia risk in patients with long QT intervals. *Br Heart J* 1990; **63**: 342–344.

50. Barr CS, Naas A, Freeman M et al. QT dispersion and sudden unexpected death in chronic heart failure. *Lancet* 1994; **343**: 327–329.

51. Pinsky DJ, Sciacca RR, Steinberg JS. QT dispersion as a marker of risk in patients awaiting heart transplantation. *J Am Coll Cardiol* 1997; **29**: 1576–1584.

52. Fu G-S, Meissner A, Simon R. Repolarization dispersion and sudden cardiac death in patients with impaired left ventricular function. *Eur Heart J* 1997; **18**: 281–289.

53. Grimm W, Steder U, Menz V et al. Clinical significance of increased QT dispersion in the 12-lead standard ECG for arrhythmia risk prediction in dilated cardiomyopathy. *Pacing Clin Electrophysiol* 1996; **19**: 1886–1889.

54. Fei L, Goldman JH, Prasad K et al. QT dispersion and RR variation on 12-lead ECGs in patients with congestive heart failure secondary to idiopathic dilated cardiomyopathy. *Eur Heart J* 1996; **17**: 258–263.

55. Statters DJ, Malik M, Ward DE, Camm AJ. QT dispersion: problems of methodology and clinical significance. *J Cardiovasc Electrophysiol* 1994; **5**: 672–685.

56. Murray A, McLaughlin NB, Campbell RWF. Measuring QT dispersion: man versus machine. *Heart* 1997; **77**: 539–542.

57. Richards DAB, Byth K, Ross DL, Uther JB. What is the best predictor of spontaneous ventricular tachycardia and sudden death after myocardial infarction? *Circulation* 1991; **83**: 756–763.

58. Stevenson WG, Stevenson LW, Weiss J, Tillisch JH. Inducible ventricular arrhythmias and sudden death during vasodilator therapy of severe heart failure. *Am Heart J* 1988; **116**: 1447–1454.

59. Sager PT, Choudhary R, Leon C et al. The long-term prognosis of patients with out-of-hospital cardiac arrest but no inducible ventricular tachycardia. *Am Heart J* 1990; **120**: 1334–1342.

60. Lindsay BD, Osborn JL, Schechtman KB et al. Prospective detection of vulnerability to sustained ventricular tachycardia in patients awaiting cardiac transplantation. *Am J Cardiol* 1992; **69**: 619–624.

61. Chen X, Shenasa M, Borggrefe M et al. Role of programmed ventricular stimulation in patients with idiopathic dilated cardiomyopathy and documented sustained ventricular tachyarrhythmias: inducibility and prognostic value in 102 patients. *Eur Heart J* 1994; **15**: 76–82.

62. Stevenson WG, Woo MA, Moser DK, Stevenson LW. Late potentials are unaltered by ventricular filling pressure reduction in heart failure. *Am Heart J* 1991; **122**: 473–477.

63. Carlson MD, Schoenfeld MH, Garan H et al. Programmed ventricular stimulation in patients with left ventricular dysfunction and ventricular tachycardia: effects of acute hemodynamic improvement due to nitroprusside. *J Am Coll Cardiol* 1989; **14**: 1744–1752.

64. Bashir Y, Sneddon JF, O'Nunain S et al. Comparative electrophysiological effects of captopril or hydralazine combined with nitrate in patients with left ventricular dysfunction and inducible ventricular tachycardia. *Br Heart J* 1992; **67**: 355–360.

65. Kulick DL, Bhandari AK, Hong R et al. Effect of acute hemodynamic decompensation on electrical inducibility of ventricular arrhythmia in patients with dilated cardiomyopathy and complex nonsustained ventricular arrhythmias. *Am Heart J* 1990; **119**: 878–883.

66. The CONSENSUS Trial Study Group. Effects of enalapril on mortality in severe congestive heart failure. Results of the Cooperative North Scandinavian Enalapril Survival Study (CONSENSUS). *N Engl J Med* 1987; **316**: 1429–1435.

67. The SOLVD Investigators. Effect of enalapril on survival in patients with reduced left ventricular ejection fractions and congestive heart failure. *N Engl J Med* 1991; **325**: 293–302.

68. Cohn JN, Johnson G, Ziesche S et al. A comparison of enalapril with hydralazine-isosorbide dinitrate in the treatment of chronic congestive heart failure. *N Engl J Med* 1991; **325**: 303–310.

69. Cleland JGF, Dargie HJ, Hodsman GP et al. Captopril in heart failure. A double blind controlled trial. *Br Heart J* 1984; **52**: 530–535.

70. Webster MWI, Fitzpatrick A, Nicholls G et al. Effect of enalapril on ventricular arrhythmias in congestive heart failure. *Am J Cardiol* 1985; **56**: 566–569.

71. Fletcher RD, Cintron GB, Johnson G et al. Enalapril decreases prevalence of ventricular tachycardia in patients with chronic congestive heart failure. *Circulation* 1993; 83(Suppl VI): 49–55.

72. Captopril Multi-center Research Group. A placebo-controlled trial of captopril in refractory chronic congestive heart failure. *J Am Coll Cardiol* 1983; **2**: 755–766.

73. Newman TJ, Maskin CS, Dennick LG et al. Effects of captopril on survival in patients with heart failure. *Am J Med* 1988; 84(Suppl 3A): 140–144.

74. Pfeffer MA, Braunwald E, Moyé LA et al. Effect of captopril on mortality and morbidity in patients with left ventricular dysfunction after myocardial infarction. Results of the Survival and Ventricular Enlargement Trial. *N Engl J Med* 1992; **327**: 669–677.

75. Cleland JGF, Erhardt L, Murray G et al. Effect of ramipril on morbidity and mode of death among survivors of acute myocardial infarction with clinical evidence of heart failure. *Eur Heart J* 1997; **18**: 41–51.

76. Køber L, Torp-Pedersen C, Carlsen JE et al. A clinical trial of the angiotensin-converting-enzyme inhibitor trandolapril in patients with left ventricular dysfunction after myocardial infarction. *N Engl J Med* 1995; **333**: 1670–1676.

77. Fonarow GC, Chelimsky-Fallick C, Stevenson LW et al. Effect of direct vasodilation with hydralazine versus angiotensin-converting enzyme inhibition with captopril on mortality in advanced heart failure: the Hy-C Trial. *J Am Coll Cardiol* 1992; **19**: 42–50.

78. Pitt B, Segal R, Martinez FA et al. Randomised trial of losartan versus captopril in patients over 65 with heart failure (Evaluation of Losartan in the Elderly Study, ELITE). *Lancet* 1997; **349**: 747–752.

79. Cleland JGF, Bristow MR, Erdmann E et al. Beta-blocking agents in heart failure. Should they be used and how? *Eur Heart J* 1996; **17**: 1629–1639.

80. CIBIS-II Investigators and Committees. The Cardiac Insufficiency Bisoprolol Study II (CIBIS-II): a randomised trial. *Lancet* 1999; **353**: 9–13.

81. Leclerq J-F, Coumel P, Denjoy I et al. Long-term follow-up after sustained monomorphic ventricular tachycardia: causes, pump failure, and empiric antiarrhythmic therapy that modify survival. *Am Heart J* 1991; **121**: 1685–1692.

82. Hallstrom AP, Cobb LA, Yu BH et al. An antiarrhythmic drug experience in 941 patients resuscitated from an initial cardiac arrest between 1970 and 1985. *Am J Cardiol* 1991; **68**: 1025–1031.

83. Eichhorn EJ. The paradox of β-adrenergic blockade for the management of congestive heart failure. *Am J Med* 1992; **92**: 527–538.

84. Waagstein F, Bristow MR, Swedberg K et al. Beneficial effects of metoprolol in idiopathic dilated cardiomyopathy. *Lancet* 1993; **342:** 1441–1446.

85. CIBIS Investigators and Committees. A randomized trial of β-blockade in heart failure. The Cardiac Insufficiency Bisoprolol Study (CIBIS). *Circulation* 1994; **90:** 1765–1773.

86. Bristow MR, Gilbert EM, Abraham WT et al. Carvedilol produces dose-related improvements in left ventricular function and survival in subjects with chronic heart failure. *Circulation* 1996; **94:** 2807–2816.

87. Packer M, Bristow MR, Cohn JN et al. The effect of carvedilol on morbidity and mortality in patients with chronic heart failure. *N Engl J Med* 1996; **334:** 1349–1355.

88. Lechat P, Packer M, Chalon S et al. Clinical effects of beta-adrenergic blockade in chronic heart failure. *Circulation* 1998; **98:** 1184–1191.

89. Doughty RN, Rodgers A, Sharpe N, MacMahon S. Effects of beta-blocker therapy on mortality in patients with heart failure. A systematic overview of randomized controlled trials. *Eur Heart J* 1997; **18:** 560–565.

90. Packer M. Effects of beta-adrenergic blockade on survival of patients with chronic heart failure. *Am J Cardiol* 1997; **80:** 46L–54L.

91. Yee KM, Struthers AD. Can drug effects on mortality in heart failure be predicted by any surrogate measure? *Eur Heart J* 1997; **18:** 1860–1864.

92. Feldman AM, Bristow MR, Parmley WW et al. Effects of vesnarinone on morbidity and mortality in patients with heart failure. *N Engl J Med* 1993; **329:** 149–155.

93. Packer M, Carver JR, Rodeheffer RJ et al. Effect of oral milrinone on mortality in severe chronic heart failure. *N Engl J Med* 1991; **325:** 1468–1475.

94. Kuchar DL, Rottman J, Berger E et al. Prediction of successful suppression of sustained ventricular tachyarrhythmias by serial drug testing from data derived at the initial electrophysiological study. *J Am Coll Cardiol* 1988; **12:** 982–988.

95. The ESVEM Investigators. Determinants of predicted efficacy of antiarrhythmic drugs in the Electrophysiologic Study Versus Electrocardiographic Monitoring Study. *Circulation* 1993; **87:** 323–329.

96. Swerdlow CD, Winkle RA, Mason JW. Determinants of survival in patients with ventricular tachyarrhythmias. *N Engl J Med* 1983; **308:** 1436–1442.

97. Poole JE, Mathison TL, Kudenchuk PJ et al. Long-term outcome in patients who survive out of hospital ventricular fibrillation and undergo electrophysiologic studies: evaluation by electrophysiologic subgroups. *J Am Coll Cardiol* 1990; **16:** 657–665.

98. Packer M. Hemodynamic consequences of antiarrhythmic drug therapy in patients with chronic heart failure. *J Cardiovasc Electrophysiol* 1991; **2**(Suppl): S240–S247.

99. Podrid PJ, Schoenberger A, Lown B. Congestive heart failure caused by oral dysopyramide. *N Engl J Med* 1980; **302:** 614–617.

100. Ravid S, Podrid P, Lampert S, Lown B. Congestive heart failure induced by six of the newer antiarrhythmic drugs. *J Am Coll Cardiol* 1989; **14:** 1326–1330.

101. Echt DS, Liebson PR, Mitchell LB et al. Mortality and morbidity in patients receiving encainide, flecainide, or placebo. *N Engl J Med* 1991; **324:** 781–788.

102. Hallstrom AP, Anderson JL, Carlson M et al. Time to arrhythmic, ischemic, and heart failure events: exploratory analyses to elucidate mechanisms of adverse drug effects in the Cardiac Arrhythmia Suppression Trial. *Am Heart J* 1995; **30:** 71–79.

103. Greenberg HM, Dwyer EM, Hochman JS et al. Interaction of ischaemia and encainide/flecainide treatment: a proposed mechanism for the increased mortality in CAST I. *Br Heart J* 1995; **74:** 631–635.

104. Flaker GC, Blackshear JL, McBride R et al. Antiarrhythmic drug therapy and cardiac mortality in atrial fibrillation. *J Am Coll Cardiol* 1992; **20:** 527–532.

105. Pratt CM, Eaton T, Francis M et al. The inverse relationship between baseline left ventricular ejection fraction and outcome of antiarrhythmic therapy: a dangerous imbalance in the risk-benefit ratio. *Am Heart J* 1989; **118:** 433–440.

106. Sheldon RS, Mitchell LB, Duff HJ et al. Right and left ventricular function during chronic

amiodarone therapy. *Am J Cardiol* 1988; **62:** 736–740.

107. Cleland JGF, Dargie HJ, Findlay IN, Wilson JT. Clinical, haemodynamic, and antiarrhythmic effects of long-term treatment with amiodarone of patients in heart failure. *Br Heart J* 1987; **57:** 436–445.

108. Nicklas JM, McKenna WJ, Stewart RA et al. Prospective, double-blind, placebo-controlled trial of low-dose amiodarone in patients with severe heart failure and asymptomatic frequent ventricular ectopy. *Am Heart J* 1991; **122:** 1016–1021.

109. Hamer AWF, Arkles LB, Johns JA. Beneficial effects of low dose amiodarone in patients with congestive cardiac failure: a placebo-controlled trial. *J Am Coll Cardiol* 1989; **14:** 1768–1774.

110. Doval HC, Grancelli HO, Perrone SV et al. Randomised trial of low-dose amiodarone in severe heart failure. *Lancet* 1994; **334:** 493–498.

111. Nul DR, Doval HC, Granceilli HO et al. Heart rate is a marker of amiodarone mortality reduction in severe heart failure. *J Am Coll Cardiol* 1997; **29:** 1199–1205.

112. Singh S, Fletcher RD, Fisher SG et al. Amiodarone in patients with congestive heart failure and asymptomatic ventricular arrhythmia. *N Engl J Med* 1995; **333:** 77–82.

113. Massie BM, Fisher SG, Deedwania PC et al. Effect of amiodarone on clinical status and left ventricular function in patients with congestive heart failure. *Circulation* 1996; **93:** 2128–2134.

114. Pfisterer M, Kiowski W, Burckhardt et al. Beneficial effect of amiodarone on cardiac mortality in patients with asymptomatic complex ventricular arrhythmias after acute myocardial infarction and preserved but not impaired left ventricular function. *Am J Cardiol* 1992; **69:** 1399–1402.

115. Navarro-López F, Cosin J, Marrugat J et al. Comparison of the effects of amiodarone versus metoprolol on the frequency of ventricular arrhythmias and on mortality after acute myocardial infarction. *Am J Cardiol* 1993; **72:** 1243–1248.

116. Cairns JA, Connolly SJ, Roberts R, Gent M, for the Canadian Amiodarone Myocardial Infarction Arrhythmia Trial Investigators. Randomised trial of outcome after myocardial infarction in patients with frequent or repetitive ventricular premature depolarisations: CAMIAT. *Lancet* 1997; **349:** 675–682.

117. Julian DG, Camm AJ, Frangin G et al. Randomised trial of effect of amiodarone on mortality in patients with left-ventricular dysfunction after recent myocardial infarction: EMIAT. *Lancet* 1997; **349:** 667–674.

118. Janse MJ, Malik M, Camm AJ et al on behalf of the EMIAT Investigators. Identification of post acute myocardial infarction patients with potential benefit from prophylactic treatment with amiodarone. A substudy of EMIAT (The European Myocardial Infarct Amiodarone Trial). *Eur Heart J* 1998; **19:** 85–95.

119. Sim I, McDonal KM, Lavori PW, Norbatus CM, Hlatky MA. Quantitative overview of randomized trials of amiodarone to prevent sudden cardiac death. *Circulation* 1997; **96:** 2823–2829.

120. Waldo AL, Camm AJ, de Ruyter H et al. Effect of *d*-sotalol on mortality in patients with left ventricular dysfunction after recent and remote myocardial infarction. *Lancet* 1996; **348:** 7–12.

121. Kelly PA, Cannom DS, Garan H et al. The automatic implantable cardioverter-defibrillator: efficacy, complications and survival in patients with malignant ventricular arrhythmias. *J Am Coll Cardiol* 1988; **11:** 1278–1286.

122. Winkle RA, Mead RH, Ruder MA et al. Long-term outcome with the automatic implantable cardioverter-defibrillator. *J Am Coll Cardiol* 1989; **13:** 1353–1361.

123. Bardy GH, Johnson G, Poole JE et al. A simplified, single-lead unipolar transvenous cardioversion-defibrillation system. *Circulation* 1993; **88:** 543–547.

124. Zipes DP, Roberts D for the Pacemaker-Cardioverter-Defibrillator Investigators. Results of the International Study of the Implantable Pacemaker-Cardioverter-Defibrillator. A comparison of epicardial and endocardial lead systems. *Circulation* 1995; **92:** 59–65.

125. Powell AC, Fuchs T, Finkelstein DM et al.

Influence of implantable cardioverter-defibrillator on the long-term prognosis of survivors of out-of-hospital cardiac arrest. *Circulation* 1993; **88**: 1083–1092.

126. Newman D, Sauve J, Herre J et al. Survival after implantation of the cardioverter defibrillator. *Am J Cardiol* 1992; **69**: 899–903.

127. Fogoros RN, Elson JJ, Bonnet CA et al. Efficacy of the automatic implantable cardioverter-defibrillator in prolonging survival in patients with severe underlying cardiac disease. *J Am Coll Cardiol* 1990; **16**: 381–386.

128. Kim SG, Maloney JD, Pinski SL et al. Influence of left ventricular function on survival and mode of death after implantable defibrillator therapy (Cleveland Clinic Foundation and Montefiore Medical Center experience). *Am J Cardiol* 1993; **72**: 1263–1267.

129. Mehta D, Saksena S, Krol RB. Survival of implantable cardioverter-defibrillator recipients: role of left ventricular function and its relationship to device use. *Am Heart J* 1992; **124**: 1608–1614.

130. Kim SG, Fisher JD, Choue CW et al. Influence of left ventricular function on outcome of patients treated with implantable defibrillators. *Circulation* 1992; **85**: 1304–1310.

131. Böcker D, Bansch D, Heinecke A et al. Potential benefit form implantable cardioverter-defibrillator therapy in patients with and without heart failure. *Circulation* 1998; **98**: 1636–1643.

132. Sweeney MO, Ruskin JN, Garan H et al. Influence of the implantable cardioverter/defibrillator on sudden death and total mortality in patients evaluated for cardiac transplantation. *Circulation* 1995; **92**: 3273–3281.

133. Moss AJ, Hall WJ, Cannom DS et al. Improved survival with an implanted defibrillator in patients with coronary disease at high risk for ventricular arrhythmia. *N Engl J Med* 1996; **335**: 1933–1940.

134. Bigger JT for the Coronary Artery Bypass Graft (CABG) Patch Trial Investigators. Prophylactic use of implanted cardiac defibrillators in patients at high risk for ventricular arrhythmias after coronary artery bypass graft surgery. *N Engl J Med* 1997; **337**: 1569–1575.

135. The Antiarrhythmic Versus Implantable Defibrillators (AVID) Investigators. A comparison of antiarrhythmic-drug therapy with implantable defibrillators in patients resuscitated from near-fatal ventricular arrhythmias. *N Engl J Med* 1997; **337**: 1576–1583.

136. Nisam S, Mower M. ICD trials: an extraordinary means of determining patient risk? *Pacing Clin Electrophysiol* 1998; **21**: 1341–1346.

137. Garratt CJ. A new evidence base for implantable defibrillator therapy. *Eur Heart J* 1998; **19**: 189–191.

18

Calcium channel blockers in heart failure: has the bridge been crossed?

John J Smith and Marvin A Konstam

Introduction

Our understanding of the pathophysiology of cardiomyopathy and heart failure has evolved considerably over the past two decades. We have learned that the progression of asymptomatic left ventricular dysfunction to symptomatic heart failure involves a complex interaction of myocardial and systemic factors, which cannot be altered solely by altering the loading conditions of the heart. Acute improvement of the haemodynamics of the left ventricle with vasodilating medications does not necessarily translate into long-term clinical improvement, particularly if the direct and indirect neurohormonal effects are unfavourable.

The calcium channel blockers as a class, are an excellent example of pharmacological agents with complex physiological effects, particularly in heart failure patients. They have considerable diversity as a chemical class, but they all are effective vasodilators, and several agents have been studied extensively in heart failure and cardiomyopathy. The net pharmacological activity of these vasodilators is influenced by direct and indirect neurohormonal modulation. The resultant effect of each of these agents on heart failure symptoms and survival has neither been easy to predict nor consistent across the therapeutic class.

Calcium channel blockers have certainly been one of the most controversial classes of agents used in the treatment of cardiovascular disease during the 1990s. The safety of these agents, specifically of the short-half-life dihydropyridine calcium channel blockers, has been questioned in meta-analyses of the early placebo controlled trials.[1] The therapeutic and adverse effects of one agent cannot necessarily be extrapolated to another. The results of appropriately powered and designed trials with cardiovascular morbidity and all-cause mortality as primary endpoints are critical pieces of data, which are lacking for most of these agents.

There are several rationales for considering the use of calcium channel blockers in the treatment of patients with heart failure. The most common use of these agents currently is the treatment of conditions associated with heart failure, such as coronary disease and hypertension. They are effective anti-ischaemic and antihypertensive agents, and it would seem logical that treating these background diseases early in the natural history of ischaemic and hypertensive cardiomyopathy may favourably alter their clinical course. The efficacy of this 'early intervention' strategy may be demonstrated in the large prospective primary prevention trials now in progress.

Pharmacology of the calcium channel blockers

Calcium channel blockers are commonly grouped together in a single therapeutic class for most discussions, but we have learned that there is no 'class effect' for them particularly with regard to their effects in heart failure patients. They can be grouped by chemical class (benzothiazepines, phenylalkylamines, dihydropyridine, tetralol); by site of action (L 'long' or T 'transient' channel); or by the primary pharmacological effect (cardiac, peripheral, selective vascular bed, etc). The scope of this discussion will be limited to calcium channel blockers now available clinically in most countries although some of the uses discussed must be considered investigational. In distinction from their clinical actions, the cellular pharmacological effects of the calcium channel blockers may be discussed as a class. Virtually all of the currently available calcium channel blockers block the slow inward calcium current through the L- (long) calcium channel. The L-channel is widely distributed throughout the body, particularly in the heart and smooth muscle cells. The singular exception to L-channel blockade is mibafradil, which has T- (transient) channel blocking activity. The T-channels are similarly distributed in vascular smooth muscle and to a much lesser degree, cardiac myocytes.

The dihydropyridine (nifedipine-like) agents have been the most extensively studied class of calcium channel blockers in patients with heart failure. The members of this class differ primarily in pharmacokinetics, which accounts for many of the striking differences observed among members of this therapeutic class in heart failure patients. Nifedipine has a short elimination half-life in comparison with other members of the group, leading to a rapid onset and offset of action. Wide swings in peak and trough activity result in reflex neurohormonal activation and worsening of heart failure symptoms. In contrast, amlodipine is a very lipid soluble agent with a long elimination half-life and more favourable neurohormonal

effects. The remaining dihydropyridine agents are intermediate between these two extremes.

The cellular pharmacology of the calcium channel blockers continues to be elucidated. In a strict pharmacokinetic sense, these agents are calcium channel blockers and not 'calcium antagonists'. The L-channel blocking agents reversibly bind distinct binding sites on the transmembrane spanning region of the L-channel. A tetrad of α-1 subunit proteins forms the 'pore' of the L-channel and is the 'receptor' for calcium channel blockers. Binding is 'use-dependent' meaning that quiescent channels will not bind drug. By partially inhibiting the slow inward calcium, contractile activity of the smooth muscle cell or cardiac myocyte is inhibited.

Much of our data on the activity of calcium channel blockers comes from studies in normal tissue. Their cellular activity in the failing circulation may not be predicted by studies in normal animals or subjects. Calcium homeostasis is altered in the failing myocytes by a number of mechanisms that include altered Na^+/Ca^{2+} exchanger expression and sarcoplasmic reticulum Ca^{2+} ATPase activity.[2] We also now know that hypertrophy and stress on the sarcolemma result in reductions in the L-channel current which is the active site of clinically available calcium channel blockers.[3]

New data have suggested that some calcium channel blockers have an endothelial-dependent activity which had not been previously appreciated. Zhang and Hintze recently reported that the dihydropyridine calcium channel blocker amlodipine increased nitric oxide release from canine coronary microvessels.[4] This property was not observed with nifedipine or diltiazem. This finding supports the observations of Lyons and co-workers who observed that amlodipine influenced forearm blood flow through a nitric oxide-dependent mechanism.[5] In the rat myocardial infarct model with established heart failure, deVries and co-workers found no evidence that amlodipine influenced endothelial-dependent vasodilatation, casting doubt on the importance of endothelium-dependent actions of the calcium channel blockers.[6]

Potential benefits and risks of calcium channel blockers in heart failure

There are several hypothetical and practical reasons why calcium channel blockers may be of benefit for patients with heart failure (summarized in Table 18.1). All of the available calcium channel blockers are potent vasodilators, which should 'unload' the failing heart. Most calcium channel blockers have favourable effects on haemodynamics with acute administration, but this finding is not predictive of long-term clinical benefit. Patients with heart failure and preserved systolic function would benefit from favourable effects on diastolic function and prolongation of the diastolic filling period with slowing of the heart rate. Individuals with supernormal systolic function may benefit from the negative inotropic effect of selected calcium channel blockers. Reduction in contractility may be accompanied by reflex neurohormonal activation which may neutralize any clinical benefit of calcium channel blocker therapy (Table 18.2). Calcium channel blockers do not appear to have the anti-remodeling effects of the beta-adrenergic blockers and the ACE inhibitors.

Sixty per cent or more of patients with heart failure have underlying ischaemic heart disease, which is either responsible for, or contributes to, their ventricular dysfunction. All patients presenting for evaluation of heart failure should undergo an assessment for active

- Afterload reduction
- Improvement of diastolic function
- Prolongation of diastolic filling period (selected agents)
- Negative inotropic effects (selected agents)
- Relief of ischaemia

Table 18.1
Potential therapeutic benefits of calcium channel blockers in patients with heart failure.

- Negative inotropic effects
- Impairment of calcium delivery to the contractile apparatus
- Direct or indirect neurohormonal activation

Table 18.2
Potential adverse effects of calcium channel blockers in heart failure.

coronary artery disease and be treated, if appropriate. Patients with hypertrophic cardiomyopathy and normal epicardial coronary arteries may have objective evidence of ischaemia on perfusion imaging.[7] Patients in either group may benefit from the anti-ischaemic effects of calcium channel blockers, although this has yet to be confirmed in a controlled clinical trial.

Neuroendocrine and baroreceptor effects of calcium channel blockers

Early investigators hypothesized that calcium channel blockers would have a favourable effect on patients with left ventricular dysfunction by virtue of their vasodilatory effect. In these early studies, deterioration of clinical status observed in some patients was thought to be secondary to the negative inotropic effects of these agents. Later investigations discovered that calcium channel blockers have both direct and reflex effects on the neuroendocrine system, which explains, in part, the adverse clinical response in some patients.

Pharmacokinetics play an important role in the neuroendocrine effects of some agents. Peak and trough effects of potent vasodilators may lead to compensatory activation of the renin-angiotensin and sympathetic nervous systems, which may be detremental to patients who already have these systems activated.[8] These neuroendocrine effects of the calcium channel blockers may negate the beneficial effects, as evidenced by the failure of felodipine to reduce left ventricular mass when the sympathetic nervous system is activated.[9]

The data on the effects of calcium channel blockers on baroreceptor function are scant. In a relatively small, acute study involving normal subjects, no effect of amlodipine or felodipine on resting heart rate, mean arterial pressure, plasma norepinephrine or norepinephrine spillover was observed.[10] This finding would not exclude an effect of calcium channel blockers in patients with abnormal baroreceptor function at baseline. There is a potentially significant direct neuroendocrine effect of calcium channel blockade. Calcium has an inhibitory effect on renin release and administration of calcium channel blockers blocks this inhibitory mechanism facilitating renin release.[11] It is unclear whether this direct physiological effect is predominantly responsible for the increase in renin levels seen with some calcium channel blockers or if this is merely a compensatory response to altered haemodynamics. Calcium channel also inhibits aldosterone production.

Calcium channel blockers may have a clinically relevant effect on the production of cytokines. Heart failure is a disease of cytokine activation, as first described by Levine and co-workers.[12] Tissue macrophages and endothelial cells, as well as the myocardium, produce tumor necrosis factor alpha (TNF-α). Interleukin-6 (IL-6) is a related cytokine, the production of which is closely linked to TNF-α. These two cytokines are produced in excessive amounts in a number of cardiovascular conditions including heart failure. Cytokine levels are higher as symptoms and functional class worsen.[13]

In a PRAISE trial substudy, the effect of amlodipine therapy and placebo on TNF-α and IL-6 levels in advanced heart failure patients was assessed.[14] TNF-α and IL-6 levels were elevated when compared to matched subjects without heart failure at baseline. Six months of active treatment had no impact on TNF-α levels when compared to placebo. In contrast, 6 months of amlodipine therapy resulted in a significant reduction of IL-6 levels with adverse endpoints more likely to occur in the patients with elevated IL-6 levels.

Calcium channel blockers and diastolic dysfunction

The presence of left ventricular hypertrophy (LVH) increases the probability that patients will subsequently develop heart failure or die of cardiovascular causes.[15] In this population, the presence of LVH is associated with abnormal exercise haemodynamics[16] and ischaemia in the absence of coronary disease.[17] Several authors have reported that up to 40% of patients presenting for evaluation of heart failure symptoms will have preserved left ventricular systolic function.[18,19]

Disorders other than hypertension and coronary artery disease, which may contribute to diastolic dysfunction include: renal dysfunction, infiltrative cardiomyopathies such as amyloidosis, diabetes, hypertrophic cardiomyopathy and aortic valve disease.[20] Furthermore, this phenomenon is more common in elderly individuals[21] and may be further exacerbated by the presence of coronary artery disease.[22] Given the diverse aetiologies of diastolic dysfunction and the resulting heart failure symptoms, it is not surprising that therapy may be ineffectual in some patient subsets. Furthermore, predicting which patients will respond to therapy is difficult and may require an individualized therapeutic trial for each patient.

The use of calcium channel blockers in 'diastolic dysfunction' has been based primarily on acute administration studies with virtually no data on chronic administration and outcomes available. On a cellular level, they may correct myocardial relaxation abnormalities due to the delay in the removal of cystolic calcium for hypertrophied myocytes associated with cardiomyopathy.[23]

The presence of LVH should prompt the use of antihypertensive therapy with efficacy in reducing left ventricular mass. There is little doubt that calcium channel blockers are effective in reducing left ventricular mass in patients with LVH. In a recent meta-analysis of 39 placebo-controlled trials, they were second only to the ACE inhibitors in reducing left ventricular mass in patients with hypertension.[24] A smaller study in patients with LVH and hypertension suggest that regression of left ventricular mass is positively correlated with improvement in indices of left ventricular diastolic function.[25] There were no functional endpoints in this small study so one cannot conclude whether patients realized a clinical benefit from this therapy. Improvement in maximal exercise capacity has been reported in patients with heart failure and preserved

ventricular function treated with verapamil.[26] Calcium channel blocker-induced regression of left ventricular mass may not be a characteristic of all agents in this class since reflex sympathetic nervous system activation may negate the benefit of selected members of this class.[9]

Patients with hypertrophic cardiomyopathy and symptoms of heart failure may benefit from calcium channel blocker therapy. Abnormalities of calcium handling have been identified in this condition.[27,28] The acute haemodynamic response to calcium channel blockers has been studied in small studies of patients with hypertrophic cardiomyopathy. Lorell and co-workers demonstrated that nifedipine administration to this patient subset could accelerate relaxation and normalize the relationship between diastolic pressure and ventricular volume (Figure 18.1).[29]

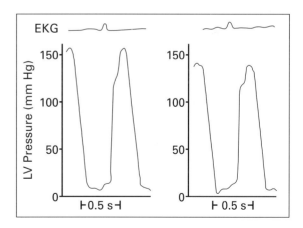

Figure 18.1

Left ventricular pressure recordings from a patient with hypertrophic cardiomyopathy before (left) and after (right) administration of nifedipine. Tracings suggest a normalization of left ventricular relaxation with nifedipine. (From Lorell et al[29] with permission.)

Patients with coronary disease complicating diastolic function may benefit from the anti-ischaemic properties of calcium channel blockers. In patients with ischaemic heart disease and heart failure symptoms, the benefits of calcium channel blockers may depend on the particular agent employed. In the Prospective Randomized Amlodipine Survival Evaluation (PRAISE), amlodipine added to ACE inhibitor therapy had no significant impact on the combined endpoint of all-cause mortality and cardiovascular morbidity in patients with an ischaemic aetiology (discussed further below).[30] In contrast, a small randomized pilot study of verapamil and trandolapril in a less ill population suggested that the combination of the ACE inhibitor and calcium channel blocker had a lower cardiovascular event rate when compared to the ACE inhibitor alone.[31,32] This provocative finding must be confirmed in a large randomized trial with long-term follow-up to be of clinical utility.

Diastolic dysfunction is a common cause of heart failure symptoms in the elderly population,[33] exceeding 10% in patients in their eighth decade of life. The causes of heart failure symptoms in this population are diverse and include many of the conditions listed above. Many of these patients have preserved left ventricular systolic function but abnormal indices of diastolic function.[21,33,34] The mechanisms contributing to abnormal diastolic function are complex but include myocardial ischaemia, collagen deposition in the heart, or impaired calcium translocation to the sarcoplasmic reticulum during diastole. These abnormalities may be further accentuated by exercise, particularly as the heart rate accelerates and diastole shortens.[35] Elderly patients with this heart failure syndrome with preserved left ventricular systolic function may benefit from calcium channel blocker therapy with verapamil or diltiazem. Figure 18.2

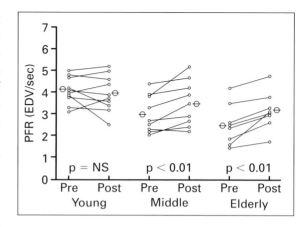

Figure 18.2
Peak filling rates before and after verapamil therapy in young, middle aged and elderly patients. There is improvement in ventricular filling in the middle aged and older patients with calcium channel blockers. (From Arrighi et al[36] with permission.)

demonstrates the effect of verapamil on left ventricular filling in young, middle aged and elderly hearts compared with the pretreatment period. A significant improvement in peak filling rate was observed in the older but not younger individuals indicating that verapamil treatment may have utility in treating the diastolic abnormalities accompanying the aging process.[36]

Calcium channel blockers and haemodynamics/systolic performance

Calcium influx in excitable tissue is critical in excitation–contraction coupling. The translocation of calcium from the cytoplasm to the sarcoplasmic reticulum is similarly important in the termination of contraction. Abnormalities in calcium handling are found in car-

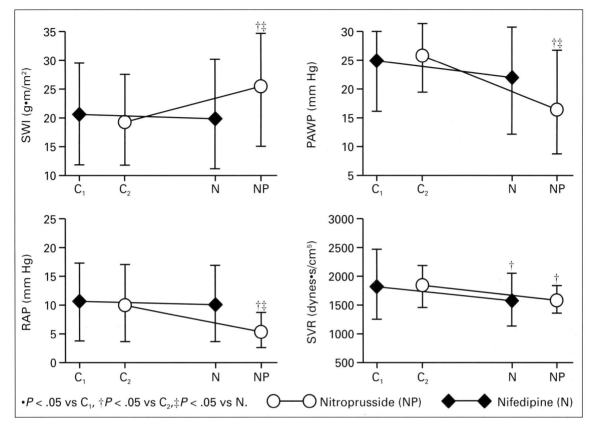

Figure 18.3
Comparative acute haemodynamic effects of nitroprusside (NP) and nifedipine (N) in patients with heart failure. There is comparable reduction in systemic vascular resistance (SVR) (lower right panel) but a greater improvement in stroke work index (SWI), and reductions in pulmonary artery wedge pressure (PAWP) and right atrial pressure (RAP) with nitroprusside suggesting effects of nitrates independent of afterload reduction not shared by nifedipine. (From Elkayam et al[37] with permission.)

diomyopathy and may be associated with ageing as well.[23] These investigators reported that isolated muscle from failing hearts had reduced capacity to reduce intracellular calcium levels during diastole in comparison to muscle from normal subjects. This finding would suggest that further modification of calcium homeostasis in failing cardiac muscle with pharmacological agents might lead to clinical decompensation.

As predicted by their cellular activity, the pharmacodynamic effects of calcium channel blockers in the cardiovascular system are vasodilatation of the vasculature and reduction in contractility of the heart. Despite its potent vasodilator activity, nifedipine has not demonstrated as potent an effect as sodium nitroprusside on the haemodynamics of heart failure patients (Figure 18.3). The purely arterial vasodilatation of the calcium channel blocker may stimulate the sympathetic nervous system and the renin–angiotensin systems to a greater degree than the nitrate preparations. The net haemodynamic effect of the calcium channel blockers in patients with left ventricular dysfunction reflects the balance of direct vasodilatory and negative intropic actions with the reflex activation of the neuroendocrine system.

Calcium channel blockers differ from other therapeutic classes of vasodilators used in patients with heart failure. In contrast to the nitrates and ACE inhibitors, they are purely arterial vasodilators, devoid of venodilatory effects in heart failure patients.[37] Nicardipine,[38] nitredipine,[39] nisoldipine[40] and felodipine[41] have all been found to have short-term salutary effects on haemodynamics and cardiac performance but long-term improvement has not been demonstrated with any of these agents.

Nifedipine has been the most extensively studied first-generation dihydropyridine calcium channel blocker, with two acute haemodynamic trials showing mixed results. Acute administration of 20–50 mg of oral nifedipine was associated with a greater than 15% reduction of cardiac index in one-third of patients with half of these patients classified as having a 'severe' reduction of cardiac index.[42] There were no clinical or haemodynamic predictors for which patients would have a favourable or unfavourable response to the calcium channel blocker. Similar findings were observed in a second study where over half of the patients developed unfavourable haemodynamics by predefined criteria and was associated with further neurohormonal activation.[43] In this latter study, five patients receiving study drug, developed sufficient haemodynamic compromise to require pressor support. The findings of these trials and clinical experience dictates that patients with haemodynamic compromise

due to systolic dysfunction are unlikely to derive any haemodynamic benefit from vasodilatory calcium channel blockers and may be acutely harmed by these agents.

Calcium channel blocker following acute myocardial infarction

There has been an extensive experience with calcium channel blockers following myocardial infarction (MI) with morbidity and mortality endpoints. These studies tested the primary hypothesis that calcium channel blockers would reduce mortality and reinfarction. Several of these trials did not specifically exclude patients with left ventricular dysfunction although retrospective analysis of the data suggested that this patient subset did not benefit and may be harmed by this therapy. The most compelling post-MI data come from the Diltiazem Multicenter Post-infarction trial, where patients were randomized to placebo or diltiazem at the time of the acute infarction. Patients with evidence of pulmonary congestion who were randomized to diltiazem, had a significantly greater chance of developing heart failure or having a clinical endpoint.[44] Evidence of reduced left ventricular ejection fraction (< 0.40) was predictive of a rapid progression to clinical heart failure in the patients randomized to diltiazem (Figure 18.4).[45]

Studies with the dihydropyridine calcium channel blockers have been similarly disappointing with the possible exception of nisoldipine. In the DEFIANT-II study involving a total of 542 completed patients with an average left ventricular ejection fraction of 0.40, nisoldipine therapy initiated within days following myocardial infarction increased the time to develop ischaemic electrocardiographic changes compared with placebo on exercise

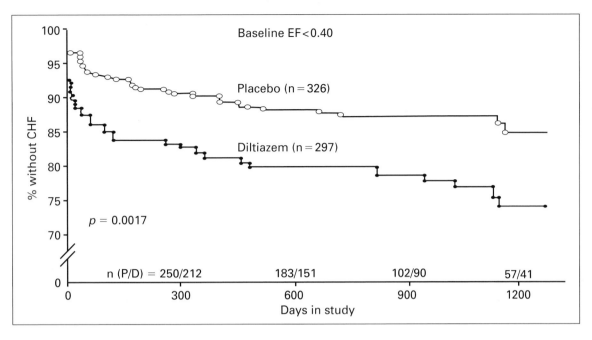

Figure 18.4
Results from the Multicenter Diltiazem Post-infarction trial showing that patients with left ventricular ejection fraction less than 0.40 following myocardial infarction had a more rapid progression to clinical heart failure. (From Goldstein et al[45] with permission.)

testing.[46] Nisoldipine also improved echocardiographic indices of diastolic function and appeared to be well tolerated for 6 months.

The Danish Verapamil Infarction Trial (DAVIT I) investigated the utility of early treatment with verapamil in patients presenting with acute myocardial infarction.[47] There was no significant differences in mortality or reinfarction rates in the verapamil and placebo groups after 6 months of therapy. Like the Diltiazem Multicenter Post Infarction trial, patients with heart failure in the DAVIT I trial had a worse clinical outcome with calcium channel blocker therapy. Examination of time points earlier than six months in a post hoc analysis suggested a reduction in mortality and reinfarction with verapamil therapy. Data from

DAVIT I suggested that initiation of treatment with verapamil after the acute phase of the MI, treating patients for a longer time period and excluding patients with clinical heart failure may be beneficial when compared to placebo. This hypothesis was the basis of the DAVIT II trial. In a trial design which was similar to the Diltiazem Multicenter Post-infarction trial, investigators in the DAVIT II trial reported that reinfarction-free survival was improved in patients randomized to verapamil, although this trial specifically excluded patients with heart failure, based on DAVIT I results.[48] In a post hoc analysis, these investigators reported that the benefit was seen only in patients without heart failure but heart failure progression indicators such as diuretic use were reduced in the patients receiving verapamil on a chronic basis.[49] A reduction in recurrent ischaemia has been proposed as a potential explanation for this finding.[50] In an open label pilot study, this group has proposed that verapamil combined with the ACE inhibitor trandolapril, will be superior to verapamil alone in patients with ischaemic heart disease and systolic dysfunction. A preliminary study of this strategy has shown promise.[31] In contrast, a retrospective analysis of the Survival and Ventricular Enlargement (SAVE) trial, there was no beneficial or adverse effect of open label calcium channel blocker use in patients with asymptomatic left ventricular dysfunction.[51] These disparate findings must be resolved with an appropriately designed and powered trial of calcium channel blocker/ACE inhibitor combination therapy versus ACE inhibitor alone in asymptomatic left ventricular dysfunction.

Calcium channel blockers and exercise capacity in heart failure

Several investigations have been performed with various calcium channel blockers in patients with all classes of heart failure to assess the impact of these agents on exercise capacity and clinical symptoms. Short-acting nifedipine preparations were studied extensively in several early trials during the 1980s. Despite some early enthusiasm suggesting a favourable effect on exercise tolerance, subsequent studies confirmed that the clinical status deteriorated in significantly more patients on nifedipine than in those receiving non-calcium channel blocker regimens (Figure 18.5). As previously discussed, this clinical deterioration was associated with neurohormonal activation which apparently neutralized any favourable effects of this potent vasodilator.

An early multicentre trial of amlodipine versus placebo in patients with moderate heart failure, there was a significant improvement in exercise time compared with placebo patients.[52] This trial prompted a number of follow-up studies, including the PRAISE trial discussed below. In a single-centre trial of amlodipine versus placebo in patients with ischaemia cardiomyopathy, mean treadmill exercise time increased 96 seconds compared with a 50-second increase in the placebo group — a difference that did not achieve statistical significance.[53] There were also no treatment differences in regional blood flow to the kidneys or the limb in this same patient subset. One may conclude from the published reports of exercise tolerance in heart failure patients that exercise capacity does not deteriorate with amlodipine. The Diltiazem in Dilated Cardiomyopathy (DiDi) trial assessed exercise capacity in 186 patients, 92 of whom were randomized to diltiazem. There was a significant improvement in exercise time in the group randomized to diltiazem for 24 months.

Felodipine is a second-generation dihydropyridine calcium channel blocker with minimal cardiac depressant activity which was studied in the placebo-controlled V-HeFT III trial. This trial enrolled 450 males with moderate heart failure, left ventricular ejection fraction less than 0.45 or enlarged heart on echocardiogram or chest X-ray and already receiving ACE inhibitor therapy. Of interest, less than 10% of the patients screened for this trial were enrolled with the most common exclusion criteria being active angina (requiring calcium channel blockers, nitrates or beta-blockers–34% of excluded patients) or pulmonary disease (16% of excluded patients). Patients were randomized to felodipine or placebo, and efficacy was assessed by exercise capacity, clinical signs of heart failure,

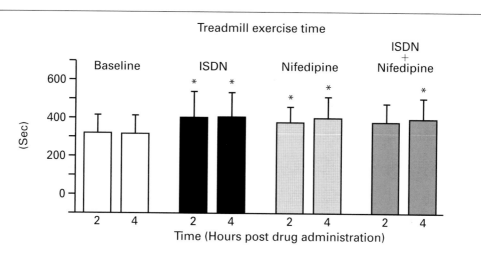

Treadmill exercise time

Episodes of hospitalizations and increase in diuretics for worsening congestive heart failure

Treatment	Patients (n)			CHF episodes (n)
	Hospitalizations	Increase in diuretics dose	Total	
Nifedipine (NIF) (n = 21)	5*	3	8	9 †
Isosorbide dinitrate (ISDN) (n = 20)	0	3	3	3
NIF + ISDN (n = 23)	6*	2	8	21 ‡§

CHF, congestive heart failure.
*$p<0.05$ versus ISDN; † $p<0.09$ versus ISDN; ‡ $p<0.0001$ versus ISDN; § $p<0.001$ versus NIF.

Figure 18.5

Comparative effects of nifedipine, isosorbide dinitrate, and the combination in patients with compensated heart failure 4 and 6 hours after drug administration after 8 weeks of therapy. All active therapies improved exercise time compared with baseline. Table indicates incidence of hospitalization and increase in diuretic use during this study indicating that active therapy led to clinical deterioration. (From Elkayam et al,[58] with permission.)

ejection fraction and other clinical indicators of heart failure at 12 and 42 weeks. This study was not powered to detect differences in mortality between the felodipine and placebo groups. There was no difference in exercise capacity, quality of life, or need for hospitalization in the active therapy group when compared with placebo. There was a reduction in blood pressure and slight improvement in ejection fraction in the long-term follow-up period, the slight improvement in ejection fraction did not persist but active therapy prevented the deterioration of exercise tolerance seen in the placebo limb.

Effect on survival

Survival has become the critical endpoint in heart failure studies in the past two decades. At the present time, no calcium channel blocker carries an indication for 'heart failure' in the US, although several have undergone extensive study in heart failure patients. Diltiazem has been studied in a relatively small group of patients (by heart failure trial standards) already on background therapy of ACE inhibitors, digoxin and diuretics in the Diltiazem in Dilated Cardiomyopathy (DiDi) trial. The endpoints of this trial included transplant-listing-free survival, exercise capacity and haemodynamics. There was no impact on this somewhat subjective 'survival' endpoint but statistically significant improvement in the other parameters was observed.[54] These data would need to be reproduced in an appropriately powered study in order to support using diltiazem in this patient population.

One of the most extensive studies of calcium channel blockers in heart failure was the PRAISE trial, which was a randomized trial of amlodipine versus placebo in patients with New York Heart Association (NYHA) class III or IV heart failure.[30] In this trial, 1153 patients with either ischaemic (63%) or nonischaemic (37%) cardiomyopathy with left ventricular ejection fractions of less than 30% despite therapy with ACE inhibitors, digoxin and diuretics were randomized. 'Non-ischemic cardiomyopathy' in PRAISE was a clinical classification, assigned by the local principle investigator. This population included a variety of patients, including those with coronary artery disease which was not felt by the investigator, to be the cause of the cardiomyopathy. The primary endpoint in this trial was the combination of all-cause mortality and strictly defined cardiovascular morbidity. Randomization was stratified a priori for aetiology of heart failure using clinical discrimination between an ischaemic (731 patients) or non-ischaemic aetiology (421 patients). There was no statistically significant treatment effect on the primary endpoint when the ischaemic and non-ischaemic patients were analysed together. In a subsequent, predefined analysis, the investigators determined that there was a significant reduction in mortality and the combined endpoint of mortality and cardiovascular morbidity in patients randomized to amlodipine (Figure 18.6) with a non-ischaemic aetiology of heart failure. Adverse events which occurred with greater frequency in the amlodipine group included pulmonary and peripheral oedema which are worrisome considering the population under study.

There are several potential explanations for the observations of the PRAISE trial. First, there may be a pathophysiological aspect particular to dilated cardiomyopathy not found in ischaemic cardiomyopathy that is particularly sensitive to the action of amlodipine. A second potential explanation proposes that some aspect of ischaemic cardiomyopathy physiology neutralizes a favourable effect of amlodipine. Finally, there may be an unidentified covariate that segregates with nonischaemic heart failure aetiologies and is responsible for the beneficial therapeutic effect. This latter hypothesis is supported by previous trials with amiodarone[55] where a favourable response to active therapy was seen only in nonischaemia cardiomyopathy populations. These findings with amlodipine must be confirmed in the ongoing PRAISE II trial before broadly applying to patients with non-ischaemic cardiomyopathies.

A trial of mibafradil versus placebo has been completed and a preliminary report indicates no significant difference between treatment group 3 years after randomization. There was

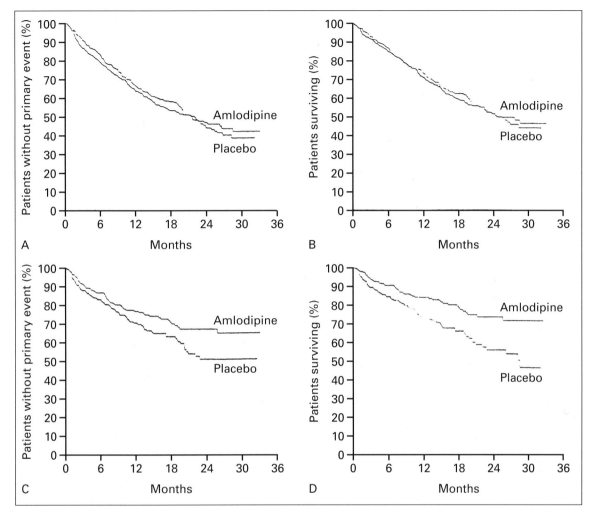

Figure 18.6
Kaplan–Meier plots of the time to first primary event (A) and survival (B) in patients with ischaemic cardiomyopathy compared with time to first primary event (C) and survival (D) in patients with nonischemic cardiomyopathy randomized to amlodipine or placebo in the PRAISE trial. (From Packer et al[30] with permission.)

evidence of a drug interaction between mibafradil and drugs which predispose to the potentially fatal arrhythmia, torsade de pointes.[53,56] The future of this medication is in doubt following its voluntary withdrawal from the US market because of multiple drug interactions and a potential for proarrhythmia.

Ongoing research

Despite the concern regarding calcium channel blockers as a therapeutic class, there is considerable interest in selected agents for supplemental therapy in patients with congestive heart failure. There are several agents that continue to be investigated to achieve formal approval for heart failure therapy. Amlodipine is currently under study in the PRAISE II trial, enrolling patients with advanced symptomatic heart failure due to systolic dysfunction due to non-ischaemic aetiologies. This trial is designed to confirm the provocative findings of the PRAISE trial discussed above and will be completed within 2 years.

There is a large 'unmet need' for therapeutic agents with lusitropic activity. Heart failure due to diastolic dysfunction will increase in prevalence as the world population grows older and there is, as yet, no effective therapy for this condition. Unfortunately the design of prospective, randomized, placebo-controlled therapeutic trials is limited by the heterogeneity of the affected population. Patients with diastolic dysfunction may have LVH, ischaemia, infiltrative cardiomyopathy, age-related myocardial changes, or a combination of several of these factors, confusing and diluting the therapeutic advantage directed against any single aetiology. Precisely defining the entry criteria for such a trial would be critical but not easily accomplished. At present, therapy should be directed against the treatable components of diastolic abnormalities such as LVH and ischaemia although it is unknown if this treatment strategy will alter the natural history of the condition.

Have we crossed the bridge?

Based on the data presented above, how may we view the use of calcium channel blockers in patients with heart failure? Calcium channel blocker use in heart failure patients varies around the world. Among patients enrolled in a recent international heart failure trial, baseline therapy with calcium channel blockers ranged from a low of 9% in several countries to a high of 18% in the UK and Ireland.[57] Cer-

tainly in the acute setting, there are no studies that support the use of any calcium channel blocker in patients with acutely decompensated heart failure, regardless of aetiology. The one exception to this recommendation is the cautious use of diltiazem in patients with rapid atrial fibrillation when the rate cannot be controlled with digoxin and the physician believes that control of the ventricular response is paramount in the treatment of the patient. Patients with left ventricular dysfunction early after myocardial infarction should not be treated with diltiazem or verapamil as well-designed trials have failed to demonstrate benefit and they may in fact harm this patient subset.

Patients with compensated heart failure who are receiving medical therapy with ACE inhibitors at effective doses and who have hypertension or symptomatic coronary disease may be treated with selected calcium channel blockers. Results from the first PRAISE trial support the safety of amlodipine in patients with ischaemic heart disease and severe heart failure. One may argue that such patients may also be candidates for treatment with beta-adrenergic blockers, including the 'vasodilating' alpha-beta blockers such as carvedilol. At the present time, the data suggest that the beta-blockers favourably alter the natural history of cardiomyopathy whereas further proof is required to make a similar claim for the calcium channel blockers.

Sir William Osler has written that 'a physician without physiology flounders in an aimless fashion, never able to gain any accurate conception of disease, practising a sort of popgun pharmacy, hitting now the malady and again the patient, himself not knowing which.' Our simplistic view of cardiovascular disease and heart failure in the past has led to the misuse of calcium channel blockers in some patient populations. As we learn more about the complex relationship of myocardial and systemic factors and complete appropriately powered and designed clinical trials, we will be able to use calcium channel blockers more effectively and safely in patients with heart failure. Each agent is unique and requires an independent investigation for efficacy and safety and each agent must 'cross the bridge' individually, if at all.

References

1. Furberg C, Psaty B, Meyer J. Nifedipine: dose-related increase in mortality in patients with coronary heart disease. *Circulation* 1995; **92**: 1326–1331.

2. Barry W, Bridge J. Intracellular calcium homeostasis in cardiac myocytes. *Circulation* 1993; **87**: 1806–1815.

3. Nuss H, Houser S. Voltage dependance of contraction and calcium current in severely hypertrophied feline ventricular myocytes. *J Mol Cell Cardiol* 1991; **23**: 717–26.

4. Zhang X, Hintze T. Amlodipine releases nitric oxide from canine microvessels. An unexpected mechanism of action of a calcium channel blocking agent. *Circulation* 1998; **97**: 576–580.

5. Lyons D, Webster J, Benjamin N. The effect of antihypertensive therapy on responsiveness to local intra-arterial N-monomethyl–l–arginine in patients with essential hypertension. *J Hypertens* 1994; **12**: 1047–1052.

6. deVries R, Anthonio R, Veldhusien DV et al. Effects of amlodipine on endothelial function in rats with chronic heart failure after experimental myocardial infarction. *J Cardiovasc Pharmacol* 1997; **30**: 683–689.

7. Perrone-Filardi P, Bacharach S, Dilsizian V et al. Regional systolic function, myocardial blood flow and glucose uptake at rest in hypertrophic cardiomyopathy. *Am J Cardiol* 1993; **72**: 199–204.

8. Opie L. Calcium channel antagonists in the treatment of coronary artery disease: fundamental pharmacological properties relevant to clinical use. *Prog Cardiovasc Dis* 1996; **38**: 273–290.

9. Leenen F, Hollowell D. Antihypertensive effect of felodipine associated with persistent sympathetic activation and minimal regression of left ventricular hypertrophy. *Am J Cardiol* 1992; **69**: 639–645.

10. Goldsmith S. Effect of amlodipine and felodipine on sympathetic activity and baroreflex function in normal humans. *Am J Hypertens* 1995; **8**: 902–908.

11. Naftilan A, Oparil S. The role of calcium in the control of renin release. *Hypertension* 1982; **4**: 670–675.

12. Levine B, Kalman J, Mayer L et al. Elevated levels of circulating tumor necrosis factor in severe chronic heart failure. *N Engl J Med* 1990; **323**: 236–241.

13. Testa M, Yeh M, Lee P et al. Circulating levels of cytokines and their endogenous modulators in patients with mild to severe congestive heart failure due to coronary disease of hypertension. *J Am Coll Cardiol* 1996; **28**: 964–971.

14. Mohler E, Sorensen L, Ghali J et al. Role of cytokines in the mechanism of action of amlodipine: the PRAISE heart failure trial. *J Am Coll Cardiol* 1997; **30**: 35–41.

15. Levy D, Garrison R, Savage D et al. Prognostic implications of echocardiographically determined left ventricular mass in the Framingham Heart Study. *N Engl J Med* 1990; **322**: 1561–1566.

16. Cuocolo A, Sax F, Brush J et al. Left ventricular hypertrophy and impaired diastolic filling in essential hypertension. Diastolic mechanisms for systolic dysfunction during exercise. *Circulation* 1990; **81**: 978–986.

17. Cannon R, Rosing D, Maron B et al. Myocardial ischemia in patients with hypertrophic cardiomyopathy: contribution of inadequate vasodilator reserve and elevated left ventricular filling pressures. *Circulation* 1985; **71**: 234–243.

18. Dougherty A, Naccerelli G, Gray E et al. Congestive heart failure with normal systolic function. *Am J Cardiol* 1984; **54**: 778–782.

19. Soufer R, Wohgelernter D, Vita N et al. Intact systolic left ventricular function in clinical congestive heart failure. *Am J Cardiol* 1985; **55**: 1032–1036.

20. Tresch D, McGough M. Heart failure with normal systolic function: a common disorder in older people. *J Am Geriatr Soc* 1995; **43**: 1035–1042.

21. Miller T, Grossman S, Schechtman K et al. Left ventricular diastolic filling and its association with age. *Am J Cardiol* 1986; **58**: 531–553.

22. Aronow W, Ahn C, Kronszon I. Prognosis of congestive heart failure in elderly patients with normal versus abnormal left ventricular systolic function associated with coronary artery disease. *Am J Cardiol* 1990; **66**: 1257–1259.

23. Gwathmey JK, Copelas L, MacKinnon R et al. Abnormal intracellular calcium handling in myocardium from patients with end-stage heart failure. *Circ Res* 1987; **61**: 70–76.

24. Schmeider R, Martus P, Klingbiel A. Reversal of left ventricular hypertrophy in essential hypertension: a meta-analysis of randomized, double-blind studies. *JAMA* 1996; **275**: 1507–1513.

25. Schulman S, Weiss J, Becker L et al. The effects of antihypertensive therapy on left ventricular mass in elderly patients. *N Engl J Med* 1990; **322**: 1350–1356.

26. Setaro J, Zaret B, Schulman D et al. Usefulness of verapamil for congestive heart failure associated with abnormal left ventricular diastolic filling and normal left ventricular systolic performance. *Am J Cardiol* 1990; **66**: 981–986.

27. Bonow R, Ostrow H, Rosing D et al. Effects of verapamil on left ventricular systolic and diastolic function in patients with hypertrophic cardiomyopathy: pressure–volume analysis with a non-imaging scintillation probe. *Circulation* 1983; **68**: 1062–1073.

28. Wagner J, Sax F, Weisman H et al. Calcium antagonist receptors in the atrial tissue from patients with hypertrophic cardiomyopathy. *N Engl J Med* 1989; **320**: 755–761.

29. Lorell B, Paulus W, Grossman W et al. Modification of abnormal left ventricular diastolic properties by nifedipine in patients with hypertrophic cardiomyopathy. *Circulation* 1982; **65**: 499–507.

30. Packer M, O'Connor C, Ghali J et al. Effect of amlodipine on morbidity and mortality in severe chronic heart failure. *N Engl J Med* 1996; **335**: 1107–1114.

31. Hansen J, Group DS. Congestive heart failure and ischemic heart disease treated with trandolapril and verapamil. *J Hypertens* 1998; **16** (Suppl 1): S71–S74.

32. Hansen J, Hagerup L, Sigurd B et al. Treatment with verapamil and trandolapril in patients with congestive heart failure and myocardial infarction. *J Hypertens* 1997; **15**: S119–S122.

33. Bonow R, Udelson J. Left ventricular diastolic dysfunction as a cause of congestive heart failure: mechanisms and management. *Ann Intern Med* 1992; **117**: 502–510.

34. Bonow R, Vitale D, Bacharach S et al. Effects of aging on asynchronous left ventricular regional function and global ventricular filling in normal human subjects. *J Am Coll Cardiol* 1988; **11**: 50–58.

35. Schulman S, Lakatta E, Fleg F et al. Age-related decline in left ventricular filling at rest and exercise. *Am J Physiol* 1992; **263**: H1932–H1938.

36. Arrighi J, Dilsizian V, Perrone-Filardi P et al. Improvement in age-related impairment of diastolic filling with verapamil in the normal human heart. *Circulation* 1994; **90**: 213–219.

37. Elkayam U, Webber L, Torkam B et al. Comparison of the hemodynamic responses to nifedipine and nitroprusside in severe chronic congestive heart failure. *Am J Cardiol* 1984; **53**: 1321–1325.

38. Ryman K, Kubo S, Lystash J et al. Effect of nicardipine on rest and exercise hemodynamics in chronic congestive heart failure. *Am J Cardiol* 1986; **58**: 583–588.

39. Olivari M, Levine T, Cohn J. Acute hemodynamic effects of nitrendipine in congestive heart failure. *J Cardiovasc Pharmacol* 1984; **6** (Suppl): S1002–S1004.

40. Lewis B, Shefer A, Merdler A et al. Effects of the second generation calcium channel blocker nisoldipine on left ventricular contractility in cardiac failure. *Am Heart J* 1988; **115**: 1238–1244.

41. Timmis A, Campbell S, Monaghan M et al. Acute hemodynamic and metabolic effects of felodipine in congestive heart failure. *Br Heart J* 1984; **51**: 445–451.

42. Elkayam U, Webber L, McKay C, Rahimtoola S. Spectrum of acute hemodynamic effects of nifedipine in severe congestive heart failure. *Am J Cardiol* 1985; **56**: 560–566.

43. Packer M, Lee W, Medina N et al. Prognostic importance of the immediate hemodynamic response to nifedipine in patients with severe

left ventricular dysfunction. *J Am Coll Cardiol* 1987; **9**: 622–630.

44. Diltiazem Multicenter Post-infarction group. The effect of diltiazem on mortality and reinfarction after myocardial infarction. *N Engl J Med* 1988; **319**: 385–392.

45. Goldstein R, Boccuzzi S, Cruess D, Nattel S. Diltiazem increases late-onset congestive heart failure in post-infarction patients with early reduction in ejection fraction. *Circulation* 1991; **83**: 52–60.

46. DEFIANT-II Research Group. Doppler flow and echocardiography in functional cardiac insufficiency: assessment of nisoldipine therapy. *Eur Heart J* 1997; **18**: 31–40.

47. The Danish Study Group on Verapamil in Myocardial Infarction. Verapamil in myocardial infarction. *Eur Heart J* 1984; **5**: 516–528.

48. DAVIT Investigators. The effect of verapamil on mortality and major events after myocardial infarction: the Danish Verapamil Infarction Trial (DAVIT) II. *Am J Cardiol* 1990; **66**: 779–785.

49. Jesperson CM. The effect of verapamil on major events in patients with impaired cardiac function recovering from acute myocardial infarction. The Danish Study Group on Verapamil in Myocardial Infarction. *Eur Heart J* 1993; **14**: 540–545.

50. Vaag-eNilsen M, Rasmussen V, Hollader N et al. Prevalence of myocardial ischemia during the first year after a myocardial infarction. Effect of treatment with verapamil. *Eur Heart J* 1992; **13**: 666–670.

51. Hager W, Davis B, Riba A et al. Absence of a deleterious effect of calcium channel blockers in patients with left ventricular dysfunction after myocardial infarction: the SAVE study experience. *Am Heart J* 1998; **135**: 406–413.

52. Packer M, Nicod P, Khandheria B et al. Randomized, multicenter, double blind, placebo-controlled evaluation of amlodipine in patients with mild to moderate heart failure. *J Am Coll Cardiol* 1991; **17**: 274A.

53. Walsh J, Andrews R, Curtis S et al. Effects of amlodipine in patients with chronic heart failure. *Am Heart J* 1997; **134**: 872–878.

54. Figulla H, Gietzen F, Zeymer U et al. Diltiazem improves cardiac function and exercise capacity in patients with idiopathic dilated cardiomyopathy. *Circulation* 1996; **94**: 346–352.

55. Singh S, Fletcher R, Fisher S et al. Amiodarone in patients with congestive heart failure and asymptomatic ventricular arrhythmia. *N Engl J Med* 1995; **333**: 77–82.

56. Levine TB. MACH-1 Trial Results, 2nd Scientific Meeting of the Heart Failure Society of America, Boca Raton, Florida, USA, 1998.

57. Massie B, Cleland J, Armstrong P et al. Regional differences in the characteristics and treatment of patients participating in an international heart failure trial. *J Card Fail* 1998; **4**: 3–8.

58. Elkayam U, Amin J, Mehra A et al. A prospective, randomized, double blind crossover study to compare the efficacy and safety of chronic nifedipine therapy with that of isosorbide dinitrate and their combination in the treatment of congestive heart failure. *Circulation* 1990; **82**: 1954–1961.

19

Surgical treatment for heart failure
Stephen Westaby

Introduction

In 1990 heart failure accounted for 5% of all hospital admissions in Britain at a cost to the NHS of £360 million. In the United States where 400 000 new cases are diagnosed annually, treatment costs exceed $34 billion. While a small proportion of these patients may benefit from conventional surgical methods for most these are inappropriate and other interventions must be considered. Emerging surgical strategies for advanced heart failure increasingly address the inherent cellular and humoral mechanisms. Eventually the ultimate surgical option, cardiac transplantation, may be required only when initial treatment options fail.

Pathological processes which underlie new surgical strategies

Heart failure begins with a pathological insult which may be ischaemic, immunological, toxic or infective. Left ventricular contractile dysfunction and the resulting haemodynamic sequelae activate neurohumoral systems to cause vasoconstriction and increased left ventricular wall stress.[1] Altered loading conditions eventually cause the myocardium to change its form and function resulting in cavity dilatation (Figure 19.1).[2] Early conventional surgical

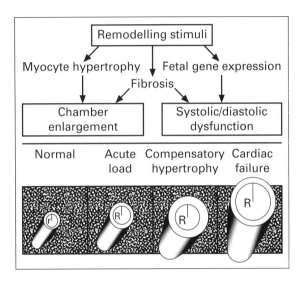

Figure 19.1
Remodelling stimuli which affect the shape and function of the heart.

procedures may prevent further deterioration but ineffective treatment allows progressive decline.

As the heart dilates both systolic and diastolic wall stress increase through their physical relationship with diameter and intracavity pressure. Compensatory hypertrophy occurs when the heart wall thickens in an attempt to normalize wall stress but in the vast majority of patients with systolic dysfunction myocyte hypertrophy does not prevent further deterioration. The left ventricle continues to dilate,

Phenotype	Adult	Fetal	Hypertrophy/ failure
Cardiac α actin	+++	+	+
Skeletal α actin	+	+++	+++
Smooth muscle α actin	+	+++	+++
α Myosin heavy chain	+++	+	+
β Myosin heavy chain	+	+++	+++
SR Ca^{2+} ATPase	+++	+	+

Table 19.1
Myocardial phenotype in adult, fetal and hypertrophic hearts.

diastolic filling pressures rise, afterload increases due to vasoconstriction and wall stress becomes exceptionally high. With cellular hypertrophy there are changes in myocyte genetic expression. Normally as the fetal heart matures to an adult form changes in myocardial phenotype occur. In contrast genetic expression in remodelled myocardium reverts to fetal type with downregulation of those genes functional in the adult heart (Table 19.1). Cardiac fibroblasts also begin to produce large amounts of extracellular matrix causing interstitial fibrosis in the myocardium.[3] The progression of morphological changes (dilatation) and reduction in ejection fraction are closely linked. The dilated ventricle suffers elevated wall tension because myocardial thickness does not increase to compensate for the greater radius. An increase in myocardial oxygen demand coincides with impairment of subendocardial bloodflow through high filling pressures.

Exercise capacity has a poor relationship with left ventricular function although ejection fraction is an important determinant of survival.[4] Patients with an ejection fraction (EF) greater than 40% have modest annual mortality rates (less than 10%) while those with EF less than 30% have annual mortality over 25%.[5,6] For patients with EF 15–40% there is an almost linear relationship between EF and annual mortality rate. The condition of the left ventricle is therefore an important determinant of survival independent of the severity of the symptoms. A low EF (<30%) indicates that the ventricle has remodelled but a dilated chamber with low EF can eject the same stroke volume as a normal ventricle with an EF of 60%. As EF decreases it does not necessarily reflect an impairment of contraction, but rather a remodelling of the ventricle. Consequently an important goal of both medical and surgical therapy for chronic heart failure is to prevent progression of the remodelling process. Neurohumoral agents including angiotensin, norepinephrine, endothelin, aldosterone and cyclic guanosine monophosphate (GMP) influence the remodelling process (Figure 19.2). In particular the relationship between plasma norepinephrine

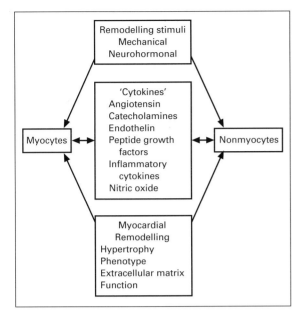

Figure 19.2
Actions of mechanical and neurohormonal remodelling stimuli on myocytes and nonmyocytes.

and mortality is clearly defined.[7] Patients with a plasma norepinephrine less than 600 pg/ml have the lowest cumulative mortality rate compared with those whose plasma norepinephrine levels exceed 900 pg/ml who have a short life expectancy. Activation of the sympathetic nervous system is therefore an important contributor to mortality.

New surgical treatments for heart failure now focus on preventing progressive left ventricular dysfunction and promoting symptomatic relief. Currently, moderation of left ventricular remodelling in coronary disease, dilated cardiomyopathy, long standing valvular disease, or hypertension is first attempted with ACE inhibitors, nitrates, calcium channel or beta-blockers.[8,9] When these measures fail to control symptoms or progressive cardiac enlargement, surgical methods should be considered.

Conventional operations in heart failure

A number of primary cardiac defects which cause heart failure are amenable to conventional surgical techniques. Coronary artery disease is the leading cause of heart failure in most Western countries and improvements in the treatment of myocardial infarction result in more patients who survive long enough to develop symptoms. Those with angina or silent reversible ischaemia (Figure 19.3) even with ejection fractions less than 20%, are amenable to coronary bypass surgery at low risk (<5%) given the benefits of intra-aortic balloon counter pulsation and inotropic support in the postoperative period. Many potential transplant patients are now managed by more aggressive coronary surgery given the shortage of donor hearts. Valvular heart disease responds to valve replacement or repair as long as left ventricular remodelling is not rendered irreversible by excessive dilatation or myocardial fibrosis. For instance the 'cor bovinum' of end-stage aortic stenosis or chronic aortic regurgitation has an inordinately high risk of surgical mortality and little functional rehabilitation in operative survivors. Similarly patients with chronic mitral regurgitation and severely impaired left ventricular function (EF < 25%) may not survive restoration of mitral competence particularly if the subvalvar apparatus is excised. While the importance of an intact mitral subvalvar apparatus is well known, the effort expended to preserve this varies from surgeon to surgeon. Both operative and event-free survival are greater after valve repair than replacement, although valve replacement (in mitral regurgitation) with preservation of the cordal apparatus provides similar results.[10]

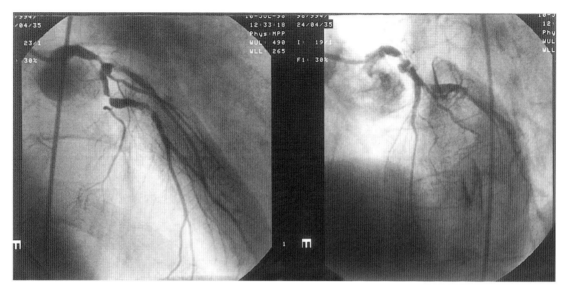

Figure 19.3
Severe proximal occlusive disease of the left coronary artery. The patient had no angina but presented with breathlessness, mitral regurgitation and ejection fraction less than 20%. Hibernating myocardium responded to surgical coronary revascularization with improvement in symptoms and mitral valve function.

Mitral annular dilatation occurs secondary to the left ventricular dilatation in ischaemic and dilated cardiomyopathies.[11] This causes incomplete mitral leaflet coaption which may be exacerbated by papillary muscle scarring and elongation in ischaemic cases. In this context a number of distinct clinical patterns are recognized where mitral valve repair, with or without coronary bypass, provides symptomatic improvement.[12] These are:

1. Ischaemia manifest by angina and variable mitral regurgitation which becomes significantly worse during an acute ischaemic episode causing dyspnoea at rest or acute left ventricular failure with pulmonary oedema;
2. Acute myocardial ischaemia or infarction located inferobasally (right coronary or dominant circumflex distribution) which causes sudden posteromedial papillary muscle dysfunction and mitral regurgitation;
3. Acute catastrophic pulmonary oedema due to papillary muscle rupture (inferobasal in 75% of cases) several days after acute myocardial infarction;
4. Chronic progressive dyspnoea (New York Heart Association (NYHA) III or IV) associated with previous myocardial infarction, an enlarged dysfunctional left ventricle mitral regurgitation and varying degrees of pulmonary hypertension. This comprises the largest group;
5. Patients with idiopathic dilated cardiomyopathy and annular dilatation producing moderate to severe mitral regurgitation through inadequate leaflet coaptation.

The recommended threshold for mitral repair in ischaemic regurgitation is a left ventricular end-systolic volume index greater than 80 ml per/m^2.[13] A calculated regurgitant fraction greater than 50% of the forward EF is also an indication for mitral repair. In ischaemic patients with left ventricular failure both the coronary arteries and mitral valve must be investigated before surgery. Patients with angina, good target vessels, mild to moderate mitral regurgitation and reversible ischaemia posterolaterally on the thallium scan should be treated by myocardial revascularization alone. Mitral valve surgery should be performed together with coronary bypass in cases where regurgitation is moderate to severe and repair is more likely than replacement. Should replacement prove necessary then as much of the subvalvar apparatus as possible should be retained to conserve left ventricular geometry and function.

After myocardial infarction resection of a left ventricular aneurysm usually improves global left ventricular function.[14] Although aneurysms may form in the circumflex and right coronary territories the vast majority follow complete proximal occlusion of the left anterior descending coronary. Fifty per cent develop within 48 hours of acute infarction and most of the remainder are established within 2 weeks. Besides left ventricular failure many patients have new or persisting angina, ventricular arrhythmias or thromboembolism. Resection of the aneurysm is performed in conjunction with coronary artery bypass and is achieved with low operative mortality as long as the EF is more than 20% with a pulmonary artery pressure less than 40 mmHg and cardiac index greater than 2.0 litres/min/m^2.[15] The indication for surgery in asymptomatic patients is less clear although those enrolled in the Coronary Artery Surgery Study (CASS) registry had a much worse prognosis if they had poor ventricular function regardless of symptomatic status. Also patients with large asymptomatic aneurysms eventually develop global left ventricular dysfunction by the time symptoms appear.

Dynamic cardiomyoplasty

Because the muscle fibres in the myocardium are syncytial a single electrical impulse such as that delivered by an ordinary cardiac pacemaker will illicit an all or none contraction of the whole heart. In contrast, skeletal muscle requires a burst stimulator to recruit the separate motor units to generate sufficient power. This constraint led to the development of the programmable burst stimulator which is synchronized with cardiac systole by R-wave sensing (Medtronic, MN, USA, now withdrawn).

In dynamic cardiomyoplasty the latissimus dorsi muscle is mobilized from the left chest wall, brought with its vascular pedicle between the ribs, and wrapped around the ventricles of the failing heart or an alternative pumping chamber (Figure 19.4).[16] The muscle then undergoes low frequency electrical stimulation for several weeks to confer fatigue resistance. It is then stimulated using a synchronizable burst stimulator to contract during cardiac systole. Several weeks of low frequency electrical stimulation alters the phenotypic expression of skeletal muscle to produce an almost pure type I muscle which is highly resistant to fatigue.

Dynamic cardiomyoplasty was conceived as an alternative to cardiac transplantation. However for patients in NYHA IV operative mortality was prohibitively high, rendering the technique unsuitable for those patients who might benefit most.[17] Even for experienced surgical teams treating NYHA III patients there was an early hospital mortality of 12–15% and an additional major morbidity

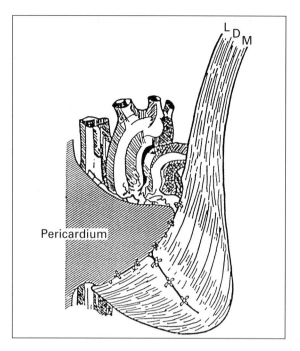

Figure 19.4
The principles underlying the use of programmed skeletal muscle for cardiac assist. The latissimus dorsi muscle is transposed to encircle the native left ventricle, the aorta or an auxiliary pumping chamber to augment blood flow.

rate of about 20%. Most cardiologists consider this unacceptably high for patients who can be effectively managed by medical treatment. In short those who need it don't survive it and those who survive it don't need it.[18] However protagonists of the technique claimed symptomatic benefit in up to 80% of cases (mean improvement 1.3 NYHA classes) but objective improvement in left ventricular systolic function (including LVEF, ventricular/work indices and mean wall motion scores) was difficult to demonstrate.[16] In effect, with negligible improvement in exercise capacity, the results fell short of those recently described for current drug regimes. Because placebo therapy can evoke improvement in clinical sta-

tus (NYHA class) and exercise capacity in heart failure patients, the modest objective findings after cardiomyoplasty are difficult to interpret.[19] There can be no satisfactory prospective randomized trial with a sham operation to assess NYHA status, quality of life or hospital admission rates between the groups. Similarly the use of nonrandomized reference groups raises concern about patient selection and proper case matching.

Several mechanisms might account for subjective improvement after cardiomyoplasty. Synchronized squeezing of the heart during systole has been shown to be effective in laboratory animals but not in patients. By adding another layer of muscle to the ventricular wall cardiomyoplasty may be regarded as iatrogenic cardiac hypertrophy. By LaPlace's law the increase in wall thickness may reduce myocardial wall tension. Also the passive muscle wrap may delay ventricular dilatation by attenuating the remodelling process. In ischaemic cardiomyopathy the muscle graft may induce neovascularization to the myocardium comparable with historical attempts at revascularization by Beck, Vineberg and others. However, with improvements in drug therapy and emerging surgical strategies cardiomyoplasty seems similarly destined to the museum of medicine.

Partial left ventriculectomy

Partial left ventriculectomy was conceived by the Brazilian Randas Batista (1994) to address the imbalance between ventricular mass and diameter in heart failure patients with left ventricular cavity dilatation.[20] LaPlace's law dictates that an enlarged ventricle will generate more wall tension to achieve a fixed intracavity pressure. As wall stress increases so does myocardial oxygen demand so the dilated ventricle is mechanically disadvantaged by its own size. Hypothetically a decrease in radius should lower wall tension with improved mechanical advantage to the failing myocardium. Surgical reduction of the ventricular cavity to near normal size is achieved by excision of the lateral wall between the anterolateral and posteromedial papillary muscles. This removes the territory of the first marginal circumflex coronary artery. The limits of the wedge shaped excision extend from the left ventricular apex between the inner aspects of the papillary muscles to the mitral annulus. The marginal artery is oversewn and the ventriculotomy closed in two or three layers. In very large ventricles (end diastolic diameter of 9–10 cm) resection of the interpapillary segment may prove inadequate. In this case a larger excision is performed and the mitral valve replaced through the ventriculotomy. Alternatively one or both papillary muscles are explanted and translocated allowing preservation of the native valve and a more physiological operation. For those patients with significant mitral regurgitation through a dilated annulus, it is helpful to perform mitral repair.[21] This can be undertaken through the ventriculotomy by sewing the free edges of the anterior and posterior leaflets together (Alfieri technique).

Left ventriculectomy has been applied successfully to patients with end-stage aortic valve disease (in South America), but predominantly for those with idiopathic dilated cardiomyopathy. A left ventricular end-diastolic dimension greater than 7.0 cm and an EF less than 25% are arbitrary criteria for patient selection. In most cases the patients are not transplant candidates and usually those with ischaemic cardiomyopathy, extensive myocardial fibrosis, or active myocarditis are excluded. Pulmonary hypertension, right ventricular failure or incidental minor coronary disease are not contraindications. In Oxford, we have applied the technique to patients with

ischaemic cardiomyopathy in conjunction with coronary bypass (Figure 19.5). While marked improvement in EF can be obtained, these patients are susceptible to ventricular dysrhythmias as the anastomotic site stretches.[22]

The results of left ventricular reduction vary between spectacular (allegedly!) to unremarkable with substantial hospital mortality. Intraoperative pressure–volume loop analysis shows that the reduction in left ventricular cavity volume (approximately 40%) to improve all indices of systolic function. However, diastolic function tends to worsen with elevated left ventricular end-diastolic pressure, decreased external work, and a fall in total energy consumption. There appears to be no initial increase in stroke volume or fall in pulmonary artery wedge pressure suggesting that an increase in cardiac output depends solely on heart rate. In Batista's series those who underwent extended lateral ventriculectomy had a 43% hospital mortality.[20] Six-month follow-up in selected survivors showed that end-systolic volume was then reduced more than end-diastolic volume with a resulting increase in stroke volume. Ejection fraction was improved at this stage but end-diastolic and pulmonary artery wedge pressures remained elevated. The best results were achieved in patients with valvular heart disease then dilated cardiomyopathy. Results for coronary artery disease and Chagas disease were less satisfactory.

The substantial mortality from extended ventriculectomy with mitral valve excision is a serious limitation of this approach. Papillary muscle continuity with the valve anulus plays an important role in left ventricular systolic function. Loss of annuloventricular interaction causes a decrease of up to 12% in stroke volume and elongation of the left ventricle. Elongation then impairs diastolic function.

The Cleveland Clinic has restricted use of ventriculectomy to patients with idiopathic

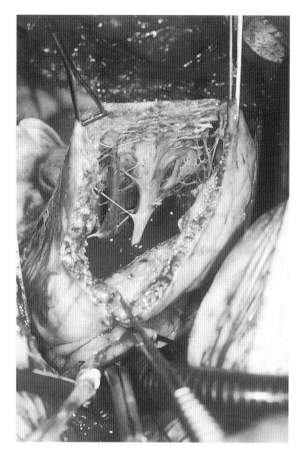

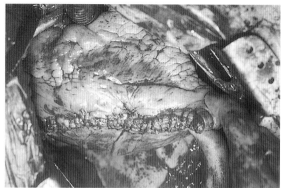

Figure 19.5

Partial left ventriculectomy in an ischaemic cardiomyopathy patient with EF = 15%. (a) Resection of the anterolateral territory of a chronically occluded left anterior descending coronary preserving the subvalvar apparatus. (b) Primary closure to produce a small vigorous left ventricle.

dilated cardiomyopathy and specifically excluded those with coronary disease.[23] All patients were NYHA class III or IV, many were inotrope dependent and most were listed for transplantation. Detailed echocardiographic studies showed reduction in left ventricular end-diastolic diameter from 8.3 ± 1.1 cm to 6.0 ± 0.7 cm and reduction in left ventricular end-diastolic volume from 238 ± 76 ml to 116 ± 45 ml on intraoperative measurements. EF increased from $15 \pm 5.0\%$ to $33 \pm 10.7\%$, although stroke volume remained virtually unchanged from 33 ± 8.7 ml preoperatively to 36 ± 7.5 ml after ventricular resection. Three

months postoperatively there had been a slight increase in left ventricular end-diastolic diameter to 6.5 ± 0.9 cm and an increase in left ventricular end-diastolic volume to 170 ± 50 ml. Stroke volume remained constant but EF fell to $26 \pm 8.0\%$. While left atrial pressure fell from 22 ± 7.6 to 12 ± 3.4 mmHg, cardiac index was only modestly improved from 2.1 ± 0.4 to 2.2 ± 0.4 ($P = 0.04$). Of thirty-two patients, seven required either a left ventricular assist device (LVAD) or cardiac transplant to achieve survival. Postoperative morbidity was also considerable with many patients requiring prolonged inotropic support, intra-aortic balloon counter pulsation, or haemofiltration. Histological findings showed that active myocarditis or excessive myocardial fibrosis mitigated against survival.

In summary, many patients with idiopathic dilated cardiomyopathy show symptomatic and metabolic improvement after left ventricular reduction. However in some patients the ventricle redilates and the improvement is not sustained perhaps due to adverse underlying pathology. Outcome is unpredictable and facilities for rescue by LVAD or transplantation are advisable.

Long-term mechanical circulatory support and bridge to myocyte recovery

An understanding of the maladaptive aspects of left ventricular remodelling and the mechanisms of pharmacological improvement has provided insight into new surgical methods to treat heart failure. Twenty years ago, Burch reported that reduction in cardiac work load by prolonged bed rest in heart failure could achieve a partial left ventricular recovery.[24] Nevertheless this approach was limited by the adverse consequences to the peripheral musculature, vasculature and autonomic nervous system of prolonged inactivity. Both ACE inhibitors and nitroglycerin attenuate left ventricular dilatation after myocardial infarction suggesting that reduction in wall stress may be an important therapeutic manoeuvre.[25,26] Other studies show that chronic beta-blockade reduces ventricular mass and improves left ventricular shape in heart failure patients.[27]

Although ventricular remodelling may be modestly attenuated by drugs whilst the heart supports the circulation, the extent to which ventricular recovery can be achieved by complete haemodynamic unloading is of greater interest. LVAD use in end-stage dilated car-

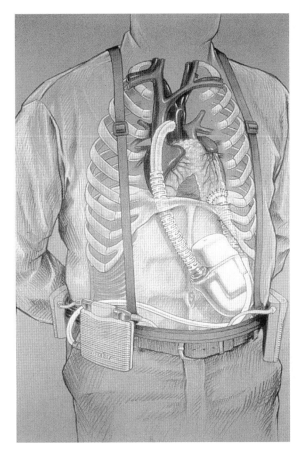

Figure 19.6
The Novacor LVAD with electric driveline and portable battery power supply mounted on a belt.

diomyopathy patients awaiting transplantation (bridge to transplant) has suggested that complete off-loading can reverse dilatation and normalize the end diastolic pressure volume relationship.[28]

If myocardial rest could be combined with whole body exercise training the combined effects might prove beneficial. This is precisely the situation achieved during long-term bridge to transplantation with the implantable Thermocardio Systems (TCI) and Novacor

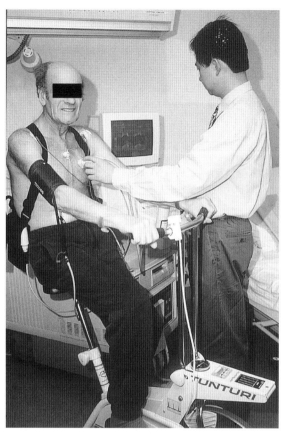

Figure 19.7
Oxford Thermo-Cardio systems LVAD patient with dilated cardiomyopathy NYHA I and living at home. Serial exercise echocardiography showed progressive improvement in left ventricular function.

LVADs.[29,30] These 'pusher plate' blood pumps function in series with the patients left ventricle, are implanted into the abdominal cavity (or extraperitoneal space) and powered by a percutaneous electric driveline (Figure 19.6). The improved systemic blood flow with LVAD support reverses multisystem organ failure enabling resumed physical activity (Figure 19.7). Use of an LVAD in so-called Status I

patients awaiting transplant greatly increases survival both before the donor organ becomes available and after transplantation.[31] Hepatic and renal failure improve whilst serum aldosterone levels, plasma renin activity, atrial natriuretic peptide and noradrenaline revert to normal.

At the time of transplantation some chronically offloaded hearts had reverted towards normal size and weight.[28,32] Some indices of left ventricular function had approached normal values by the time a donor heart became available. This stimulated planned investigation of left ventricular recovery at the Columbia Presbyterian Medical Center and the Texas Heart Institute. Levin et al studied end-diastolic pressure volume relations (EDPVR) in seven excised hearts from transplant recipients with idiopathic dilated cardiomyopathy.[32] Four had received optimal medical therapy while three who deteriorated on medical treatment underwent LVAD support for 4 months. They were compared with three normal human hearts that were harvested but technically unsuitable for transplantation. LVAD use reduced the left ventricular end-diastolic dimension from over 6 cm to less than 3 cm and reduced pulmonary capillary wedge pressure from 29 ± 4 to 13 ± 2 mmHg ($P < 0.001$ measured 30 days after implantation). The LVAD increased cardiac output from 2.2 ± 0.4 to 5.1 ± 0.11/min and increased mean systemic blood pressure from 71 ± 9 to 93 ± 10 mmHg ($P < 0.001$). Hearts from the medically treated patients had EDPVRs with much larger volumes compared with those of normal hearts. After LVAD support for 127 ± 20 days the EDPVRs were shifted towards much lower volumes, similar to those obtained from the normal hearts. Ventricular mass was also reduced. Normal hearts weighed between 250 and 350 g. The LVAD-supported hearts weighed 270 to

290 g, while medically treated hearts weighed from 393 to 905 g. The study suggested that severe ventricular dilatation in idiopathic cardiomyopathy could be substantially reversed. Histologically the process was accompanied by normalization of fibre-orientation and regression of myocyte hypertrophy.[33]

Frazier et al retrospectively analysed data from 31 NYHA Class IV heart patients (30 men and 1 woman), who had been supported for more than 30 days (mean 137 days, range 31–505 days) with either a pneumatic or vented electric 'Heartmate' LVAD.[28] The mean age of the patients was 46 years (range 22–64).

Seventeen had idiopathic cardiomyopathy and fourteen had ischaemic cardiomyopathy. The patients had been in heart failure for an average of 33.5 ± 39 months before implantation of the device. Radiographic cardiothoracic ratio and echocardiographic measurements of left ventricular end-diastolic volume and ejection fraction were measured serially with the native heart assuming the entire cardiac load (LVAD switched off). In addition, tissue samples from the core of the left ventricular apex removed at the time of implant were compared with myocardium from the explanted heart at the time of transplant. These were examined for extent of myocytolysis. Calcium uptake and binding studies of isolated sarcoplasmic reticulum vesicles were performed on five pre- and post-LVAD samples. The cardiothoracic ratio improved from 0.62 ± 0.04 to 0.55 ± 0.03 ($P < 0.0001$). Echocardiography performed with the pump switched off showed a significant decrease in left ventricular end-diastolic dimension (6.81 ± 0.87 to 5.30 ± 1.08 cm, $P < 0.0005$), a significant improvement in ejection fraction (11.2 ± 5.4 to $22.5 \pm 16.7\%$, $P < 0.02$). Cardiac index increased from 1.96 ± 0.52 to 2.93 ± 0.73 litres/min/m^2

($P < 0.0001$). Pulmonary capillary wedge pressure decreased from 24.18 ± 6.27 to 14.48 ± 3.01 mmHg ($P < 0.0001$) and pulmonary vascular resistance decreased from 3.34 ± 2.0 to 2.51 ± 0.88 Wood units ($P < 0.05$). Plasma noradrenaline decreased to near normal levels. The histological studies showed a marked reduction in myocytolysis while deranged calcium uptake and binding rates in the sarcoplasmic reticulum normalized. In one of Frazier's patients who died from a stroke after 505 days of support, the LVAD was turned off. The native heart continued to maintain the circulation with satisfactory blood pressure and cardiac output until ventilation was discontinued. Our own experience in dilated cardiomyopathy suggests that recovery begins much sooner than anticipated, although changes in ventricular morphology do not necessarily imply sustainable improvement in left ventricular function. Reduction in left ventricular volume reduces wall stress but cannot be expected to reverse defects in the myocardial contractile process. Nevertheless normalization of calcium metabolism is promising.

In the United States it has been mandatory to transplant the patient after committal to bridge to transplantation with an LVAD. These restrictions do not apply elsewhere and LVAD removal without transplantation has been utilized by Hetzer's group in Germany, by Nakatani in Japan and the Westaby group in the UK.[34–36] In Berlin recovery has been sustained for periods of up to 2 years in four dilated cardiomyopathy patients who were supported for 160–347 days and there has been complete recovery in three infants with viral myocarditis treated with biventricular support. In Osaka, four patients were explanted after between 26 and 94 days LVAD support. Two dilated cardiomyopathy patients are well 20 months afterwards,

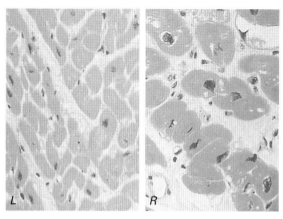

Figure 19.8
Hypertrophied myocytes in dilated cardiomyopathy (L) which revert to normal morphology (R) after months of left ventricular off-loading with an LVAD.

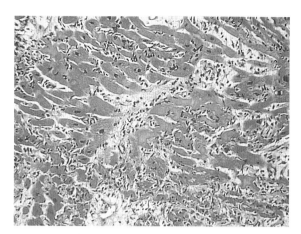

Figure 19.9
Myocardial histology in acute fulminant lymphocytic myocarditis. This moribund patient was resuscitated by conventional cardiopulmonary bypass for implantation of an AB180 LVAD. She was weaned from LVAD support 6 days later and was NYHA I 3 months later.

whereas two ischaemic patients died. In Oxford we have also documented substantial recovery in dilated cardiomyopathy (Figure 19.8) and complete recovery in fulminant viral myocarditis (Figure 19.9). If hearts were treated before absolute end-stage the prospects of recovery would be even better.

The scope of bridge to recovery (the keep-your-own-heart strategy)

When the pacemaker evolved to treat heart block during cardiac surgery 40 years ago, the ultimate scope of the technology was unforeseen. Similarly it is only a matter of time before a user-friendly blood pump emerges as a substitute for the left ventricle in heart failure. There is considerable scope for 'mechanical bridge to recovery' in both acute and chronic left ventricular failure depending upon aetiology. In acute myocardial infarction an implantable centrifugal pump such as the AB-180 (Figure 19.10) can reverse cardiogenic

shock or sustain the patient through a period of myocardial stunning after cardiac surgery. In myocarditis, dilated cardiomyopathy, or ischaemic heart disease, an implantable device should be used before multisystem failure while the potential for recovery still exists.

There are two requirements for a 'bridge to recovery' programme. First, some reliable biochemical markers are needed to indicate sustainability of ventricular recovery. The Berlin group used disappearance from the serum of the autoantibody against the β_1-adrenergic receptor, suggesting that the autoantibody reflects an immune process causing functional impairment.[34] The Texas group suggest normalization of noradrenaline levels.[28] The second requirement is a user-friendly device which can be removed easily or simply switched off. The TCI 'Heartmate' and Nova-

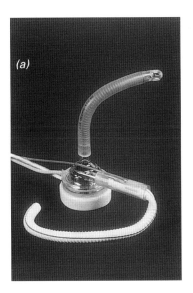
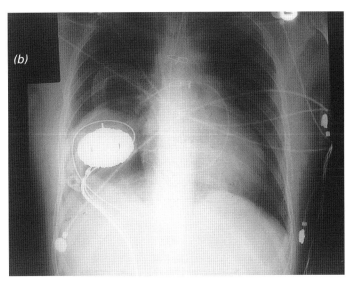

Figure 19.10
(a) The AB-180 implantable centrifugal pump; (b) CXR showing the LVAD in the right pleural cavity during bridge to myocardial recovery in a myocarditis patient.

cor LVADs have an acceptable record of mechanical reliability and have been used for permanent implantation in patients not suitable for transplantation. However both the Heartmate and the Novacor LVADs are bulky devices implanted in the abdomen with stiff percutaneous powerlines which constitute a permanent infection risk. The operation to remove these devices whilst leaving a functioning heart in situ is technically difficult. Efforts are therefore directed towards the design of a less obtrusive blood pump for widespread use in various settings of acute and chronic heart failure.

We are currently developing a system based on the Jarvik 2000 axial flow impeller pump that is inserted through a sewing cuff into the apex of the left ventricle (Figure 19.11).[37] An impervious dacron graft conveys blood from the failing left ventricle to the descending thoracic aorta. The electromagnetic pump con-

sists of a rotor with impeller blades encased in a titanium shell and supported at each end by tiny blood-immersed ceramic bearings less than 1 mm in diameter. The adult model measures 2.5 cm in diameter by 5.5 cm in length, the weight is 85 g and the displacement volume 25 ml. Jarvik has also developed a paediatric device 1.4 cm in diameter and one-fifth the size of the larger model (Figure 19.12). Power is delivered by a fine percutaneous wire and regulated by a pulse width, modulated, brushless, direct current motor controller to determine motor speed. At the site of exit through the skin, the fine electric cable is transmitted through a titanium button which will be secured to the patient's skull. The combination of immobility and highly vascular scalp skin is known to resist infection in a percutaneous system for artificial hearing. The Jarvik 2000 Heart can deliver up to 10 litres/min flow but at normal operating speeds

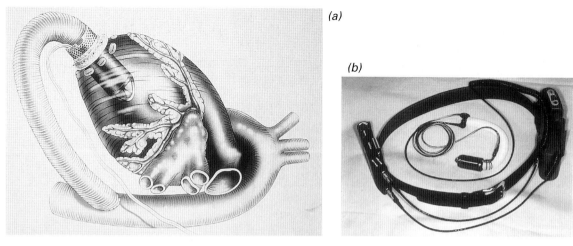

Figure 19.11
(a) The Jarvik 2000 Heart implanted into the apex of the left ventricle and transmitting blood to the descending thoracic aorta. (b) The pump, electrical system, external controller and battery pack which clips onto a belt.

of between 10 000 and 18 000 rpm flow rates of between 3 and 6 litres/min are obtained at a mean aortic pressure of 80 mmHg. The device has the capacity to capture all the flow through the mitral valve so that the aortic valve does not open. At lower speeds left ventricular contraction transmits a pulse through the device. Despite speeds up to 18 000 rpm, the device is silent, haemolysis is insignificant and the propensity for thrombosis is low, even in animals without anticoagulation. The intraventricular site resists infection to which other LVADs are vulnerable.

The Jarvik 2000 Heart has the potential for use in permanent support, bridge to transplantation or bridge to recovery. The paediatric pump with a displacement volume of 5 ml and the capacity for 3 litres/min blood flow could be implanted for post-infarction cardiogenic shock or after coronary bypass with poor left ventricular function, then switched off if the

ventricle recovers. The vascular graft would then be closed through a small thoracotomy or by a percutaneous balloon. For infants and children with viral myocarditis or dilated cardiomyopathy, a period of left ventricular off-loading might allow myocardial recovery thereby avoiding transplantation. For adults with potentially recoverable left ventricular failure (dilated cardiomyopathy, acute myocarditis or ischaemic cardiomyopathy treated by coronary bypass), the pump flow could be adjusted according to physical activity or ventricular recovery. The pump is removed simply by cutting the retaining ligatures in the silicone cuff, then withdrawing the device and oversewing the apex. We have achieved this through a small thoracotomy with survival in an animal model. Use of the device does not preclude transplantation should it prove necessary. Suggestions that resting the myocardium would cause atrophy

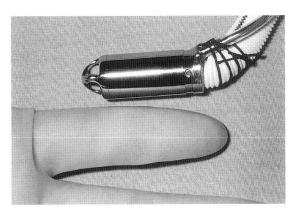

Figure 19.12
Paediatric Jarvik 2000 Heart.

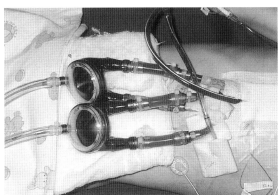

(a)

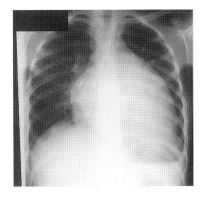

(b)

Figure 19.13
(a) External 'Berlin BIVAD' used for bridge to transplant in a 10-year-old dilated cardiomyopathy patient (b).

are not supported by clinical experience. The Jarvik 2000 will allow scarce donor hearts to be used for well-defined cases, while others keep their own heart, treated temporarily or permanently by a mechanical device. Advances in genetic engineering and molecular biology should be directed towards a supportive role in the quest for myocardial recovery.

Cardiac transplantation

In the past 30 years more than 45 000 heart transplants have been performed worldwide. With time, some problems have been resolved but many outstanding issues continue to restrict cardiac transplantation to the realms of a novelty procedure. The principal problem is that access to transplantation is extremely difficult. In the USA at least 700 000 new cases of heart failure are diagnosed each year resulting in more than 40 000 deaths.[38] In the UK, 100 000 new cases occur annually accounting for 5% of all hospital admissions.[39] The number of transplants performed respectively in these countries are 2200 and 300. Given that the National Co-operative Transplant Study estimates that 41 000

patients in the USA could benefit from cardiac transplantation, the operation clearly does not address the problem.[40] Consequently transplant recipients are highly selected on the bases of young age (<65) and absence of comorbid conditions in order to achieve satisfactory outcomes. Even so the waiting list mortality is at least 30% and the number of donors fatal head injuries is falling progressively.[41] Transplant activity can be sustained only by accepting older or marginal donors. Bridge to transplantation with left or biventricular (Figure 19.13) support may sustain urgent cases but further increases the demand for a donor organ.

Data from the 1997 report of the Registry of the International Society for Heart and Lung Transplantation (ISHLT) showed encouraging 1-, 5-, and 10-year survival of 80, 65, and 45%, respectively.[42] At 1 year, 90% of heart transplant recipients have returned to full activity with no physical limitation. There are now 20-year transplant survivors. These results compare favourably with maximum medical management where the 1- and 5-year survival rates are in the order of 57% and 25%, respectively.[43] Considerable morbidity persists through lack of specific, nontoxic immunosuppression, infective complications and allograft coronary artery disease.[44] The standard immunosuppressive regime comprises cyclosporin, azathioprine and corticosteroids. These agents are nonspecific in their actions and more effective drugs with less end-organ toxicity and fewer unwanted side-effects are currently sought. Tacrolimus (FK506) inhibits the expression of interleukin-2 in T cells together with T cell growth and proliferation.[45] Tacrolimus has been tested as an alternative to cyclosporin in both liver and cardiac transplantation resulting in fewer rejection episodes, lower risk of hypertension and lower steroid maintenance dose. Mycophenolate myofetil has been tested as an alternative inhibitor of cellular purine synthesis to azathioprine.[46] Lymphocyte function is suppressed more than that of neutrophils or macrophages and the patient suffers fewer rejection episodes or bone marrow suppression. New monoclonal antibodies of the IgM subtype have been developed to treat steroid-resistant cardiac allograft rejection as an alter-native to OKT III, the monoclonal antibody of IyG subtype which is directed against the CDIII receptors on the surface of human T cells.[47] Current experimental effort is directed to the development of antiadhesion molecule monoclonal antibodies and to induction of donor-specific tolerance in transplant recipients.[48] Bone marrow transplantation and the creation of microchimerism are thought to be promising methods to achieve this goal. The eventual aim is to limit increased susceptibility to infection, end-organ toxicity or the development of malignancy which continue to blight the long-term outlook of transplant recipients.

Cardiac allograft vasculopathy

This obliterative vasculopathy resembles diffuse concentric coronary artery disease and is the predominant cause of death in those who survive more than 12 months.[49] At 5 years the incidence is virtually 50% although only 12% of patients experience a mild equivalent to angina through reinnervation. Silent ischaemia manifests as rhythm disturbances, acute myocardial infarction, heart failure or sudden death. The pathogenesis of obliterative vasculopathy involves both chronic rejection and nonimmunological factors. The lesions consist of smooth muscle proliferation with collagen and ground substance accumulation rather than classic atheromatous plaques. Since the disease affects the entire length of the vessel, coronary artery bypass grafting or percutaneous transluminal coronary angioplasty are seldom useful. Rather than retransplantation which carries a 1-year survival of 55–62%, therapy is focused on pharmacological intervention. There is some evidence that the severity of vasculopathy may be reduced by the calcium channel blocker diltiazem and the HMGCoA reductase inhibitor pravastatin.[50,51]

Is xenotransplantation an option?

The solution to an inadequate supply of donor organs resides in either axial flow impeller pumps such as the Jarvik 2000 or hearts from animals. Xenotransplantation can be performed by using a donor that is closely related phylogenetically to humans such as the great apes or old world monkeys.[52] This relationship is termed concordant. New world monkeys and lower nonprimate mammals such as the pig have a more distant relationship with humans and are termed discordant donors. The important feature that differentiates the immunological response to concordant versus discordant organs relates to donor vascular endothelial oligosaccharide epitopes that have a terminal alpha I/III galactosile molecule (Gal). Humans apes and old world monkeys do not have this Gal epitope but express the ABO oligosaccharide antigens instead. Because these species lack Gal they develop antiGal antibodies.[53] New world monkeys and lower mammals express Gal on the surface of all their vascular endothelia and on certain other tissues. Their organs are at risk of destruction when transplanted into species that have anti-Gal antibodies. Transplantation of a pig heart into a human leads to rapid destruction by hyperacute rejection. The histopathological picture shows capillary congestion and endothelial wall destruction with interstitial haemorrhage and oedema.[54] This reaction usually occurs within minutes leading to rapid termination of cardiac activity. It is mediated by antiGal antibody antigen binding which activates the complement cascade. Although baboon organs have already been implanted into humans and are rejected less rapidly, the pig is believed to be a preferable choice for a potential clinical transplant programme.

Considerable resources have been directed towards overcoming hyperacute rejection. The two alternatives are modification of the immune state of the potential recipient or modification by genetic engineering of the donor organ. Extracorporeal immunoadsorption (EIA) of antiGal antibody from the potential recipient can be achieved over 3–4 days.[55] When coordinated with standard pharmacological immunosuppressive therapy EIA will delay rejection for a few days. This may allow a state of accommodation in which organ function continues satisfactorily despite new production of antibody and normal complement levels. Currently however the mechanism of accommodation is unknown and there is no evidence that this will occur after discordant xenotransplantation. An alternative method to modify the immune state of a potential recipient involves inhibition of complement by cobra venom factor or soluble complement receptor I.[56] This has resulted in extended (4–7 week) graft survival. If antiGal antibody is not removed a slower form of antibody-mediated rejection known as delayed xenograft rejection or acute vascular rejection will destroy the graft within this period.

Genetic engineering techniques or gene therapy allow downregulation of Gal expression by the vascular endothelium.[57] This can be achieved by introducing a gene for an enzyme that will compete with agalactosyltransferase. Such attempts have focused on introducing the gene responsible for H fucosyltransferase which leads to the expression of universal donor blood group O on the vascular endothelium. Such pigs express about 90% less Gal than normal pigs. Under most circumstances human organs are protected from human complement by human complement inhibiting proteins on their cell surfaces. While pig organs are protected by the porcine equivalent they have very poor resistance to human complement. Pigs that are transgenic for human complement inhibiting proteins have some protection against hyperacute rejection although most organs survive only 4–8 weeks in experimental conditions. These organs are also still susceptible to delayed xenograft rejection which is antibody related and complement independent. Even if hyperacute rejection could be overcome the problem of delayed xenograft rejection remains. Cellular rejection of a xenograft organ is likely to be quantitatively more severe than a human equivalent. The amount of immunosuppressive therapy required to suppress the cellular response is likely to prove prohibitive through an unacceptable rate of serious complications including infection and cancer. Also the potential exists for transfer of infectious organisms from the pig to the immunosuppressed recipient. The doubt also arises as to whether pig organs can function adequately in the human body.[58] Hearts of corresponding size can be obtained but so far pig hearts have been transplanted only in a nonworking heterotopic position with cessation of cardiac action as an endpoint in less than 2 months. Consequently claims in 1997 that pig hearts were ready for human transplantation were overtly misleading.

Summary

Considerable effort is currently expended to develop surgical solution for advanced heart failure. A range of conventional cardiac operations can arrest the remodelling process and rehabilitate the left ventricle. For greatly dilated hearts both cardiomyoplasty and left ventricular reduction surgery have provided disappointing results. Cardiac transplantation provides the gold standard for surgical treatment but numbers are decreasing through lack of donor organs. Problems inherent in xenotransplantation currently render this option unlikely for orthotopic cardiac transplantation. In contrast new strategies of mechanical circulatory support aimed at myocyte recovery may eventually allow scarce human organs to be used for young patients in whom mechanical blood pumps are inappropriate.

References

1. Kaye DM, Lefkovits J, Jennings GL et al. Adverse consequences of high sympathetic nervous activity in the failing human heart. *J Am Coll Cardiol* 1995; **26**: 1257–1263.

2. Swynghedauw B. The biological limits of cardiac adaption to chronic overload. *Eur Heart J* 1990; **11** (Suppl G): 87–94.

3. Calderone A, Thaik CM, Takahashi N, Colucci WS. Norepinephrine-stimulated DNA and protein synthesis in cardiac fibroblasts are inhibited by nitric oxide and atrial natriuretic factor. *Circulation* 1995; **92** (Suppl I): 1384 (abst).

4. Cohn JN, Johnson G, Ziesche S et al. A comparison of enalapril with hydralazine-isosorbide dinitrate in the treatment of chronic congestive heart failure. *N Engl J Med* 1991; **325**: 303–310.

5. Cohn JN, Archibald DG, Ziesche S et al. Effect of vasodilator therapy on mortality in chronic congestive heart failure: results of a Veterans Administration Cooperative Study. *N Engl J Med* 1986; **314**: 1547–1552.

6. Cohn JN, Johnson GR, Shabetai R et al. Ejection fraction, peak exercise oxygen consumption, cardiothoracic ratio, ventricular arrhythmias, and plasma norepinephrine as determinants of prognosis in heart failure. *Circulation* 1993; **87** (Suppl VI): V15–VI16.

7. Francis GS, Cohn JN, Johnson G et al. Plasma norepinephrine, plasma renin activity, and congestive heart failure: relations to survival and the effects of therapy in V-HeFT II. *Circulation* 1993; **87** (Suppl VI): V140–V148.

8. Hall SA, Cigarroa CG, Marcoux L et al. Time course of improvement in left ventricular function, mass, and geometry in patients with congestive heart failure treated with β-adrenergic blockade. *J Am Coll Cardiol* 1995; **25**: 1154–1161.

9. Pfeffer MA, Braunwald E, Moye LA et al the SAVE investigators. Effect of captopril on mortality and morbidity in patients with left ventricular dysfunction after myocardial infarction: results of the Survival and Ventricular Enlargement Trial. *N Engl J Med* 1993; **327**: 669–677.

10. Atkins CW, Hilgenberg AD, Buckley MJ et al. Mitral valve reconstruction versus replacement for degenerative or ischaemic mitral regurgitation. *An Thorac Surg* 1994; **58**: 668–675.

11. Boltwood CM, Tei C, Wong M, Shah PM. Quantative echocardiography of the mitral complex in dilated cardiomyopathy: the mechanism of functional mitral regurgitation. *Circulation* 1983; **68**: 498–508.

12. Oury JH, Cleveland JC, Duran CG, Angell WW. Ischaemic mitral valve disease: classification and systemic approach to management. *J Thorac Cardiovasc Surg* 1994; **9** (Suppl): 262–273.

13. Cohn LH, Rizzo RJ, Adams DH et al. The effect of pathophysiology on the surgical treatment of ischaemic mitral regurgitation: operative and late risks of repair versus replacement. *Eur J Thorac Cardiovasc Surg* 1995; **9**: 568–574.

14. Cooley DA, Frazier OH, Duncan JM et al. Intracavitary repair of ventricular aneurysm and regional dyskinesia. *Ann Thorac Surg* 1992; **215**: 417–424.

15. Mangschau AS, Simonsen S, Abdelnoor M et al. Evaluation for left ventricular aneurysm resection: a prospective study of clinical and haemodynamic characteristics. *Eur J Thorac Cardiovasc Surg* 1989; **3**: 58–64.

16. Carpentier A, Chachques JC, Acar C et al. Dynamic cardiomyoplasty at seven years. *J Thorac Cardiovasc Surg* 1993; **106**: 42–52.

17. Furnary AP, Jessup M, Moreira LFP for the American Cardiomyoplasty Group. Multicenter trial of dynamic cardiomyoplasty for chronic heart failure. *J Am Coll Cardiol* 1996; **28**: 1175–1180.

18. Leier CV. Cardiomyoplasty: is it time to wrap it up? *J Am Coll Cardiol* 1996; **28**: 1181–1182.

19. Packer M. The placebo effect in heart failure.

Am Heart J 1990; **120**: 1579–1582.

20. Batista RJ, Verde J, Nery P et al. Partial left ventriculectomy to treat end-stage heart disease. *Ann Thorac Surg* 1997; **64**: 634–638.

21. Bach DS, Bolling SF. Early improvement in congestive heart failure after correction of secondary mitral regurgitation in end-stage cardiomyopathy. *Am Heart J* 1995; **129**: 1165–1170.

22. Katsumata T, Westaby S. Left ventricular reduction surgery in ischaemic cardiomyopathy: a note of caution. *Ann Thorac Surg* 1997; **64**: 1154–1156.

23. McCarthy PM, Starling RC, Wong J et al. Early results with partial left ventriculectomy. *J Thorac Cardiovasc Surg* 1997; **114**: 755–765.

24. Burch GE, DePasquale NP. On resting the human heart. *Am J Med* 1968; **44**: 165–167.

25. Pfeffer MA, Braunwald E. Ventricular remodelling after myocardial infarction: experimental observations and clinical implications. *Circulation* 1990; **81**: 1161–1172.

26. Judgutt BL, Warnica JW. Intravenous nitroglycerine therapy to limit myocardial infarct size, expansion and complications: effect of timing, dosage and infarct location. *Circulation* 1988; **78**: 906–919.

27. Hall S, Cigassoa C, Marcouz L et al. Regression of hypertrophy and alteration in left ventricular geometry in patients with congestive heart failure treated with beta-adregenic blockade. *Circulation* 1994; **90** (Suppl I): 543 (abst).

28. Frazier OH, Benedict CR, Radovancevic B et al. Improved left ventricular function after chronic left ventricular unloading. *Ann Thorac Surg* 1996; **62**: 675–682.

29. Frazier OH, Rose EA, MacMannus Q et al. Multicenter clinical evaluation of the Heartmate 1000 IP left ventricular assist device. *Ann Thorac Surg* 1992; **53**: 1080–1090.

30. McCarthy PM, Portner PM, Tobler HG et al. Clinical experience with the Novacor ventricular assist system. *J Thorac Cardiovasc Surg* 1991; **102**: 573–581.

31. Frazier OH, Rose EA, McCarthy P et al. Improved mortality and rehabilitation of transplant candidates treated with a long term implantable left-ventricular assist system. *Ann Thorac Surg* 1995; **222**: 327–338.

32. Levin HR, Oz MC, Chen JM et al. Reversal of chronic ventricular dilation in patients with end stage cardiomyopathy by prolonged mechanical offloading. *Circulation* 1995; **91**: 2717–2720.

33. McCarthy PM, Nakatani S, Vargo R et al. Structural and left ventricular histologic changes after implantable LVAD insertion. *Ann Thorac Surg* 1995; **59**: 609–613.

34. Müller J, Wallukat G, Weng Y et al. Weaning from mechanical cardiac support in patients with idiopathic dilated cardiomyopathy. *Circulation* 1997; **96**: 542–549.

35. Nakatani S, McCarthy PM, Kottke-Marchant K et al. Left ventricular echocardiographic and histologic changes: impact of chronic unloading by an implantable ventricular assist device. *J Am Coll Cardiol* 1996; **27**: 894–901.

36. Westaby S, Jiu XY, Katsumata T et al. Mechanical support in dilated cardiomyopathy: signs of early left ventricular recovery. *Ann Thorac Surg* 1997; **64**: 1303–1308.

37. Westaby S, Katsumata T, Houel R et al. Jarvik 2000 Heart. Potential for bridge to myocyte recovery. *Circulation* 1998; **98**: 1568–1574.

38. Massie B, Packer M. Congestive heart failure: current controversies and future prospects. *Am J Cardiol* 1990; **66**: 429–430.

39. Sutton G. Epidemiologic aspects of heart failure. *Am Heart J* 1990; **120**: 1538–1550.

40. Evans R. *Executive summary: the National Cooperative Transplantation Study.* BHARC-100-91-020. Seattle WA: Battelle Seattle Research Centre, 1991.

41. Sharples L, Roberts M, Parameshwar J et al. Heart transplantation in the United Kingdom: who waits the longest and why? *J Heart Lung Transplant* 1995; **14**: 236–243.

42. Hosenpud J, Bennett L, Keck B et al. The Registry of the International Society for Heart and Lung Transplantation: fourteenth official report — 1997. *J Heart Lung Transplant* 1997; **16**: 691–712.

43. Ho K, Anderson K, Kannel W et al. Survival after the onset of congestive heart failure in Framingham Heart Study subjects. *Circulation* 1993; **88**: 107–151.

44. Johnson D, Gao S, Schroeder J et al. The spectrum of coronary artery pathologic finding in human cardiac allograft. *J Heart Transplant* 1989; **8**: 349–359.

45. Pham S, Kormos R, Hattler B et al. Aprospective trial of tacrolimus (FK506) in clinical heart transplantation: intermediate-term results. *J Thorac Cardiovasc Surg* 1996; **111**: 764–772.

46. Taylor D, Ensley R, Olsen S et al. Mycophenolate myofetil: preclinical, clinical and three year experience in heart transplantation. *J Heart Lung Transplant* 1994; **13**: 571–582.

47. Kirkman R, Shapiro M, Carpenter C et al. A randomised prospective trial of anti-TAC monoclonal antibody in human renal transplantation. *Transplantation* 1991; **51**: 107–113.

48. Odorico J, Barker C, Posselt A, Naji A. Induction of donor-specific tolerance to rat cardiac allografts by intrathymic inoculation of bone marrow. *Surgery* 1992; **112**: 370–376.

49. Billingham M. Cardiac transplant atherosclerosis. *Transplant Proc* 1987; **19**: 19–25.

50. Schroeder J, Gao S, Alderman E et al. A preliminary study of diltiazem in the prevention of coronary artery disease in heart transplant recipients. *N Engl J Med* 1993; **328**: 164–170.

51. Kobashigawa J, Katznelson S, Laks H et al. Effect of pravastatin on outcome after cardiac transplantation. *N Engl J Med* 1995; **333**: 621–627.

52. Galili U, Shohet SB, Kobrin E et al. Man, apes and Old World monkeys differ from other mammals in the expression of galactosyl epitopes on nucleated cells. *J Biol Chem* 1988; **263**: 17755–17762.

53. Oriol R, Ye Y, Koren E, Cooper DKC. Depletion of natural antibodies as potential targets for hyperacute vascular rejection in pig-to-man organ xenotransplantation. *Transplantation* 1993; **56**: 1433–1442.

54. Rose AG, Cooper DKC, Human PA et al. Histopathology of hyperacute rejection of the heart: experimental and clinical observations in allografts and xenografts. *J Heart Transplant* 1991; **10**: 223–234.

55. Cooper DKC. Depletion of natural antibodies in nonhuman primates — a step towards successful discordant xenografting in humans. *Clin Transplant* 1992; **6**: 178–183.

56. Kobayashi T, Taniguchi S, Ye Y et al. Delayed xenograft rejection in C3-depleted discordant (pig-to-baboon) cardiac xenografts treated with cobra venom factor. *Transplant Proc* 1996; **28**: 560.

57. Cozzi E, White DJG. The generation of transgenic pigs as potential organ donors for humans. *Nature Med* 1995; **1**: 964–966.

58. Bach FH, Robson FC, Winkler H et al. Barriers to xenotransplantation. *Nature Med* 1995; **1**: 869–873.

20

Non-pharmacological treatment of heart failure: just as important?
Michael W Rich

Introduction

The primary goals of therapy in patients with heart failure are as follows: prevent or slow disease progression, maximize functional capacity and quality of life, reduce resource utilization and cost of care, and prolong survival. As discussed in preceding chapters, dramatic advances in both the pharmacological and surgical management of heart failure have occurred in the past 20 years. However, despite the availability of many new therapies, the prognosis in patients with established heart failure remains poor. Moreover, heart failure is a major cause of chronic disability and impaired quality of life, and it remains the leading cause of hospitalization and rehospitalization in individuals over 65 years of age.[1] Furthermore, heart failure is currently the most costly medical illness in the United States, with estimated annual expenditures in excess of $38 billion.[2]

Clearly, medications and surgical procedures alone are not enough, and this begs the question: is there anything else that can be done? Ultimately, the answer to this question lies in the development of new and more effective strategies for the prevention of ventricular hypertrophy and contractile dysfunction. In the meantime, there is a growing body of evidence suggesting that non-pharmacological and non-surgical interventions can signifi-

cantly improve exercise tolerance and quality of life, while reducing hospitalizations and cost of care in patients with chronic heart failure. In this chapter, the nonpharmacological aspects of heart failure management are reviewed, available data from clinical studies are summarized and the effects of non-pharmacological treatment on clinical outcomes are compared with the effects of pharmacotherapy.

Non-pharmacological aspects of treatment

Factors confounding heart failure management

Heart failure rarely occurs as an isolated disease process and there are often multiple coexistent factors which may confound heart failure management (Table 20.1). In Western countries, hypertension and/or coronary heart disease account for over 70% of heart failure cases,[3] and the prevalence of diabetes, dyslipidaemia, chronic lung disease, renal insufficiency, and peripheral arterial disease are quite high in the heart failure population. Arthritis, gastrointestinal disturbances, and neurological disorders (including Alzheimer's disease) are also common, particularly in older patients. Thus, heart failure management must often be undertaken in the context of multiple comor-

High prevalence of comorbid illnesses and other conditions

Polypharmacy
- Noncompliance
- Drug interactions

Dietary issues

Psychosocial and financial concerns
- Depression
- Social isolation
- High cost of care, including medications

Physical limitations
- Exercise intolerance
- Arthritis
- Neuromuscular disorders (e.g. stroke)
- Sensory deficits (e.g. visual, auditory)

Cognitive dysfunction

Table 20.1
Factors confounding heart failure management.

bid conditions, many of which may directly impact on the success of therapy. For example, optimal utilization of angiotensin-converting enzyme (ACE) inhibitors and diuretics may be limited by pre-existing renal insufficiency and, conversely, aggressive use of these agents may worsen renal function. Similarly, beta-blockers may be poorly tolerated in patients with diabetes or peripheral arterial disease.

In addition to the above concerns, the presence of multiple comorbid conditions contributes to a high prevalence of polypharmacy in heart failure patients. Individuals with advanced illness are often taking three or four heart failure medications (e.g., digoxin, diuretic, ACE inhibitor, beta-blocker), as well as several additional medications for other chronic illnesses. Polypharmacy has two potentially serious adverse consequences. First,

it is well recognized that medication compliance varies inversely with the number of medications prescribed and with the number of daily dosing intervals.[4] Thus, the more medications prescribed, the less likely that the patient is taking the medications correctly. Second, polypharmacy increases the risk of adverse drug–drug and drug–disease interactions. For example, nonsteroidal anti-inflammatory drugs (NSAIDs) are widely used to treat arthritis and other musculoskeletal syndromes. However, NSAIDs antagonize the effects of ACE inhibitors and other antihypertensive agents (i.e. drug–drug interactions),[5] and they also promote renal sodium and water retention which may directly exacerbate congestive symptoms (i.e. drug–disease interaction).

Dietary sodium intake is another factor which may confound heart failure management. Many heart failure patients, especially those with diastolic dysfunction, are highly 'salt-sensitive'; moderate excesses in dietary sodium intake may precipitate an acute heart failure exacerbation, even in otherwise compliant and well compensated patients. This issue may be further complicated by the fact that patients often have a poor understanding of which foods are high in salt. In addition, patients who do not prepare their own meals or who eat out frequently may have little direct control over sodium intake. Similarly, elderly patients with physical or financial limitations may subsist on prepared, packaged or canned foods with very high sodium contents.

Psychosocial and financial issues may also compromise heart failure management. Major depression occurs in 15–20% of patients with heart failure and may contribute to medical and dietary noncompliance.[6] In addition, for reasons which have not yet been fully elucidated, depression may be associated with more frequent heart failure exacerbations and increased mortality.[6] Anxiety disorders are also common in patients with cardiovascular disease and may give rise to increased resource utilization. Additionally, since heart failure is a chronic debilitating disorder, patients often require assistance in performing routine activities, including meal preparation and the dispensing of medications. Social isolation, which is particularly prevalent in elderly women, may limit the patient's ability to comply with therapy and, in advanced cases, may necessitate placement in a long-term care facility. In the United States, medication costs for heart failure and other conditions may be as high as several hundred dollars each month, and this factor may severely limit compliance, especially in patients living on fixed incomes and those with inadequate insurance coverage.

Physical limitations such as arthritis and neuromuscular disorders may make it difficult for patients to prepare meals, dispense medications, and carry out routine daily activities. Severe exercise intolerance due to advanced heart failure may further impair functional capacity. In addition, sensory deficits, including impaired visual and auditory acuity, may result in confusion or uncertainty about the medication regimen, proper diet, and follow-up arrangements. And finally, the presence of significant cognitive impairment may further confound heart failure management.

Impact on clinical outcomes

Although the impact of confounding factors on clinical outcomes is difficult to quantify, several studies have shown that noncompliance and psychosocial factors are a major cause of heart failure exacerbations requiring hospitalization.[7–11] In 1988, Ghali et al reported that noncompliance with medications or diet contributed to 64% of heart failure exacerbations in an urban black population.[7] Similarly, environmental and emotional factors contributed to readmission in 26% of cases.[7] In 1990, Vinson et al reported that among 140 patients over 70 years of age hospitalized with heart failure, 47% were readmitted within 90 days of initial hospital discharge.[8] Factors contributing to readmission included noncompliance with medications (15%) or diet (18%), inadequate discharge planning (15%) or follow-up (20%), social isolation or inadequate social support (21%), and failure to seek medical attention promptly when symptoms recurred (20%).[8] More recent studies have confirmed that in 15–30% of cases noncompliance is a major factor contributing to heart failure decompensation.[9–11]

Non-pharmacological aspects of care

Due to the fact that multiple behavioural, psychosocial, and situational factors often confound heart failure management and contribute to recurrent hospitalizations and impaired quality of life, it is apparent that these issues must be addressed if optimal clinical outcomes are to be achieved. Table 20.2 lists non-pharmacological interventions which may facilitate heart failure management in selected patients. Among these, patient education and close-follow-up are perhaps the most important. Patient education should include general information about heart failure, a discussion of common symptoms and signs, instructions on when to contact the physician or nurse if symptoms worsen, and detailed information about all medications and dietary restrictions, emphasizing the importance of compliance. Patients should also be instructed to weigh themselves on a daily basis, and to record their weights on a chart or in a log. Detailed information concerning activity restrictions should be provided, and most patients should be encouraged to remain

Patient education
- Symptoms and signs of heart failure
- Specific information about when and how to contact the nurse or physician if symptoms worsen
- Detailed discussion of all medications
- Emphasize importance of compliance
- Involve family/significant other as much as possible

Dietary consultation
- Individualized and consistent with needs/lifestyle
- Sodium restriction (1.5–2 g/day)
- Weight loss, if appropriate
- Low fat, low cholesterol, if appropriate
- Adequate caloric intake
- Emphasize compliance while allowing flexibility

Medication review
- Eliminate unnecessary medications
- Simplify regimen whenever possible
- Consolidate dosing schedule

Social services
- Assess social support structure
- Evaluate emotional and financial needs
- Intervene pro-actively when feasible

Daily weight chart
- Specific directions on when to contact nurse or physician for changes in weight

Support stockings to reduce edema

Activity prescription

Intensive follow-up
- Telephone contacts
- Home visits
- Outpatient clinic

Contact information
- Names and phone numbers of nurse and physician
- 24-hour availability

Table 20.2
Nonpharmacological aspects of heart failure management.

active and to engage in an appropriate level of regular exercise. Whenever possible, family members should be included in the education process in order to promote their active involvement in the management program.

To minimize polypharmacy, the physician or pharmacist should critically review all of the patient's medications, eliminating all non-essential drugs and simplifying or consolidating the medication regimen and dosing schedule wherever possible. In selected cases, social service evaluation to identify and manage social, emotional, and financial concerns is appropriate. All patients should be followed closely during the first few months after an acute heart failure exacerbation using a combination of home health services, telephone contacts, and office visits based on individual patients needs. The patient should also be encouraged to contact the physician, nurse, or other health care professional promptly whenever questions or problems occur.

Multi-disciplinary heart failure management

To address the myriad nonmedical issues which frequently arise, a multi-disciplinary approach to heart failure management is advocated. The concept of a multi-disciplinary heart failure team is not new; indeed, heart transplant programs worldwide have been utilizing a multi-disciplinary approach for over two decades. In addition to the patient and the patient's family, core members of the heart failure team typically include a nurse coordinator or case manager, dietician, social worker, primary care physician and cardiology consultant. In selected cases, the addition of a home health nurse, pharmacist, physical therapist, or rehabilitation specialist may be appropriate. Ideally, the nurse case manager should oversee all aspects of the patient's care to ensure proper coordination of services.

There have now been several trials assessing the impact of multidisciplinary heart failure management on clinical outcomes (Table 20.3).[12–21] Section I of Table 20.3 includes trials which did not include a pharmacological component,[12–19] whereas Section II includes two recent trials which combined pharmacological and nonpharmacological aspects of care.[20,21]

As early as 1983, Cintron et al reported that a heart failure clinic directed by a nurse-practitioner improved patient satisfaction and reduced hospitalizations and costs in a small number of individuals with advanced heart failure.[12] More recently, several observational studies have confirmed that various non-pharmacological interventions may be associated with fewer hospital admissions, lower costs, improved functional capacity, and better quality of life.[14,16,18,19] Most of these studies have been limited, however, by the small number of patients treated and the lack of a suitable control group.

In 1995, our group reported the results of a prospective, randomized trial involving 282 patients 70 years of age or older hospitalized with heart failure.[17] Patients received routine care, as directed by their regular physicians, or routine care supplemented by a nurse-directed multi-disciplinary intervention. The intervention included intensive patient education, dietary and social service consultation, detailed medication analysis, and close follow-up after hospital discharge by a home health nurse and through telephone contacts. Patients in both groups were followed for 90 days, during which patients in the intervention group experienced a 44% reduction in all-cause readmissions, 56% reduction in heart failure readmissions, and 29% reduction in readmissions not due to heart failure. In addition, quality of life improved to a greater extent in patients receiving multidisciplinary care, and the total cost of care during the study period was $460 lower per patient in the intervention group, reflecting the marked reduction in readmissions.[17] Patients in the intervention group also demonstrated improved compliance with both medications and diet,[22] as well as a greater understanding of heart failure and its treatment. After completing the 90-day follow-up period, all patients were observed for an additional 9 months. Despite the fact that no additional intervention was undertaken during this period, all-cause readmissions and heart failure readmissions remained 11% and 29% lower in patients randomized to multidisciplinary care. These findings provide compelling evidence that a non-pharmacological, nurse-directed intervention is not only cost-effective, but that it is also associated with significant improvements in quality of life and resource utilization. Moreover, the beneficial effects appear to persist for at least 1 year. Study limitations include the fact that the sample size was relatively small and somewhat selected (only 21% of elderly heart failure patients were enrolled), and the fact that the study was conducted at a single academic medical centre. The generalizability of these findings to other settings thus requires further study.

Since the publication of our trial, two additional observational studies have combined non-pharmacological treatment with an effort to optimize medical therapy (Table 20.3).[20,21] The results of these studies, both of which showed significant reductions in hospitalizations and health care costs accompanied by improved exercise tolerance, symptoms, and quality of life, provide further validation of the benefits of multi-disciplinary case management, and suggest that the combination of optimal medical management and non-pharmacological treatment may be associated with the most desirable clinical outcomes. This

Author/year	Study design	No. of patients	Intervention	Duration of follow-up	Results	Comments
I. Trials without a pharmacological component						
Cintron et al 1983[12]	Observational pre-post intervention	15	Nurse practitioner-based clinic with physician referral as needed, average of 18 clinic visits/year	Mean of 24 months	61% reduction in hospitalizations 85% reduction in hospital days Cost reduction of $8000/patient/year	Mean age 65 years NYHA class III–IV patients Improved patient satisfaction
Rich et al 1993[13]	Randomized pilot study	98	Nurse-directed team with patient education, dietary counselling, social services, homecare, telephone follow-up	90 days	27% reduction in readmissions 25% reduction in hospital days	All patients 70 years or older Mean NYHA class 2.8
Lasater 1996[14]	Observational pre-post intervention	80	Nurse-managed heart failure clinic with access to physician, dietician, and social worker	6 months	14% reduction in hospitalizations 22% reduction in length of stay Hospital costs reduced $500/patient	No information provided on patient population
Kostis et al 1994[15]	Randomized parallel groups	20	Exercise, cognitive therapy, stress management, dietary counselling	12 weeks	Improved exercise tolerance Reduced anxiety, depression Enhanced weight loss	Age range 54–77 years Digoxin group and placebo group as controls
Kornowski et al 1995[16]	Observational pre-post intervention	42	Intensive homecare surveillance by internist and paramedical team, at least 1 visit/week	1 year	62% reduction in hospitalizations 77% reduction in hospital days 72% reduction in CV admissions Improved ability to perform ADLs	Mean age 78 years NYHA class III–IV patients
Rich et al 1995[17]	Randomized clinical trial	282	Nurse-directed team with patient education, dietary counselling, social services, homecare, telephone follow-up	90 days	44% reduction in readmissions 56% reduction in HF admissions Improved quality of life Improved compliance Cost reduction of $460/patient	Mean age 79 years High-risk population Benefits persisted up to 1 year
Dennis et al 1996[18]	Retrospective chart review	24	Home health nurse, teaching, clinical assessments	1 year	Frequency and intensity of visits inversely correlated with readmissions	Age, other demographic data not specified
Martens and Mellor 1997[19]	Retrospective chart review	924	Home health nurse, teaching, clinical assessments	90 days	36% fewer readmissions in patients receiving home care	Mean age 71 years
II. Trials with a pharmacological component						
West et al 1997[20]	Observational pre-post intervention	51	Physician-supervised, nurse-mediated home-based system with frequent telephone contacts targeting medication dosing, compliance, activities, symptom status	Mean of 138 ± 44 days	74% reduction in hospitalizations 87% reduction in HF admissions Fewer office and ER visits Improved symptoms, quality of life, exercise tolerance Improved ACE inhibitor dosing and salt restriction	Mean age 66 years NYHA class I–II, 60%; class III–IV, 40% Initial clinic visit, subsequent follow-up by phone
Fonarow et al 1997[21]	Observational pre-post intervention	214	Comprehensive management by HF/transplant team, including diet, exercise, teaching, medications	6 months	35% reduction in hospitalizations Improved NYHA class and exercise tolerance Improved medication dosing Cost reduction of $9800/patient	Mean age 52 years NYHA class III–IV patients

ACE, angiotensin-converting enzyme; ADLs, activities of daily living; CV, cardiovascular; ER, emergency room; HF, heart failure; NYHA, New York Heart Association.

Table 20.3
Trials of multidisciplinary heart failure management.

conclusion is reinforced by two new randomized controlled trials of nurse-led intervention. Stewart et al, as part of a larger clinical trial,[23] randomized hospitalized heart failure patients with impaired left ventricular systolic function, exercise intolerance and a history of at least one admission for acute heart failure to usual care (N = 48) or a home-based intervention (N = 49).[24] The home-based intervention comprised a single home visit 1 week after discharge by either a nurse or a pharmacist. The purpose of this visit was to optimize medication management, identify early clinical deterioration, and intensify medical follow-up/caregiver vigilance where appropriate. The primary endpoint of the study was the frequency of unplanned readmission plus out-of-hospital death within 6 months of discharge. Home-based intervention patients had both fewer unplanned readmissions (36 versus 63; P = 0.03) and out-of-hospital deaths (1 versus 5; P = 0.11), equating to a mean (SD) of 0.76 (0.91) versus 1.4 (1.8) events per patients in the usual care and home-based intervention groups, respectively (P = 0.03).[23,24] Home-based intervention patients also had fewer days of hospitalization (261 versus 452; P = 0.05) and fewer multiple (≥3) readmissions for heart failure (P = 0.02).[23,24] Moreover, the benefits of home-based treatment have now been shown to persist through an extended follow-up period of 18 months, during which unplanned readmissions, mortality, and hospital costs were all significantly lower in the intervention group.[25]

Cline et al added further evidence in favour of nurse-led multidisciplinary intervention following admission to hospital with heart failure.[26] These authors randomized 206 patients aged 65–84 years hospitalized with heart failure to intervention by specially trained nurses or to usual care. The special intervention included an educational programme for patients and their families, concentrating on treatment. Guidelines on adjusting treatment in response to sodium and water overload and fluid depletion were also provided. This programme was carried out over two 30-minute visits to the patient in hospital and a 1-hour visit to the patient and family 2 weeks after discharge. A special diary was provided. Close, easily accessible, patient-initiated follow-up was provided at a nurse-run, hospital-based clinic and through telephone contact.

One-year mortality did not differ between groups. However, time to first readmission over the same period however was 33% longer in the intervention group (106 versus 141 days; P < 0.05). The mean number of hospitalizations was 36% lower (0.7 versus 1.1; P = 0.08) and the total days hospitalized 49% lower (8.2 versus 4.2; P = 0.07) in the intervention group. Total annual costs of care also tended to be lower in the intervention group (US$2294 versus US$3594; P = 0.07). It should be noted that this study recruited patients with a much lower rate of readmission than those in the previous two studies.

Exercise training

In recent years there has been increasing interest in the role of exercise training as an additional non-pharmacological intervention for improving functional capacity and quality of life in heart failure patients. In the past, exercise has been considered to be potentially hazardous in the heart failure population. However, it is now recognized that excessive activity restriction leads to muscular deconditioning and disuse atrophy which contribute directly to the progressive decline in exercise tolerance occurring in heart failure patients. As a result, most experts now recommend that the majority of patients engage in an appropriate level of regular physical activity.[27,28]

Author/year	No. of patients	Duration	Intervention	Results	Comments
Coats et al 1990[30]	11	8 weeks	Stationary bike, 20 min 5 days/week, 70–80% of peak HR	Exercise time increased 2 min Peak VO_2 increased 3.2 ml/min/kg	NYHA class II–III Improved symptoms
Jette et al 1991[31]	18	4 weeks	Jogging, calisthenics, cycling, walking 90–120 min 5 days/week, 70–80% peak HR	Peak VO_2 increased 200 ml/min	NYHA class I–III Post-MI study 30% dropout rate
Coats et al 1992[32]	17	8 weeks	Stationary bike, 20 min 5 days/week, 70–80% of peak HR	Exercise time increased 2.6 min Peak VO_2 increased 2.4 ml/min/kg	NYHA class II–III Improved symptoms
Belardinelli et al 1995[33]	55	2 months	Stationary bike 40 min 3 days/week, 60% peak VO_2	Peak VO_2 increased 12% Peak workload increased 8.5%	Mean age 55 years NYHA class II–III Improved diastolic function
Keteyian et al 1996[34]	29	24 weeks	Treadmill, stationary bike, rowing 43 min 3 days/week, 60—80% HR reserve	Exercise time increased 2.3 min Peak VO_2 increased 2.0 ml/min/kg Peak power output increased 18W	Mean age 54 years NYHA class II–III 85% of benefit within 12 weeks
Meyer et al 1997[35]	18	3 weeks	Treadmill, stationary bike, 15–25 min 5 days/week, interval training	Peak VO_2 increased 2.4 ml/kg/min	Interval training associated with higher intensity exercise at lower cardiac stress
Dubach et al 1997[36]	25	2 months	Stationary bike 40 min 4 days/week, 70–80% peak capacity; 2 hours walking/day	Peak VO_2 increased 4.7 ml/kg/min Exercise time increased 1.9 min Peak power increased 41 W	Mean age 55 years All patients post-MI or CABG No major complications

CABG, coronary artery bypass grafting; HR, heart rate; MI, myocardial infarction; NYHA, New York Heart Association; VO_2, oxygen consumption.

Table 20.4
Randomized trials of exercise training in patients with heart failure.

Numerous observational studies have demonstrated that exercise training is associated with an increase in maximum aerobic capacity ranging from 10–25% in patients with chronic heart failure, and that this benefit is related primarily to peripheral adaptations in the skeletal muscles (i.e. increased oxygen utilization) rather than to improvements in cardiac function or haemodynamics.[29,30] To date, fewer than 200 heart failure patients have been enrolled in randomized exercise trials (Table 20.4).[31–37] None the less, the results of these trials are quite consistent with the findings from observational studies. Notably, all seven randomized trials showed an increase in exercise tolerance, as assessed by peak oxygen consumption (VO_2), exercise time, or peak power output. In addition, many patients reported an improvement in heart failure symptoms, although this was not quantified in most of the studies. In all of the trials, exercise training was considered safe, and no major complications were reported. In one study, however, there was a 30% dropout rate after just 4 weeks of training.[32]

Although the available data support a potential role for exercise training as a means for improving functional capacity and quality of life in heart failure patients, there are several unresolved issues. First, all of the studies were small and involved relatively young patients with stable symptoms. None of the studies assessed clinical outcomes (e.g. hospitalization, mortality), and, even in aggregate, there is an insufficient number of patients to adequately assess either safety or clinical efficacy. Second, the protocols used in these trials varied substantially in terms of exercise intensity, duration, frequency, and mode of exercise. The trials themselves also varied in length from 3 to 24 weeks. Thus, the generalizability of current data to other patient populations (e.g. individuals over 65 years of age, who

comprise over 75% of all heart failure patients) is unknown. In addition, further study is needed to determine the optimal parameters (i.e. frequency, duration, intensity) for achieving maximum benefit at lowest risk for the majority of heart failure patients, and to assess the effects of regular exercise on clinical outcomes. Another practical limitation is that most heart failure patients are either incapable or unwilling to exercise at the level of intensity and for the duration specified in the study protocols. In this regard, a recent report from Belardinelli et al is of considerable interest.[38] In this study, 18 patients with chronic heart failure participated in an 8 week programme of low intensity exercise, consisting of 30 minutes of stationary cycling three times per week at 40% of peak oxygen uptake. By the end of the training period, peak oxygen uptake had increased 17% and peak workload had increased 21%.[38] These changes, which are strikingly similar to those reported in other studies using higher intensity protocols, were achieved at comfortable levels of exercise that are well within the capacity of most patients with New York Heart Association class I–III symptoms.

Exercise prescription

In the absence of contraindications (Table 20.5), regular exercise is appropriate for most heart failure patients.[27,28] However, pending additional data on safety and efficacy, a low intensity, gradually progressive programme is recommended.

In general, training should include flexibility and strengthening exercises along with aerobic activities. In all cases, the frequency, duration and intensity of exercise must be individualized to accommodate differences in baseline conditioning, symptom severity, and comorbid conditions that might limit the patient's ability to exercise (e.g. arthritis or peripheral arterial dis-

- Recent acute myocardial infarction or unstable angina
- Severe, decompensated heart failure (class IV)
- Active, life-threatening arrhythmias
- Severe aortic stenosis or hypertrophic cardiomyopathy
- Any acute serious illness
- Any condition precluding safe participation

Table 20.5
Contraindications to exercise in heart failure patients.

ease). When feasible, patients should be encouraged to exercise at least five times per week. In patients with very low exercise tolerance (e.g. class III), brief bouts of exercise twice daily (or more) may be desirable.

For most patients, self-paced walking is a suitable form of aerobic activity. Stationary cycling against little or no resistance is the best alternative in patients who are unable to walk. When beginning an exercise programme, patients should be instructed to walk or cycle at 'a comfortable pace for a comfortable period of time.' The initial pace and duration of exercise may vary considerably, with some patients able to exercise for only 1 or 2 minutes, while others may be able to exercise for 15–20 minutes or longer without difficulty. In any case, patients should gradually increase the *duration* of exercise over a period of several weeks. Once the patient can exercise continuously for 20–30 minutes without undue fatigue, shortness of breath, or other symptoms, it may be appropriate to gradually increase the *intensity* of exercise (i.e. walk a little faster or up a slight incline, or add resistance to the stationary bicycle). At the present time, exercise intensities in excess of 60–70%

of heart rate reserve are not recommended for heart failure patients.

Monitoring exercise

The necessity of performing a stress test prior to initiating an exercise programme is controversial. Stress testing can be performed safely in patients with heart failure and it provides objective data regarding baseline exercise tolerance.[30] In addition, specific recommendations about exercise intensity can be derived from the stress test results. On the other hand, routine stress testing in all patients with heart failure would entail considerable costs, and it is not clear that a 'scientific approach' to exercise prescription will necessarily lead to superior clinical outcomes compared with a subjective approach based on perceived exertion. The latter approach is simple, less costly, and more widely applicable to a broad range of patients. In this author's opinion, stress testing is appropriate in patients who are at high risk of developing asymptomatic myocardial ischaemia during exercise (e.g. diabetics with known coronary artery disease). In other situations, an exercise programme guided by symptoms and level of perceived exertion is an acceptable alternative. When beginning an exercise programme, self-perceived exertion ratings of 'very light' to 'light' are recommended. With time, exercise intensity may progress into the 'moderate' range, but exercise perceived as 'moderately heavy' or 'heavy' should generally be avoided.

Another question concerns the safety of exercise in a nonmonitored setting (e.g. at home). In the United States, most insurance companies (including Medicare) do not pay for cardiac rehabilitation unless the patient has had a recent myocardial infarction or revascularization procedure. From the practical standpoint, therefore, most heart failure patients are not candidates for a formal cardiac rehabilitation programme in a monitored setting. This consideration underscores the need for a cautious approach to exercise prescription with respect to duration and intensity. In high-risk patients, initiation of exercise should be undertaken in a supervised setting whenever possible.

Comparison with pharmacological agents
Mortality

In patients with coronary heart disease, cardiac rehabilitation has been shown to reduce mortality by 20–25% following acute myocardial infarction or coronary bypass surgery.[39,40] The applicability of these findings to the heart failure population is unknown. Similarly, none of the trials of non-pharmacological treatment in heart failure patients (Table 20.3) have been of sufficient size to examine the effect on mortality. In contrast, ACE inhibitors clearly decrease mortality,[41] as do beta-blockers[42] and currently available data suggest a survival advantage for amiodarone[43] in selected heart failure patients. Digoxin, on the other hand, has no effect on survival,[44] and the merits of calcium antagonists[45] and angiotensin II receptor antagonists[46] require further study.

Readmissions and quality of life

Table 20.6 summarizes readmission and quality of life data from selected randomized clinical trials evaluating various medications commonly used in treating heart failure patients.[44-56] In most of the studies, treatment with digoxin,[43] a beta-blocker,[47-50] an ACE inhibitor,[51-54] or an angiotensin II receptor antagonist[46] was associated with a reduction in hospitalizations. However, the magnitude of benefit was similar to that seen in the nonphar-

macological studies. Although most of the drug studies have not specifically reported on quality of life, two of the beta-blocker trials[48,49] and two of the ACE inhibitor trials[51,55] found significant improvements in symptoms, functional class, exercise tolerance, and/or quality of life. Importantly, the impact of pharmacological agents on quality of life and related parameters was again similar to that seen in the non-pharmacological and exercise trials.

Summary and conclusions

Despite recent advances in the medical and surgical management of heart failure, mortality remains high and the majority of patients suffer significant impairments in quality of life. Non-pharmacological interventions, including multi-disciplinary heart failure management and exercise training, provide additional options for improving outcomes in heart failure patients. Although the impact of these interventions on mortality is currently unknown, the effects on symptoms, exercise duration, and various quality of life parameters, as well as on hospital readmissions, are highly favourable and of similar magnitude to the benefits seen with pharmacological agents.

What, then, can be said in response to the question, 'Non-pharmacological treatment: just as important?' Based on available evidence, it appears that with respect to nonfatal outcomes, non-pharmacological treatment is indeed just as important. However, it must be recognized that non-pharmacological therapy, medications, and surgery represent *complementary* rather than *competing* therapeutic strategies. Thus, optimal management of heart failure entails the careful selection and implementation of all appropriate therapeutic options, alone or in combination, on an individualized basis.

Author/year	Agent	Study design	No. of patients	Duration of follow-up	Results	Comments
DIG 1997[43]	Digoxin	Randomized trial	6800	Mean of 37 months	6% reduction in hospitalizations / 10% reduction in CV admissions / 24% reduction in HF admissions	No difference in mortality / 25% reduction in HF death or admission / Greater benefit with more severe HF
Waagstein et al 1993[46] Wiklund 1996[44]	Metoprolol	Randomized trial	383	12–18 months	41% fewer hospitalizations / Improved symptoms and NYHA class / Improved quality of life, physical activity, and exercise capacity	Mean age 49 years / Nonischaemic dilated cardiomyopathy / Predominantly NYHA class II–III / No difference in mortality
CIBIS 1994[48]	Bisoprolol	Randomized trial	641	Mean of 1.9 years	32% reduction in HF admissions / Improved NYHA class	Mean age 60 years / 95% NYHA class III / No difference in mortality
Packer 1996[49]	Carvedilol	Randomized, stratified trial	1094	Median of 6.5 months	27% reduction in CV admissions	Mean age 58 years / Predominantly NYHA class II–III / 65% reduction in mortality
CMRG 1983[50]	Captopril	Randomized trial	92	12 weeks	24% increase in exercise time / Improved symptoms and NYHA class	Mean age 58 years / Predominantly NYHA class II–III
Pfeffer 1992[51]	Captopril	Randomized trial	2231	Mean of 42 months	22% reduction in HF admissions	Mean age 59 years / All patients 3–16 days post-MI
SOLVD 1991, 1992[52,53] Rogers 1994[54]	Enalapril	Randomized trials	6797	24–62 months	29–36% decrease in HF admissions / Improved quality of life	Mean age 59–61 years / 16% fewer deaths in treatment trial / 8% fewer deaths in prevention trial / 20–26% reduction in HF deaths and admissions
Gundersen 1995[55]	Ramipril	Randomized, parallel groups	223	12 weeks	No difference in quality of life between ramipril and placebo	Mean age 64 years / NYHA class II–III patients
Pitt 1997[45]	Losartan versus captopril	Randomized trial	722	48 weeks	26% fewer admissions with losartan / No difference in HF admissions	All patients ≥65 years of age / Predominantly NYHA class II–III
Packer 1996[44]	Amlodipine	Randomized trial	1153	Median of 13.8 months	No difference in HF admissions	Mean age 65 years / NYHA class III–IV patients / No difference in mortality

CIBIS, Cardiac Insufficiency Bisoprolol Study; CMRG, Captopril Multicenter Research Group; CT, cardiothoracic; CV, cardiovascular; DIG, Digitalis Investigation Group; HF, heart failure; MI, myocardial infarction; NYHA, New York Heart Association; SOLVD, Studies of Left Ventricular Dysfunction.

Table 20.6
Effects of pharmacological agents on readmissions, quality of life and exercise tolerance.

References

1. Graves EJ, Owings MF. *1995 Summary: National Hospital Discharge Survey. Advance data from vital and health statistics; no. 291.* Hyattsville, MD: National Center for Health Statistics, 1997.

2. O'Connell JB, Bristow MR. Economic impact of heart failure in the United States: time for a different approach. *J Heart Lung Transplant* 1994; **13**: S107–S112.

3. Ho KKL, Pinsky JL, Kannel WB, Levy D. The epidemiology of heart failure: the Framingham study. *J Am Coll Cardiol* 1993; **22** (Suppl A): 6A–13A.

4. Coons S, Sheahan S, Martin S et al. Predictors of medication noncompliance in a sample of older adults. *Clin Ther* 1994; **16**: 110–117.

5. Opie LH. Practical therapy: adverse effects of non-steroidal anti-inflammatory drugs (NSAIDs) in therapy of hypertension and congestive heart failure. *Cardiovasc Drugs Ther* 1987; **1**: 109–110.

6. Freedland KE, Carney RM, Rich MW et al. Depression in elderly patients with congestive heart failure. *J Geriatr Psychiatry* 1991; **24**: 59–71.

7. Ghali JK, Kadakia S, Cooper R, Ferlinz J. Precipitating factors leading to decompensation of heart failure. Traits among blacks. *Arch Intern Med* 1988; **148**: 2013–2016.

8. Vinson JM, Rich MW, Sperry JC et al. Early readmission of elderly patients with congestive heart failure. *J Am Geriatr Soc* 1990; **38**: 1290–1295.

9. Opasich C, Febo O, Riccardi G et al. Concomitant factors of decompensation in chronic heart failure. *Am J Cardiol* 1996; **78**: 354–357.

10. Chin MH, Goldman L. Factors contributing to the hospitalization of patients with congestive heart failure. *Am J Public Health* 1997; **87**: 643–648.

11. Happ MB, Naylor MD, Roe-Prior P. Factors contributing to rehospitalization of elderly patients with heart failure. *J Cardiovasc Nurs* 1997; **11**: 75–84.

12. Cintron G, Bigas C, Linares E et al. Nurse practitioner role in a chronic congestive heart failure clinic: in-hospital time, costs, and patient satisfaction. *Heart Lung* 1983; **12**: 237–240.

13. Rich MW, Vinson JM, Sperry JC et al. Prevention of readmission in elderly patients with congestive heart failure: results of a prospective, randomized pilot study. *J Gen Intern Med* 1993; **8**: 585–590.

14. Lasater M. The effect of a nurse-managed CHF clinic on patient readmission and length of stay. *Home Healthc Nurse* 1996; **14**: 351–356.

15. Kostis JB, Rosen RC, Cosgrove DM et al. Nonpharmacologic therapy improves functional and emotional status in congestive heart failure. *Chest* 1994; **106**: 996–1001.

16. Kornowski R, Zeeli D, Averbuch M et al. Intensive home-care surveillance prevents hospitalization and improves morbidity rates among elderly patients with severe congestive heart failure. *Am Heart J* 1995; **129**: 762–766.

17. Rich MW, Beckham V, Wittenberg C et al. A multidisciplinary intervention to prevent the readmission of elderly patients with congestive heart failure. *N Engl J Med* 1995; **333**: 1190–1195.

18. Dennis LI, Blue CL, Stahl SM et al. The relationship between hospital readmissions of Medicare beneficiaries with chronic illnesses and home care nursing interventions. *Home Healthc Nurse* 1996; **14**: 303–309.

19. Martens KH, Mellor SD. A study of the relationship between home care services and hospital readmission of patients with congestive heart failure. *Home Healthc Nurse* 1997; **15**: 123–129.

20. West JA, Miller NH, Parker KM et al. A comprehensive management system for heart failure improves clinical outcomes and reduces medical resource utilization. *Am J Cardiol* 1997; **79**: 58–63.

21. Fonarow GC, Stevenson LW, Walden JA et al. Impact of a comprehensive heart failure man-

agement program on hospital readmission and functional status of patients with advanced heart failure. *J Am Coll Cardiol* 1997; **30:** 725–732.

22. Rich MW, Gray DB, Beckham V et al. Effect of a multidisciplinary intervention on medication compliance in elderly patients with congestive heart failure. *Am J Med* 1996; **101:** 270–276.

23. Stewart S, Pearson S, Luke CG et al. Effects of a home-based intervention on unplanned readmissions and out-of-hospital deaths. *J Am Geriatr Soc* 1998; **46:** 174–180.

24. Stewart S, Pearson S, Horowitz JD. Effects of a home-based intervention among congestive heart failure patients discharged from acute hospital care. *Arch Intern Med* 1998; **158:** 1067–1072.

25. Stewart S, Vandenbroek AJ, Pearson S et al. Prolonged beneficial effects of a 'home-based intervention on unplanned readmissions and mortality among patients with congestive heart failure. *Arch Intern Med* 1999; **159:** 257–261.

26. Cline CMJ, Israelson BYA, Willenheimer RB et al. A cost effective management programme for heart failure reduces hospitalisation. *Heart* 1998; **80:** 442–446.

27. Konstam MA, Dracup K, Baker DW et al. *Heart failure: evaluation and care of patients with left ventricular systolic dysfunction. Clinical practice guideline No. 11.* Rockville, MD: Agency for Health Care Policy and Research, 1994. (AHCPR publication no. 94–0612).

28. ACC/AHA Task Force Report. Guidelines for the evaluation and management of heart failure. *J Am Coll Cardiol* 1995; **26:** 1376–1398.

29. McKelvie RS, Teo KK, McCartney N et al. Effects of exercise training in patients with congestive heart failure: a critical review. *J Am Coll Cardiol* 1995; **25:** 789–796.

30. Hanson P. Exercise testing and training in patients with chronic heart failure. *Med Sci Sports Exerc* 1994; **26:** 527–537.

31. Coats AJS, Adamopoulos S, Meyer TE et al. Effects of physical training in chronic heart failure. *Lancet* 1990; **335:** 63–66.

32. Jetté M, Heller R, Landry F, Blumchen G. Randomized 4-week exercise program in patients with impaired left ventricular function. *Circulation* 1991; **84:** 1561–1567.

33. Coats AJS, Adamopoulos S, Radaelli A et al. Controlled trial of physical training in chronic heart failure. Exercise performance, hemodynamics, ventilation, and autonomic function. *Circulation* 1992; **85:** 2119–2131.

34. Belardinelli R, Georgiou D, Cianci G et al. Exercise training improves left ventricular diastolic filling in patients with dilated cardiomyopathy. Clinical and prognostic implications. *Circulation* 1995; **91:** 2775–2784.

35. Keteyian SJ, Levine AB, Brawner CA et al. Exercise training in patients with heart failure. A randomized, controlled trial. *Ann Intern Med* 1996; **124:** 1051–1057.

36. Meyer K, Samek L, Schwaibold M et al. Interval training in patients with severe chronic heart failure: analysis and recommendations for exercise procedures. *Med Sci Sports Exerc* 1997; **29:** 306–312.

37. Dubach P, Myers J, Dziekan G et al. Effect of high intensity exercise training on central hemodynamic responses to exercise in men with reduced left ventricular function. *J Am Coll Cardiol* 1997; **29:** 1591–1598.

38. Belardinelli R, Georghou D, Scocco V et al. Low intensity exercise training in patients with chronic heart failure. *J Am Coll Cardiol* 1995; **26:** 975–982.

39. O'Connor GT, Buring JE, Yusuf S et al. An overview of randomized trials of rehabilitation with exercise after myocardial infarction. *Circulation* 1989; **80:** 234–244.

40. Juneau M, Geneau S, Marchand C, Brosseau R. Cardiac rehabilitation after coronary bypass surgery. *Cardiovasc Clin* 1991; **21:** 25–42.

41. Garg R, Yusuf S for the Collaborative Group on ACE Inhibitor Trials. Overview of randomized trials of angiotensin-converting enzyme inhibitors on mortality and morbidity in patients with heart failure. *JAMA* 1995; **273:** 1450–1456.

42. Heidenreich PA, Lee TT, Massie BM. Effect of beta-blockade on mortality in patients with heart failure: a meta-analysis of randomized clinical trials. *J Am Coll Cardiol* 1997; **30:** 27–34.

43. Pinto JV, Ramani K, Neelagaru S et al. Amiodarone therapy in chronic heart failure and myocardial infarction: a review of the mortality trials with special attention to STAT-CHF

and the GESICA trials. *Prog Cardiovasc Dis* 1997; **40**: 85–93.

44. The Digitalis Investigation Group. The effect of digoxin on mortality and morbidity in patients with heart failure. *N Engl J Med* 1997; **336**: 525–533.

45. Packer M, O'Connor CM, Ghali JK et al. Effect of amlodipine on morbidity and mortality in severe chronic heart failure. *N Engl J Med* 1996; **335**: 1107–1114.

46. Pitt B, Segal R, Martinez FA et al. Randomised trial of losartan versus captopril in patients over 65 with heart failure (Evaluation of Losartan in the Elderly Study, ELITE). *Lancet* 1997; **349**: 747–752.

47. Waagstein F, Bristow MR, Swedberg K et al. Beneficial effects of metoprolol in idiopathic dilated cardiomyopathy. *Lancet* 1993; **342**: 1441–1446.

48. Wiklund I, Waagstein F, Swedberg K, Hjalmarsson A. Quality of life on treatment with metoprolol in dilated cardiomyopathy: results from the MDC trial. *Cardiovasc Drugs Ther* 1996; **10**: 361–368.

49. CIBIS Investigators and Committees. A randomized trial of β-blockade in heart failure. The Cardiac Insufficiency Bisoprolol Study (CIBIS). *Circulation* 1994; **90**: 1765–1773.

50. Packer M, Bristow MR, Cohn JN et al. The effect of carvedilol on morbidity and mortality in patients with chronic heart failure. *N Engl J Med* 1996; **334**: 1349–1355.

51. Captopril Multicenter Research Group. A placebo-controlled trial of captopril in refractory chronic congestive heart failure. *J Am Coll Cardiol* 1983; **2**: 755–763.

52. Pfeffer MA, Braunwald E, Moyé LA et al. Effect of captopril on mortality and morbidity in patients with left ventricular dysfunction after myocardial infarction. Results of the Survival and Ventricular Enlargement trial. *N Engl J Med* 1992; **327**: 669–677.

53. The SOLVD Investigators. Effect of enalapril on survival in patients with reduced left ventricular ejection fractions and congestive heart failure. *N Engl J Med* 1991; **325**: 293–302.

54. The SOLVD Investigators. Effect of enalapril on mortality and the development of heart failure in asymptomatic patients with reduced left ventricular ejection fractions. *N Engl J Med* 1992; **327**: 685–691.

55. Rogers WJ, Johnstone DE, Yusuf S et al. Quality of life among 5025 patients with left ventricular dysfunction randomized between placebo and enalapril: the Studies of Left Ventricular Dysfunction. *J Am Coll Cardiol* 1994; **23**: 393–400.

56. Gundersen T, Wiklund I, Swedberg K et al. Effects of 12 weeks of ramipril treatment on the quality of life in patients with moderate congestive heart failure: results of a placebo-controlled trial. *Cardiovasc Drugs Ther* 1995; **9**: 589–594.

Index

cellular pathways leading to
  enhanced fibrosis 147–8
classification of types 144
dilated cardiomyopathy 168
effect on pump function 144–5
replacement 143, 144, 150
role of circulating hormones
  145–6
role of the renin—angiotensin—
  aldosterone system 146–7
therapy 148–51
normal heart 139–42
pathological consequences of
  changes 142–3
role 139–41
irbesartan 205, 206, 214
clinical outcomes in chronic heart
  failure 208, 209
pharmacology 200
ischaemic heart disease
calcium channel blockers 286
fibrosis and 145
natriuretic peptides in 61–2
ISIS 185, 216
isosorbide dinitrate
effect on exercise capacity 291
hydralazine and 183, 263, 264
nifedipine and, effect on exercise
  capacity 291

Jarvik 2000 Heart 311–13
paediatric 312–13

labetalol 247
left ventricular aneurysm, resection
  303
left ventricular assistance devices
  (LVAD)
bridge to myocardial recovery
  310–13
bridge to transplant 307–10
left ventricular dysfunction
apoptosis and 133
detection 6
diastolic *see* diastolic dysfunction
hypertension and 22
as precursor of heart failure 4, 7, 34,
  37, 127, 260
prevalence 33
progression in heart failure patients
  127–8, 130
screening for 8, 11, 33–40
  cost-effectiveness 36–7
systolic, natriuretic peptides as
  indicators 63–4
treatment
  ACE inhibitors in 184–7
  benefits 11
left ventricular function
diastolic, assessment 43–4
effects of beta-blockers 248–9
normal systolic 42–3

tests 35–36
left ventricular hypertrophy
calcium channel blocker therapy
  284–5
diastolic heart failure and 47–8
interstitial fibrosis and 145
left ventriculectomy, partial 304–7
limb-girdle muscular dystrophy,
  cardiac involvement 167
lisinopril
clinical trials 185, 187
dosage 203
effect on plasma endothelin
  concentrations 81
haemodynamic effects 206
interstitial fibrosis 148
losartan
adverse effects 215–16, 218
clinical trials 189
  ELITE study 21, 188, 206,
    210–12, 213, 265
combined with ACE inhibitor
  213–14
diastolic chronic heart failure 214
dose response studies in chronic
  heart failure 208
effects 203
  on clinical outcome in chronic
    heart failure 206–8
  electrophysiological and
    autonomic 201–2
  haemodynamic 203–4, 205–6
  neuroendocrine 206, 207
  sudden death risk 265
  uricosuric 202
pharmacology 199, 200
LVAD *see* left ventricular assistance
  devices

MADIT 272, 273
magnesium deficiency in chronic heart
  failure 96–7
management of heart failure
exercise training 327–31
follow-up services 324, 325, 327
home-based interventions 327
multidisciplinary approach 324–7
MERIT-HF trial 252
metalloproteinases, matrix, in failing
  heart 146
metavinculin deficiency, dilated
  cardiomyopathy 168
metoprolol
apoptosis modification 134
use in heart failure, clinical trials
  247, 250, 252, 253
Metoprolol in Dilated Cardiomyopathy
  (MDC) trial 247, 250
mibafradil 282, 292–3
milrinone 266
Milrinone Multicenter trial 227, 228
mitral valve repair 302–3

MOCHA trial 247, 250
molecular biology of heart failure
  163–77
MONICA coronary risk factor survey
  22
mortality rates 6, 34
plasma noripenephrine and 300–1
Multicenter Automatic Defibrillator
  Implantation trial (MADIT) 272,
  273
muscle fatigue 159
muscle LIM protein (MLP) 167–8
muscular dystrophies, cytoskeletal
  protein abnormalities 166–7, 168
mycophenolate myofetil 314
myocardial fibrosis, aldosterone and
  99–100
myocardial infarction
ACE inhibitory therapy started in
  acute phase 185, 187–8
acute, plasma ADM levels 108–9
calcium channel blockers following
  288–90
effect of amiodarone 269
heart failure and 6, 34
  ACE inhibitors 184–7
  plasma ADM levels 108–9
hypertension and 20
silent 20, 34
surgery following 302, 303
myocardial ischaemia
diastolic heart failure and 45–6
hypertension and 20
silent 20
myocardial ischaemia/reperfusion,
  apoptosis and 171–2
myocardium
hypertrophy 149–50
stiffness, influence of interstitial
  components 141, 143
stunned 143
ultrastructure 140
myocytes *see* cardiomyocytes
myofibroblasts 142, 143

natriuretic peptides 59–71
actions 62–3
clearance 62
clinical uses
  diagnostic 63–4
  prognostic 64
  as screening tests 64
  therapeutic 64–7
detection of left ventricular
  dysfunction 11, 36
effects of adrenomedullin 119
receptors 62
  nonpeptide agonists for A and B
    types 66–7
release 59–61
as screening tests 64
structure 59, 61